W9-DGJ-730

DISCARD

Ethnic Elderly and Long-Term Care

Charles M. Barresi, Ph.D., is Professor Emeritus of Sociology and Life Senior Fellow in the Institute for Life-Span Development and Gerontology, The University of Akron. He received B.A. and M.A. degrees in Anthropology/Sociology from the University of Buffalo, a Ph.D. in Sociology from the State University of New York at Buffalo, and did post-doctoral studies at the Scripps Foundation Gerontological Center, Miami University, Ohio. He was Chair of the Department of Sociology, Rosary Hill College (now Daemen College) in Buffalo for 10 years and taught for 24 years at the University of Akron. Dr. Barresi is a Fellow in the Gerontological Society of America and a member of the Minority Affairs Committee of the American Society on Aging. He has done consulting and conducted research in social gerontology for a number of years and has contributed numerous book chapters and journal articles on a variety of topics including black family caregiving, the impact of the life course on ethnic aging, and older Cubans in Miami and Tampa. His interests in long-term care are based on a 10-year involvement with adult daycare on the consulting, research, and administrative levels. He is coeditor with Donald E. Gelfand, of *Ethnic Dimensions of Aging.* Currently, he is an Adjunct Professor of Gerontology at the University of South Florida, Tampa, and resides in Palm Harbor, Florida.

Donald E. Stull, Jr., Ph.D., is Associate Professor of Sociology at The University of Akron. He received his Ph.D. from the University of Washington, Seattle. While in Seattle, he worked, for 4 years, at the Institute on Aging on research projects focusing on family caregiving, funded by the National Institute on Aging and the Administration on Aging. In 1987 he was awarded a fellowship as part of the Gerontological Society of America's Fellowship Program in Applied Gerontology. Currently, he is Principal Investigator of the ElderCare Project, a 5-year, 4-wave panel study of family caregiving funded by the National Institute on Aging. Dr. Stull is the author of many articles and book chapters on long-term care and family caregiving, and methodological issues in aging research.

ETHNIC ELDERLY AND LONG-TERM CARE

Charles M. Barresi, Ph.D.
Donald E. Stull, Ph.D.
Editors

SPRINGER PUBLISHING COMPANY
New York

To our families

Copyright © 1993 by Springer Publishing Company, Inc.

Springer Publishing Company, Inc.
536 Broadway
New York, NY 10012-3955

   95 96 97 / 5 4 3 2

Library of Congress Cataloging-in-Publication Data

Ethnic elderly and long-term care / Charles M. Barresi, Donald E.
  Stull, editors.
    p. cm.
  Includes bibliographical references and index.
  ISBN 0-8261-7370-5
   1. Minority aged—Care—United States. 2. Aged—Long-term care—
United States. 3. Minority aged—Services for—United States.
I. Barresi, Charles M. II. Stull, Donald Edgar.
HV1416.E84 1993
362.6'089—dc20   92-6066
                                                     CIP

Printed in the United States of America

Contents

Contributors

Marie-Louise Ansak, M.S.W., is Executive Director of On Lok, Inc., the parent corporation for On Lok Senior Health Services, PACE (Program for All-Inclusive Care for the Elderly, the national project to replicate the On Lok managed long-term care model) and On Lok's housing programs. Since 1971, Mrs. Ansak has directed the growth of On Lok from a small day health center serving a handful of low-income frail elderly into a nationally acclaimed comprehensive program of medical and social care funded via capitation payments from Medicare, Medicaid and the individual. Mrs. Ansak has been the recipient of the Institute of Medicine's Gustav O. Leinhard Award for outstanding achievement in health care in the United States (1988) and the recipient of the California Association of Homes for the Aging's Public Service Award (1987). She holds a M.S.W. (Smith College, 1958) and completed other training at the School of Social Work, Zurich, Switzerland; University of the Sorbonne, Paris; City of London College.

Elena Bastida, Ph.D., is Professor of Sociology at The University of Texas Pan American. Her main research interests are related to ethnicity, aging, and health. She is the author of numerous articles on the Hispanic elderly, most recently an annotated bibliography on Hispanic elderly health and a longitudinal study of Hispanic elderly health.

John Capitman, Ph.D., is Director of the National Aging Resource Center, Bigel Institute for Health Policy, Director of Long-Term Care Studies, also at the Bigel Institute, and Research Professor at the Heller School, Brandeis University. Dr. Capitman is leading a survey of selected SUAs and AAAs on issues related to community long-term care service coordination and financing as part of a Hartford Foundation project to develop consensus proposals for long-term care reform. He is also principal investigator of a study evaluating dementia care and respite service. Dr. Capitman's other projects are focused on integrated acute long-term care delivery systems and on multicultural approaches in responding to the diversity of aging service providers and consumers.

Jennie Chin-Hansen, R.N., M.S., is Director of On Lok Senior Health Services, a nationally renowned, non-profit, community-based long term care organization for the frail elderly in San Francisco. Her previous background includes clinical nursing, university teaching, and research and development. Ms. Hansen has long been an active speaker and advocate for long-term health care and issues regarding the minority elderly. Ms. Hansen received her Bachelor of Science in Nursing from Boston College, and her Master of Science from the University of California, San Francisco.

Carole Cox, D.S.W., is Associate Professor at the National Catholic School of Social Service, The Catholic University of America, Washington, D.C. Her research interests are in the areas of ethnicity, Alzheimer's disease, caregiving, and the use of informal and formal services. She is the co-author, with Abraham Monk, of *Home Care: An International Perspective*, published by Auburn House.

Lucille H. Davis, R.N., Ph.D., is Research Associate in the College of Nursing and School of Public Health at the University of Illinois at Chicago. She has been principal investigator of two research projects, "Social Factors in the Health of Black Urban Elders," funded by the National Institute on Aging (NIA), and "Self-Care Education Project for Black Elders: Hypertension, Diabetes and Arthritis," funded by the Administration on Aging (AoA). She has been dean of several schools of nursing and developed and taught in graduate programs in gerontological nursing. Since 1987, she has been a program development consultant to the Ministry of Health in Zimbabwe, Africa, supported by the Kellog Foundation.

David V. Espino, M.D., is an Assistant Professor of Family Medicine and Director of the Division of Geriatrics, Department of Family Practice at the University of Texas Health Science Center at San Antonio. He is a fellow of the American Academy of Family Practice, President of the San Antonio Geriatric Society, and President of the San Antonio Geriatrics Society Council of State Affiliates. He currently co-chair's the American Geriatrics Society's Ethnogeriatric Task Force. Currently, he is the primary investigator on two major investigations: (1) the translation and validation of the Geriatric Depression Scale in elderly Hispanics, and (2) examination of mortality differences between elderly Mexican-Americans and non-Hispanic whites.

Tracy Fedirko is a graduate student in the Department of Sociology at Case Western Reserve University, Cleveland.

Steve Folmar, Ph.D., holds a Ph.D. in anthropology, Case Western Reserve University (1985), and is a Research Associate at Bowman Gray Medical School, Wake Forest University, Winston-Salem, NC. Prior to that he was a post-doctoral fellow at the Carolina Population Center, University of North Carolina, Chapel Hill. He has collaborated on research on the elderly of Cleveland, Ohio (the GAO studies), directed the Applied Research Institute of the Menorah Park Center for the Aging, and studied the demography of the elderly in Nepal.

Genaro Gonzalez, Ph.D., is Associate Professor of Psychology at the University of Texas Pan American. He earned his Ph.D. from the University of California, Santa Cruz. He is a well-published Chicano fiction writer whose primary psychological research interests are in the area of cross-cultural psychology.

Winnie Hernandez-Gallegos, Ph.D., is Director of Research and Planning at the United Way of Massachusetts Bay, in Boston. She was the project manager of the Cultural Diversity Project described in this volume, which provided technical assistance to SUAs and AAAs by examining personnel practices and service approaches to accommodate cultural diversity. Dr. Hernandez-Gallegos' background includes experience on several research projects on organizational issues faced by home health agencies and respite service providers, as well as her previous management experience in the delivery of home-care services to elders in Dade County, Florida.

Boaz Kahana is a clinical and developmental psychologist who has done extensive research with the elderly. He is Professor of Psychology and Director of the Center on Aging at Cleveland State University.

Eva Kahana, Ph.D., is Pierce T. and Elizabeth D. Robson Professor of the Humanities, Chair of the Department of Sociology, and Director of the Elderly Care Research Center at Case Western Reserve University. She received her Ph.D. in human development from the University of Chicago. Currently Director of pre-doctoral and post-doctoral training programs in Health Research and Aging, Dr. Kahana is a recipient of a MERIT award from the National Institute on Aging for the study of Adaptation to Frailty Among Dispersed Elders (1989–94). Her current research also includes a study of illness adaptation of elderly heart attack victims and their caregivers and a study of physician–patient communication in Alzheimer's disease. She has published extensively in the area of stress, coping and health of the aged, late-life migration and environmental influences in older persons.

Jerome Kaplan, Ph.D., is Executive Director Retired (1958–1988) of Mansfield (Ohio) Memorial Homes, The University of Akron Visiting Professor of Nursing Home Administration, and The Ohio State University Adjunct Professor of Sociology. He is Honorary Editor-in-Chief of *The Gerontologist*, is past-president of The Gerontological Society of America, and served as Special Assistant on Aging to the Governor of Minnesota. He is the author of several hundred publications on aging.

Cary S. Kart, Ph.D., is Professor of Sociology at the University of Toledo. Currently a member of NIH's Human Development and Aging Study Section, he recently received funding from the AARP Andrus Foundation for a study of self-health care among the elderly. Professor Kart is author, co-author, or editor of eight books and many articles and book chapters on aging, health, and long-term care, including *Aging, Health and Society* (Jones & Bartlett, 1988) and the third edition of his text, *The Realities of Aging* (Allyn & Bacon, 1990).

Katherine Kim, R.N., Ph.D., is Associate Professor of Nursing at the Kirhof School of Nursing, Grand Valley State University. She was in charge of the Korean component in the study of Asian-American Elderly in Chicago's Congregate Housing. Her areas of interest are aging and nutrition of the minority elderly. She is a Co-Investigator in the Developmental Research on Asian-American Cancer Control Project based in Chicago.

Carmela G. Lacayo is the founder and President/CEO of the Asociacion Nacional Pro Personas Mayores (National Association for Hispanic Elderly) and El Pueblo Community Development Corporation. In 16 years she has built the Asociacion into one of the largest and best-respected national Hispanic organizations, with an annual budget of nearly $15 millon and offices in ten states and the District of Columbia. Ms. Lacayo is an internationally recognized speaker, researcher and Hispanic leader. She is a Fellow of the Gerontological Society of America and has served on many national and local boards. Ms. Lacayo has received numerous awards for more than 28 years os service on behalf of the elderly, women and minority persons, among them a Salvation Army Special Award and the National Woman of the Year Award from the Los Angeles Professional Women's Association.

William T. Liu, Ph.D., is Professor of Sociology at the University of Illinois at Chicago and Director of the Pacific/Asian American Mental Health Research Center (1974–1991). He is presently on leave and is the Dean of Social Sciences at the Hong Kong Baptist College, where he heads a collaborative study with the Bureau of the Census on the Health of the Chinese Elderly in Hong Kong. He initiated the Shanghai Study of Alzheimer's disease (1987–1991), a unique and complex research project that for the first time established the rates of Alzheimer's disease and other dementias in China, using the DSM-III Diagnostic Criteria and other standardized procedures practiced by U. S. neurologists and psychiatrists. He was the Principal Investigator of the Project, Asian-American Elderly in Chicago's Congregate Housing Units (1988–1990).

Spero M. Manson, Ph.D., is Professor in the Department of Psychiatry and Director of the National Center for American Indian and Alaska Native Mental Health Research, both located at the University of Colorado Health Sciences Center. A medical anthropologist, his major interests include the diagnosis, epidemiology, treatment, and prevention of alcohol, drug, and mental disorders among Indians and Natives, with special emphasis on older adults.

Brenda F. McGadney, M.S.W., is a doctoral candidate in the school of Social Service Administration at the University of Chicago. Her dissertation topic is Stress and the Use of Informal Social Supports of Black and White Caregivers of Elders Attending Adult Day Care Centers: Predictors of Burden. She is Assistant Professor, School of Social Work, University of Washington, Seattle. She is Director of Social Factors in the Health of Black Urban Elders research project and Self-Care Education for Urban Black Elders: Hypertension, Diabetes and Arthritis health promotion project.

Charles H. Mindel, Ph.D., is Professor of Social Work at The University of Texas at Arlington. He received his Ph.D. degree in sociology from the University of Illinois. He has served as Acting Director of the Center for Chicano Aged and is Director of the Center for Social Welfare Research, School of Social Work. He has conducted extensive research on aging and family relations, with particular focus on people of color. He has also published numerous journal articles, chapters, and books, including *Ethnic Families in America: Patterns and Variations* (1976, 1981, 1988) with R. Wright, Jr. and R. W. Haberstein, and *Aging and Ethnicity* (1987) with K. S. Markides.

Abraham Monk, Ph.D., is Professor of Social Work and Gerontology at the Columbia University School of Social Work, in New York City. He is the author or editor of six books, including the *Handbook on Gerontological Services,* currently in its second edition. Dr. Monk has also authored over 100 publications in refereed scholarly and professional journals. He has conducted research in the fields of intergenerational relations, ethnicity, planning and programming of services, long-term care, home-care services, and adjustment to retirement.

Herbert Shore, Ed.D., is Executive Vice-President of The North American Association of Jewish Homes and Housing for the Aging. He is Executive Vice-President Emeritus of The Dallas Home for Jewish Aged, where he served from 1953 to 1990, and Adjunct Professor at The Center for Studies in Aging, University of North Texas, where he teaches Long-Term Care Administration. The author of many books and publications, he was a founder and past president of the American Association of Homes for The Aging.

Carol Van Steenberg, M.S.S., is a management consultant who works with health and human services organizations in the San Francisco Bay Area. She has assisted On Lok with a variety of planning, research dissemination and development projects since 1981. She previously was a research associated at Duke University's Center for the Study of Aging in North Carolina and received her M.S.S. from Bryn Mawr College.

Gloria Sterin is a social researcher who works with the Community Federation of Cleveland. She was a Postdoctoral Fellow at the Elderly Care Research Center, Department of Sociology, Case Western Reserve University, Cleveland.

Reva Taylor is a graduate student in the Department of Sociology at Case Western Reserve University, Cleveland.

Thomas T.H. Wan, Ph.D., is Professor of Health Administration and Director of the doctoral program in Health Administrative Sciences at the Medical College of Virginia, Virginia Commonwealth University, and Director of the Williamson Institute for Health Studies at MCV/VCU. He received his Ph.D. in sociology from the University of Georgia. His current research focuses on the determinants and consequences of institutionalization, health services utilization, rural health, and gerontological health. He has published seventy articles and four books in health care and aging fields: *Promoting the Well-Being for the Elderly* (1982); *Stressful Life Events, Social Support Networks, and Gerontological Health* (1982); *Well-Being for the Elderly: Primary Preventive Strategies* (1985); and *Health Services Research and Evaluation Methods* (1989).

Siu-Chi Wong, M.S., received her degree in biostatistics from the University of Illinois at Chicago and worked with Elena Yu and William T. Liu at the Pacific/Asian American Mental Health Research Center in 1986. She is now with the Prevention Center of the School of Public Health, University of Illinois at Chicago.

Joan B. Wood, Ph.D., is Assistant Professor of Gerontology and Psychology and Educational Services Director of the Geriatric Education Center at Virginia Commonwealth University. She received a Ph.D. in developmental psychology (1987) from Virginia Commonwealth University. Her research interests include family caregiving for frail elders, ethnic and cultural issues in aging, rural aging, and aging and developmental disabilities. Her published work has appeared in numerous books and journals.

Roosevelt Wright, Jr., Ph.D., is Professor of Social Work and Dean of the School of Social Work at The University of Texas at Arlington. He received his Ph.D. degree in social welfare from the University of Wisconsin at Madison. During the past decade he has conducted extensive research on the ethnic minority aged. He is the author or co-author of over 65 journal articles, books, and chapters dealing with ethnic aging, ethnic minority alcoholism, and cultures and ethnicity. His publications include *Transcultural Perspectives in the Human Services: Organizational Issues and Trends* (1983); *Black Alcoholism: Toward a Comprehensive Understanding* (1983); *Toward Preventing Black Alcoholism: Issues and Trends* (1985); *Alcoholism and Minority Populations* (1989); and *Ethnic Families in America: Patterns and Variations* (3rd ed.) (1988) with Charles H. Mindel and Robert W. Haberstein.

Donna L. Yee, Ph.D., is a Senior Research Associate at the Bigel Institute for Health Policy. Dr. Yee is the principal investigator for the Elder Care Institute on Older Women, funded by the Administration on Aging. Her expertise includes development and implementation of quality assurance mechanisms in case-managed systems. She is currently evaluating dementia care and respite service programs in 18 day-care sites. Currently studying existing community agencies and the development of new long-term care services in the Seattle area, Dr. Yee is examining service approaches and work force diversity in the aging network in eight areas of the country as part of technical assistance to SUAs and AAAs by the National Aging Resource Center on Long-Term Care at the Bigel Institute.

Gwen W. Yeo, Ph.D., is currently Director of the Stanford Geriatric Education Center, which focuses on ethnogeriatrics, or health care for ethnic elders. She received her Ph.D. in education from Stanford University with a research emphasis in educational gerontology. She has directed three federally funded projects in the Stanford School of Medicine in geriatric education for health care providers, two of which were national programs in faculty development and curriculum development in geriatrics. In addition to research in geriatric training and post-retirement education, Dr. Yeo has been active in research in health care for older adults, including ethnic issues in long-term care. She has authored curriculum manuals for health care training in geriatrics, and published numerous articles in scientific journals.

Elena S. H. Yu, Ph.D., M.P.H., is Professor of Epidemiology at the Graduate School of Public Health, San Diego State University. She is one of the investigators in the Shanghai Study of Alzheimer's Disease and Other Dementias, a longitudinal study of the elderly begun in 1987, and also a co-investigator of the Health of the Chinese Elderly in Hong Kong, begun in 1991. She is the principal investigator of a newly funded project, and the only one thus far for Asian-Americans, called Developmental Research in Asian-American Cancer Control, based in Chicago.

Foreword

It is satisfying and encouraging to read this important volume devoted to the influence of ethnicity and long-term care. It highlights the importance of studying long-term care in terms of scientific research and public policy. The interface between these constructs has long been neglected in the social gerontology literature. The editors of this volume, Professors Charles M. Barresi and Donald E. Stull, have made an important contribution to our understanding of the relationship between ethnicity and long-term care.

Projected growth of the older population guarantees that understanding the organization, financing, and human interaction dimensions of long-term care will assume increasing importance. Within this context, the ethnic elderly will make up a proportionately larger segment of the population needing long-term care. Delivery and organization of quality long-term care services to culturally different groups has policy, practice, and scientific implications.

The volume includes a rich survey of the health issues in very diverse types of ethnic communities. In keeping with the long-standing interests of the editors, the volume addresses traditionally discriminated against minorities of color and important religious and white ethnic groups. The text ranges in content from factors related to caregiver burden, documentation of long-term care practices in different ethnic communities, as well as differences in terms of institutional care and how ethnicity may influence delivery of care and individual adaptation. I was particularly impressed with the presentation of effective modes of delivering ethnically sensitive care, ranging from small efforts in nursing homes to broad national programs, such as the On Lok care model.

Consistent with the editors' and authors' prior work, the volume does not shy away from practice and policy recommendations. There is a section devoted to policy, planning, and practice in the organization, delivery, and financing of long-term care. Undergirding the entire volume is a refreshing ethical tone, embodying a framework of respect for ethnic diversity and the need for multiculturally sensitive organization, service delivery, and public policy.

In my assessment, the volume delivers an excellent summary by a diverse set of authors on what is presently known about the influence of ethnic factors on the organization, delivery, and financing of long-term care. It points to needed gaps in our research, public policies and health-care delivery systems. I believe it provides a foundation for future research and public policy studies related to familial, institutional, and societal responsibilities in the organization, delivery, and financing of needed long-term care for the increasing numbers of the ethnic elderly.

I recommend this volume highly. It provides a documentation of what we know about ethnic factors in this important area and describes a framework of what we should seek to know over the next several decades. It is well worth the time and investment of your energy to become familiar with the contents of this volume. I would like to express my congratulations to the editors and the authors of the individual chapters for helping to move forward research, practice, and policy agendas related to the interface between ethnic factors and long-term care issues in the aging multicultural society.

James S. Jackson, Ph.D.,
Director, African–American Mental Health Research Center
Research Scientist and Professor of Psychology
Institute for Social Research
University of Michigan

Preface

It is generally understood that our society is growing older—more people are living longer. However, this growth in the elderly population is not uniform. The ethnic elderly population has been growing at a faster rate than the white elderly population. Yet we know very little about the health status, service use and needs, and kinds of long-term care programs needed for ethnic elderly. Because of issues of different languages, customs, and practices and geographical and cultural isolation, some argue that ethnic elderly require different kinds of long-term care programs than white, English-speaking elderly. These are critical issues that need addressing.

Ethnic aging and long-term care are areas that have seen tremendous scholarly activity in the last decade. Indeed, in the last few years, dozens of books and scholarly articles have been published on both of these topics. There has, however, been no systematic attempt to bring these two areas together, to take stock of what we know and what we need to know about ethnicity and long-term care.

This volume is authored by experts in their respective fields. These authors were selected for their expertise in their respective fields and invited to contribute to the effort to produce a book that represents the cutting edge of information in the long-term care of ethnic elderly. As is true of the field of gerontology in general, this book is a multidisciplinary effort. It involves experts from a variety of academic disciplines, practitioners involved in service delivery, planners, and policymakers. We believe that this broad range of perspectives will provide the reader with a variety of insights into this complex area.

The subject matter covers a broad range of issues as they relate to long-term care and aging in ethnic groups. The coverage of long-term care topics runs the full gamut, from caregiving by family and friends at home to institutional care. In addition to these more familiar areas of long-term care, it also includes formal community care, self-care, and other practices that provide elders with the necessary assistance to carry on their everyday activities of daily living. The range of groups that is included also goes beyond the usual "racial minority" groups and encompasses a broad range, including a sampling of groups based on national and religious membership. We have included discussions of several model programs designed to provide long-term care for ethnic elderly. Again, these range from the more typical, broad institutional services to those targeted at specific groups in specific places. These discussions deal with historical origins, structural components, staffing, and other relevant issues.

The book is organized into six sections. Part I starts with an introduction, written by the editors, that lays out many of the basic issues in the area of ethnicity and long-term care, including definitions, demographics on ethnic elderly, health status, and service utilization. This part includes an innovative chapter that provides important conceptual issues in the measurement of physical health status, a precursor to determining the need for long-term care. Part II deals with caregiver issues in home-based long-term care, particularly informal care to rural elders and those suffering from dementia. Part III includes chapters on long-term care in various ethnic communities, including self-care practices, the problems of determining the line of demarcation between congregate housing and institutionalization, and many issues involved in providing ethnically sensitive long-term care. Part IV looks into institutions that are currently providing care and services in ethnically oriented settings. Chapters in this section deal with both historical and current issues in a variety of groups. Part V contains four chapters that will be of particular interest to practitioners as well as policymakers, since they describe models of ethnically sensitive long-term care that are being provided in various parts of the country. These are working programs that give practical insight into the issues involved in providing care in such settings. Part VI contains articles on planning, policy, and practice issues, including a review of existing government programs, private ventures, and public–private partnerships. Readers will find this section valuable for insights into the successes and failures of programs that have attempted to provide for the long-term care needs of ethnic elderly and the needed directions for programs.

Since this book is multidisciplinary in its focus, we expect that it will be of interest to professionals in research, practice, and policy-oriented disciplines who are concerned with ethnic elderly and long-term care. We leave the judgment of the success of our endeavor to you, the reader, and hope that this volume will not only provide answers but will give rise to questions that will stimulate further research and publication in this important area of gerontology.

Acknowledgments

No undertaking of this magnitude can be accomplished without the help, support, and encouragement of many people. We would like to recognize their contributions. We owe a debt of gratitude to Ursula Springer for believing in this project when others did not. The contributors to this volume provided more than their individual chapters. They gave advice, intellectual stimulation, and direction, which spurred us on and kept us on course. We are particularly grateful to James S. Jackson for taking time from his busy schedule to contribute a foreword.

Nancy Nieswander and Karen Rice provided meticulous and painstaking bibliographic tasks, which not only contributed to the accuracy of this volume, but also helped preserve our sanity by allowing us to attend to other matters. Of course, the editors take responsibility for any errors in this work. We would also like to thank R. Frank Falk, Head of the Department of Sociology of the University of Akron, for making resources available, especially secretarial typing, photocopying, and long-distance calls. Larry C. Mullins, Head of the Department of Gerontology of the University of South Florida, provided access to the BITNET computer communications network without which this project would not have been completed in this century.

Finally, we wish to acknowledge the support and encouragement of our spouses, Lenore Barresi and Sharon Stull. They have supported this project both overtly with suggestions and advice and covertly in ways too numerous to mention.

We sincerely hope that this volume not only will contribute to the knowledge and understanding of ethnic elderly and long-term care, but will in some way make the lives of all aged persons a little better.

PART I

Introduction

The introductory chapter by the editors sets the tone for the book as a whole. It states the nature of the growing concern about ethnicity and long-term care. We provide background information on the demographics of an aging society, including the differential growth in the sizes of ethnic elderly subgroups. This chapter presents current perspectives on ethnicity and long-term care and discusses how these are being viewed in this book. This chapter also serves as an anchor for the rest of the book by providing a central place for information on health status and service utilization by ethnic elderly. Two key points are illustrated in this chapter: (1) there is tremendous diversity between elderly of different ethnicities, and (2) there is great variation in what constitutes long-term care. Both of these require us to be careful about measurement of ethnicity and long-term care.

The second chapter, by Bastida and Gonzalez, is an important contribution to the literature on ethnicity and aging and ethnicity and long-term care. The authors have previously presented these ideas in public forums, but this is the first time they have appeared in print. Responding to the need for adequate physical health measurement to precede long-term care, Bastida and Gonzalez contend that it is imperative that such measurement take cultural variations into account. Their central thesis is that variations in response to self-assessment of general health questions are culturally conditioned. They use three data sets to compare responses and illustrate that there are cross-ethnic variations in responses to questions about perceived general health. They caution against the general use of health questions without consideration of cultural variations in ethnic elders' understanding of these questions and the way in which ethnic membership affects their responses.

Ethnicity and Long-Term Care: An Overview

Charles M. Barresi
Donald E. Stull

OVERVIEW

America, the "melting pot," is growing older. The Graying of America is a fact that more and more Americans are aware of. We are experiencing a changing labor force that includes more older workers. Family demographics are changing. Household size is declining. This is due partly to couples having fewer children, and partly to more single-person households, including households with an older, widowed person. However, there are more three- and four-generation families, an unprecedented experience.

Perhaps most disturbing of all changes are the increasing costs and needs for quality health and long-term care. For example, health care expenditures in 1986 were almost 11% of the GNP, and these costs have continued to rise (U.S. Health Care Financing Administration, 1987). Almost 40% of those costs were borne by the public through programs such as Medicare and Medicaid. Health care expenditures for those 65 and older increased 700% between 1970 and 1984. Realizing that tremendous growth will be experienced in the size of the age group 65 +, policymakers, planners, practitioners, and researchers are striving to understand what implications this growth has for providing and financing health and long-term care.

The significance of this Graying of America centers around two dimensions.

The first is that of the population as a whole. The 1990 census indicates that over 31 million persons (12.6%) in the United States are 65 years of age or older. This is up from about 26 million (11.3%) in 1980. This constitutes a 22.3% increase in the older population over the 10 years. More people are living longer. The Baby Boom generation is pushing toward the middle years and beyond. This fact of societal aging alone is a profound demographic occurrence that is having a significant impact on the larger society and for large numbers of individuals themselves.

The second dimension concerns the "melting pot." Among the general population, approximately 20% are ethnic minorities (U.S. Bureau of the Census, 1991a). This does not, however, include white ethnics, such as Irish, Italians, or Poles. In 1980, among those 65 and over, approximately 2.5 million, or 10%, were non-white (U.S. Bureau of the Census, 1991b). By 1990 this figure climbed to almost 3.4 million, or approximately 11%. By 2025 it is estimated that this proportion will increase to 15%. In fact, the minority elderly population has been growing at a faster rate than the white elderly population. Yet the rate of increase is not equal for all groups of ethnic elderly. For example, the proportion of Asian/Pacific Islander elderly has grown faster than in any other minority group. Similarly, among elderly Asian/Pacific Islanders, there are more men than women. This is in contrast to the white and other ethnic groups (U.S. Bureau of the Census, 1991b).

During the period from 1820 to 1986, over 53 million immigrants entered this country. If we combine this with the several million resident and newborn Native Americans during this period, we have a tremendous portion of our population that can be classified as "other than white." Each of these groups has different languages, customs, and health problems. Many of these groups are sufficiently different that it is not justifiable to group them into a single category for purposes of analyses, planning, and policymaking. To look at "white" and "non-white" means that many white ethnics (Jews, Slavs, Italians, Irish, Poles, and the like) will be compared with blacks, Hispanics, Asians, and Native Americans combined. As this book will demonstrate, these comparisons are inadequate, incorrect, and often detrimental to the groups being compared. They also prevent us from understanding the special experiences and needs of these groups.

A great deal of research has been conducted on the elderly and the need for long-term care. Among the issues addressed are: Who are the caregivers and how do they feel about caregiving? (Horowitz, 1985; Stone, Cafferata, & Sangl, 1987) What kinds of services are they using? (Coulton & Frost, 1982; Kovar, 1986; Krout, 1983; National Center for Health Statistics, 1987) How should long-term care be organized and financed in the near and distant future? (Eisdorfer, Kessler, & Spector, 1989; Kane & Kane, 1987; Rivlin & Wiener, 1988)

A considerable amount of work is also being carried out in the area of ethnicity and aging. Numerous books, chapters and journal articles have been published is this area (for example see, Gelfand, 1982; Gelfand & Barresi, 1987; Gelfand & Kutzik, 1979; Jackson, 1980, 1985; Manuel, 1982;Markides & Mindel, 1987; McNeely & Colen, 1983). Yet there is a need for more focused and specific research on the large and growing proportion of the ethnic population that is elderly. Each ethnic group is quite different in terms of language, culture, demographics, and behaviors. It is to the advantage of researchers, practitioners, and policymakers alike to know more about how ethnic group membership affects the long-term care issues stated above.

It is important, then, to focus on the ethnic component of long-term care. In terms of long-term care needs and use, what does it mean to be white or white ethnic versus black versus Hispanic versus Asian-American versus Native American? Even more specifically, in which ways do Hispanic, Asian, and white ethnic subgroups differ? What are the difficulties in planning and implementing long-term care programs for different ethnic groups?

This book will deal with the interplay of ethnicity and long-term care. It will focus on the different needs for long-term care, patterns of long-term care and use of formal services, and special problems in planning and implementing long-term care for ethnic elderly. However, before the interface between ethnicity and long-term care can be examined, we must first clarify the issues surrounding such a relationship. Our conclusions about ethnicity and long-term care are especially dependent on how we define and measure ethnicity and long-term care.

DEFINING ETHNICITY

What is ethnicity? Which characteristics are critical in determining ethnicity? Who should be included in the study of any given ethnic group? These are important questions that raise crucial issues in the study of ethnicity and long-term care. Sound, basic definitions of both of these terms are necessary in order to carry out adequate research. The definitions one uses in research are important because of the influence they have on the direction and design, as well as the overall results.

An example of these points can be found in the effects of various definitions of ethnicity on family support studies. Rosenthal (1986) points out that some researchers approach ethnic family studies from the viewpoint of immigrant culture and models of differential assimilation of successive generations. She further notes that the results of such studies differ from those that see ethnicity as characterized by social inequality or synonymous with traditional ways. Given the variation in possible definitions and the assumptions on which they are based, it is necessary to establish working definitions of both ethnicity and long-term care as these terms will be used in this book. The issue of the definition and scope of ethnicity has been given extensive treatment in another work by the senior author (Barresi, 1990). The main arguments are summarized here. Several of the leading authors in the field rely on the classic definition of ethnicity offered by Gordon (1964), who defines an ethnic group as any group of individuals with a shared sense of peoplehood based on race, religion, or national origin (Gelfand & Barresi 1987; Gelfand & Kutzik, 1979; Markides & Mindel, 1987). Although this definition includes groups that would not generally be regarded as ethnic groups if one limited this label strictly to persons of similar national origin, it tends to be too inclusive. The breadth of this definition tends to overlook the heterogeneity found in most national groups and even in most large religious denominations. Accordingly, it does not fit the purposes of most researchers in ethnogerontology. As a matter of fact, the assumption of homogeneity in ethnic groups is one of the major errors committed by persons writing in this area.

The differential distribution of the characteristics that make up socioeconomic class differences tend to produce great variety within ethnic groups in lifestyle and other important life chances. One cannot speak of what all Jews or Catholics, for example, will do or chose to believe. The gamut of conservativism and liberalism will reflect many differences within these groups. Likewise political and regional differences in countries of origin create many dissimilarities in transplanted national groups. Greek-Americans from the mainland look down on those from the "islands." Germany, Italy, Ireland, and other countries have similar geographic differences that create heterogeneity in their migrants.

The converse of the approach that is too broad is, of course, one that is too narrow. Holzberg (1982) suggests that many researchers confuse ethnic identity with minority status. This lack of distinction focuses attention more on the effects of social discrimination and less on cultural distinctiveness, as mentioned above. Manuel (1982) provides a classic example of the confusion surrounding this issue when he incorporates race under what he considers as the wider term of ethnicity. He then goes on to discuss majority and minority groups and the relations between them and concludes that minority status is characteristic of most ethnic groups. This interweaving of the distinctive aspects of ethnic groups with minority status only contributes further to the difficulty in clarifying the definition of ethnicity and its salient characteristics.

The emphasis on racial and minority characteristics also tends to hide the fact that there are many ethnics who are "lost in the cracks" because they are identified as white. This ignoring of ethnic identity tends to treat elderly Poles, Italians, Hungarians, and other white ethnics, many of whom are minimally assimilated into the wider culture, as part of the majority. In fact, many of the generalizations that compare blacks, Hispanics, and other minority elderly with whites are making invidious comparisons. These white ethnics are in many instances as much a part of the minority as those with whom they are being compared. Interest in white ethnics has broadened in recent years as these populations have aged and many native-born Americans have moved in the direction of greater identification with their roots (Hayes, Kalish, & Guttmann 1986; Sokolovsky, 1985).

A further concern in the definition of ethnicity is the notion of a social psychological identification with the group and a commitment on the part of the individual member to the group. Group identification and a willingness to share in the fortunes of the group are central characteristics of the ethnic experience and should be incorporated into any definition. Ethnic identity is more than skin color, common national origin, or religious affiliation. It is the self-identification of the person with the group and a willingness to embrace its rules, its customs, and beliefs, or what Disman (1987) calls the experience of ethnic identity.

Therefore, for the purposes of this book, ethnicity is defined as: a large group whose members internalize and share a heritage of, and a commitment to, unique social characteristics, cultural symbols, and behavior patterns that are not fully understood or shared by outsiders. While this definition leans in the preferable direction of the broad approach of cultural distinctivness, it emphasizes individual identification with and commitment to the socially shared aspects of ethnic group membership. It goes beyond nominal identification with the group and stresses the existence of a common bond between group members.

DEFINING LONG-TERM CARE

As with ethnicity, defining long-term care is not easy. Historically, long-term care, particlularly federal and state policies, was centered around nursing homes. Even today, many people equate long-term care with nursing homes. However, long-term care is quite diverse, spanning a wide variety of health, social, and personal care services, provided by formal and informal means, and paid for by many sources. Of course, families provide the bulk of long-term care, perhaps as much as 80–90% (Doty, 1986; Horowitz, 1985; Stone, Cafferata, & Sangl, 1987).

The diversity inherent in long-term care makes it difficult to develop a concise, theoretically and operationally meaningful definition of long-term care. As Kane and Kane (1987) point out, long-term care is a hybrid of health and social services. This can include, but is not limited to, physician visits, hospital stays, nursing home stays, in-home respite care, and adult day care, among other services. More generally, long-term care can be provided formally or informally, or through both means. Oftentimes, families provide care for a relative who resides in the community while using formal services (paid or volunteer) for some aspects of the caregiving. In addition, there are services that are not directly or specifically long-term care services, yet are part of the allocation of such services, such as information and referral services, or senior centers, or nursing home ombudsman programs. Similarly, some types of care are not necessarily long-term care. For example, it is not clear whether a physician visit for a long-term care patient should be considered primary care or long-term care. Additionally, we could question whether senior centers, which may provide long-term care services such as adult day care, should be considered long-term care services. In terms of long-term care needs, some might argue that income, housing, and health care needs for functionally impaired elders should be considered long-term care needs. The extent to which long-term care should be considered a separate or distinctive set of services is unclear. Thus, long-term care can, and has been, conceptualized in terms of the type of service used or provided, the characteristics of the client (e.g., disability), and the context of service provision or care (i.e., in the home, at a physician's office, in another formal setting), or some combination of these.

Several authors have provided definitions of long-term care. For example, "Long term care encompasses a spectrum of medical, personal, and social services to aged and disabled individuals because of diminished capacity for self-care" (Rabin & Stockton, 1987, p. v). Or, "Long-term care is the help needed to cope, and sometimes to survive, when physical or mental disabilities impair the capacity to perform the basic activities of everyday life, such as eating, toileting, bathing, dressing, and moving about" (Rivlin & Wiener, 1988, p. 3). Still others have defined long-term care as "a set of health, personal care, and social services delivered over a sustained period of time to persons who have lost or never acquired some degree of functional capacity . . . Long-term care is thus a hybrid—part health and part social service" (Kane and Kane, 1987, p. 4–5).

Whereas these are definitions provided by scholars and researchers, there are providers of long-term care services, particularly those providing nursing home care, who feel that long-term care is something provided only in a nursing home setting. This suggests that some definitions of long-term care may be quite narrow and a function of special interest. At the other end of the spectrum, families may be providing long-term care according to the definitions mentioned above, but they may not define it as "long-term care." In the case of spouses, they may view this in a more developmental sense. That is, they may see this care-providing as a natural extension of their earlier roles.

ISSUES IN LONG-TERM CARE

Kane and Kane (1987) point out that long-term care presents problems of access, cost, and quality. In order to benefit elders, and in many cases caregivers and their families, long-term care must be accessible. This includes informal care provided by family and friends. In the case of formal long-term care services, which can benefit elders, and in some cases caregivers, it is not enough to be affordable. If those in need do not have access to services, the affordability issue becomes largely irrelevant. Access to long-term care is a key issue. The whole long-term care "system" is often viewed as fragmented and uncoordinated. Individuals are often uncertain about services available to them and how or whether they can pay for them. Many long-term care providers, and even information and referral services, may be unaware of other providers in the "system." Recent research has found that lower accessibility of formal long-term care services increases the risk of nursing home placement of elder care recipients (Stull, Bowman, Cosbey, McNutt, & Drum, 1990).

Quality of long-term care encompasses a wide range of issues and is not limited to assessment of the quality of services, or quality assurance. For example, a concern about the appropriateness of particular long-term care services is relevant. Do the services fit the needs of the elder, and possibly the family? In determining the quality of services, who should be the judge of whether services are providing quality care? Similarly, what criteria should be used to determine "quality care"? Since the bulk of attention has been paid to nursing home care, quality assurance has generally focused on structural aspects of facilities or programs, as well as credentials of providers. Another reasonable approach is to focus on a construct commonly used by gerontologists studying older adults in the community: well-being or quality of life (George & Gwyther, 1986).

Cost issues of long-term care represent, in many ways, a Pandora's box. These issues often center around the concern of how we are going to finance long-term care (this usually means nursing home care) with a rapidly expanding elderly population and dwindling financial resources. One way researchers have tried to address this concern is by studying family caregiving for elderly relatives. The presumption has been that the right combination of formal respite services and family involvement in the care provision will reduce the likelihood of nursing home placement. At the very least it should reduce the length of time of institutionalization, reducing the cost to families and society. However, recent research (e.g., Lawton, Brody, & Saperstein, 1989) and commentary (e.g., Callahan, 1989) indicate that it may not be appropriate to view family supports as a means of reducing long-term care costs. Respite care and other family supports may not reduce the likelihood of nursing home placement or significantly reduce the number of days in a nursing home (and thus reduce costs). Rather, they may be beneficial by maintaining or improving the quality of life (well-being) of the elder and the family.

This raises another important issue regarding long-term care. Long-term care is primarily a family issue. The bulk of care, including medically related care, for older persons is provided by family members. It is important to keep in mind families and family contexts when developing long-term care policies and programs. The intervention may be directed at the elder, but the elder's family may be affected significantly by the intervention. Family policy—and we could consider many long-term care policies as part of this—generally view the individual as the point of intervention (Moen & Schorr, 1987). It may be more appropriate to take a larger view for purposes of long-term care policies. Thus, a policy may affect the costs borne by the family and not just the elder.

There are hidden costs that are likely to increase over the next few decades. Research continually shows that women are the primary care providers for elderly relatives (Horowitz, 1985; Stone et al., 1987). As more women enter the labor force and face competing demands of work and caregiving, this may lead to more sick days taken and reduced productivity for companies. One study found that more than one-third of employed caregivers indicated a change in work status since becoming a caregiver (American Association of Retired Persons and the Travelers Foundation, 1988). Most of these either arrived late for work or were unable to come to work as a consequence of caregiving. This translates into millions of dollars lost each year because of conflicts between elder care and employment. Some of this money is lost income and lost benefits for families at a time when they have costs associated with caring for the elder. Some of this lost revenue results from lower productivity and consequently lower profits for companies. Moreover, tax revenues, one source of financing long-term care, are reduced because of lower incomes and production.

There is a need to provide elderly with detailed information regarding what Medicare does and does not cover. The vast majority of people do not have a good understanding of Medicare coverage, and for good reason. The reimbursement process is very complex and has become increasingly confusing. A recent survey of seniors in Cleveland, Ohio, found that 90% of these seniors did not have a reasonable understanding of Medicare coverage, especially with regard to long-term care coverage (Stull, 1987; also see Stull in this volume). Nearly one in seven believe that Medicare covers long-term care in a nursing home. Such misperceptions could cost elderly, their families, and society a tremendous amount of money, as well as unnecessarily high emotional costs.

Each of these issues—access, quality, and cost—is particularly relevant to our understanding of ethnicity and long-term care. For example, we know that minority elderly tend to have lower incomes than white elderly. They are also less likely than white elderly to use services. Blacks and other minority groups are generally underrepresented in nursing homes. Is the shortage of money among minority elderly a major cause of lower utilization rates? To what extent are lower utilization rates a function of wider informal networks to provide care? To what extent do language and cultural practices raise barriers to the access of such services? We could turn this last concern around and ask, to what extent do cultural practices reduce the reliance on formal providers? Although the tendency might be to view ethnicity as a barrier to long-term care services, it is not clear that this is always the case. With the increasing emphasis on volunteerism and talk of encouraging families to care for their relatives (despite overwhelming evidence that families are already providing tremendous amounts of care to older relatives), it is important to assess the role ethnicity plays in reducing long-term care service use.

A caution should be raised here. There is a conventional wisdom that ethnic families take care of their own. However, this view has been challenged by some (e.g., Cuellar & Weeks, 1980). These authors feel that this care-providing is not universal among ethnic families and that the conventional view is used by the establishment to avoid providing needed services for elderly minorities.

DEMOGRAPHICS OF ETHNIC GROUPS AND ETHNIC ELDERLY

Ethnicity in the United States

A survey of over two hundred thousand persons conducted by the U. S. Bureau of the Census in 1982 indicated that 83% of the sample reported at least one ancestry. Eleven percent did not report any ancestry and only 6% identified themselves as "American" or "United States." Clearly, we are a people who identify with an ethnic ancestry of one sort or another.

While respondents could name more than one ancestry, more than half limited their selection to only one. The most frequently reported of these were German, Afro-American or African, English, Irish, Spanish, Italian, and Mexican in that order. Other frequently reported ancestry groups, including both single and multiple choices were: Scottish, French, Native American, Polish, and Dutch (U. S. Bureau of the Census, 1982). The extent to which this self-identification is translated into ethnic social and cultural behavior is unknown, however, the potential is unquestionable.

Early figures from the 1990 census indicate that the resident population of the United States has experienced an increase in ethnic groups through the decade of the '80s. Most of this gain has come from the number of Hispanic and Asian immigrants, especially in the later half of the decade. The white population has gone from 83.1% of the resident population in 1980 to 80.3 in 1990. The respective figures for other groups are: blacks 11.7 percent to 12.1%, Hispanics 6.4% to 9.0%, Asian 1.5% to 2.9%, and native American 0.6% to 0.8% (U. S. Bureau of the Census, 1983, 1991a).

Ethnic Elderly

The study of ancestry cited above also listed the percentage of elderly persons in each ethnic group. The largest is in the English group (18%) followed by Irish (16%), Italian (16%), and German (15%) (U. S. Bureau of the Census, 1982). Figures taken from the 1980 census reveal that among self-reported white ethnics, the median age for English, French, German, and Irish varied slightly from 37.2 to 39.6 years of age. For those who identified as Italians and Polish, however, the median ages were 41.9 and 47.2 respectively. It is interesting to observe that those groups that migrated to this country in the earlier waves of migration are now "younger" in terms of generational aging. This is probably the result of the greater number of generations that have been born to these groups since their entry into the country (U. S. Bureau of the Census, 1983).

The same census report also contains figures on the number of each of these white ethnic groups, 65 years of age or older, that are in a home for the aged. Again there is a noticeable difference between the first four groups and the latter two. The English, French, German, and Irish range from 7.1% to 7.9% while 5.2% of the Polish elderly, and only 3.5% of the Italians are found in nursing homes. These figures point out again the need to exercise care when referring to white elderly as a single group. The variations among ethnic groups that are generally considered in aggregate satistics as white can sometimes be great.

Minority Elderly

Some ethnic groups are regarded as social and cultural minorities, and aged members are typically dealt with in the literature as minority elderly. At present the bulk of studies conducted on ethnic elderly have centered on these groups. Most prominent among these is the Afro-American or black elderly.[1] The second most studied group of ethnic elderly is the Spanish speaking or Hispanics. Of the 31 million elderly (persons 65 years and older) in the United States, 89% are classified as white (although as noted above this includes a number of white ethnic groups). Eight percent are black, .4% are American Indian, Eskimo, and Aleuts (AIEA), 1.5% are Asian/Pacific Islander (API), and 1% are classified as Other Race (includes API not listed separately, e.g. Cambodian, Laotian, Pakistani). Four percent are of Hispanic origin, and may be of any race (U. S. Bureau of the Census, 1991b).

Excluding whites, the elderly population in the other ethnic groups named above totals almost 3.4 million persons (Table 1.1). They make up 11% of the elderly population in the United States. This proportion has been steadily growing and currently the aged segment of ethnic groups has been growing at a faster rate than the elderly white population. This rapid growth among ethnic elderly is projected to continue well into the next century.

As can be seen in Table 1.1, the proportion of the total population of the United States that is 65 years of age or older in 1990 was 12.6%. This figure is up from 11.3% in 1980 and constitutes a 22.3% increase over the 10-year period. Whites and blacks both experienced an increase in the proportion of elderly, but in both groups the amount of change was less than that of the total population. Conversely, API elderly increased at a rate that was more than six times the norm, and the Hispanics and AIEA groups grew at a rate of triple and double the overall rate, respectively.

It is interesting to note that while the percentage of each group did not increase a great deal, the number of elderly in these groups did, hence the large percentage in-

TABLE 1.1 Number and percentage of persons 65 years and older by race and Hispanic origin, and increase, 1980 and 1990. (numbers in thousands)

		1990			1980		
	All Ages	65+	Percentage 65+	All Ages	65+	Percentage 65+	Percentage Increase 65+
Total	248,710	31,242	12.6	226,546	25,549	11.3	22.3
White	199,686	27,852	13.9	188,372	22,948	12.2	21.4
Black	29,986	2,509	08.4	26,495	2,087	07.0	20.2
AIEA[a]	1,959	114	05.8	1,420	75	05.3	52.0
ASIAN[b]	7,274	454	06.2	3,501	212	06.1	114.2
Other	9,805	312	03.2	6,758	301	04.5	NC[c]
Hispanic[d]	22,354	1,161	05.2	14,609	709	04.9	63.8

Sources: U.S. Bureau of Census. (1983). *1980 Census of population, general population characteristics, United States summary*, Vol. 1, PC 80-1-B1. Washington, DC: U. S. Government Printing Office; U. S. Bureau of the Census. (1991). Selected tables provided by the Age and Sex Statistics Branch of the Population Division. Washington, DC: U. S. Department of Commerce.

[a]American Indian, Eskimo, and Aleut.
[b]Asian and Pacific Islander.
[c]The "other" category is not comparable because different racial groups are included in 1980 and 1990.
[d]Persons of Hispanic origin may be of any race.

crease noted above. These figures reflect two trends in population growth and composition over the past decade. One is the aging of the general population and the other is the increased immigration of Hispanic and Asian persons. While these migrants are generally younger persons, many have either brought or sent for elderly parents and other relatives. This is especially true in the case of migrants who have come from countries where they have experienced political oppresion.

Average Life Expectancy

While any number of demographic statistics can be compared between whites and other racial groups, none is more revealing of basic social differences than average life expectancy. Average life expectancy for the various ethnic groups can be ranked in order from highest to lowest. Asians have the longest life expectancy of all the ethnic groups being considered here. Next are whites, followed by Hispanics, blacks, and Native Americans (U. S. Department of Health and Human Services, 1985).

The differences between average life expectancy of whites and blacks is called racial mortality crossover. Crossover effect, as it is often referred to, is the phenomenon that is observed in comparing average years of life remaining for the two groups. At all ages up to approximately 65, whites have a longer life expectancy. At that point the figures become about even, and at around age 75 blacks are observed to have a longer life expectancy (Jackson, 1985). This is explained mainly by the higher infant mortality among blacks and the superior medical treatment and nutrition enjoyed by whites. The net effect is that more whites who would have died at earlier ages survive to become "young old." However, the survivor effect culls out those persons who are more hardy and likely to endure. Hence, at the older ages, blacks are more resistant to mortality causes, and display longer life expectancy than their white counterparts.

The implications of the varied life expectancies among these ethnic groups for long-term care needs is obvious. This is particularly true for black elderly who have survived beyond 75 years of age, and for Asians with their longer life expectancy. We expect that these groups will require a greater share of long-term care facilities, if not their own exclusive facilities in the future. This point is made by a number of contributors to this volume.

Sex Ratio

The sex ratio is a measure of the number of males for every one hundred females. The sex ratio for the total United States population has been steadily decreasing since the turn of the century. This occurrence is attributed to early migration waves consisting of more men and the higher mortality among males at all ages. This trend has also held true for ethnic groups in the population. Table 1.2 shows that in 1990 the generalization of more females than males holds for the major racial and ethnic groups that were measured at all ages.

In comparing the sex ratio for all races and Hispanic origin, 65 years of age and older, between 1980 and 1990 we find that whites have had minimal change (remaining around 67 males per 100 females) while API have shown the greatest variance, from 96 to 82. Blacks have experienced a 5-point drop (68 to 63), as have Hispanics (76 to 71). The AIEA group has gone from 79 to 72 males per 100 females. These sex ratios are even smaller in the very old of these groups—those 85 year of age and older—as indicated by the numbers of males and females in this age category, as shown in Table 1.2.

When taken as a whole, more elderly men are married and more women are widowed. However, when one looks at the breakdown of these figures by ethnic group, we see that elderly blacks and AIEA have more widows of both sexes than do whites. In comparison, Hispanic groups have more widowers and fewer widows than whites, while the figures for API are reversed.

Whites have approximately 6% of males and females 65 or over who are divorced or separated, while each of the other ethnic groups mentioned above have almost double that amount for both sexes. Whites, blacks, and Hispanics have about 6% never-married among both men and women. AIEA and API men display about the same rate, while never-married women in these two groups amount to only about 3% (Barresi & Hunt, 1990).

These few examples of the differences to be found in the demographic statis-

TABLE 1.2 Persons 55 Years and Over, by Age, Sex, Race, and Hispanic Origin

Age, sex, and race/Hispanic origin	55+ years	60+ Years	65+ Years	85+ Years
Total	52,389,754	41,857,998	31,241,831	3,080,165
Male	22,546,590	17,512,220	12,565,173	857,698
Female	29,843,164	24,345,778	18,676,658	2,222,467
White	46,031,512	37,063,096	27,851,973	2,788,052
Male	19,880,504	15,549,693	11,214,909	764,450
Female	25,151,008	21,513,403	16,637,064	2,023,602
Black	4,502,919	3,470,170	2,508,551	230,183
Male	1,836,596	1,379,677	965,432	68,592
Female	2,666,323	2,090,493	1,543,119	161,591
Amer. Indian, Eskimo, & Aleut (AIEA)	227,661	165,842	114,453	9,205
Male	101,635	72,281	48,089	3,274
Female	126,026	93,561	66,364	5,931
Asian & Pacific Islander (API)	923,608	672,975	454,458	29,738
Male	412,095	298,586	204,447	12,399
Female	511,513	374,389	250,011	17,339
Other Race	704,054	485,915	312,396	22,987
Male	315,760	211,983	132,296	8,983
Female	388,294	273,932	180,100	14,004
Hispanic (any race)	2,354,233	1,714,925	1,161,283	95,564
Male	1,038,736	736,365	481,409	33,497
Female	1,315,497	978,560	679,874	61,067

Source: U.S. Bureau of the Census. (1991). Age and Sex Statistics Branch of Population Division. Washington, DC: U. S. Department of Commerce.

tics of ethnic elderly should convince the reader of the usefulness of such figures in identifying and understanding ethnic diversity. The implications for long-term care are many. A society that continues to move in the direction of having more older women than men is one that is in greater need of long-term care. Although living longer, women have more chronic illness, are sicker longer, and are thus in greater need of home care and long-term care. Moreover, women are much more likely to *provide* care to family and friends. These are especially important points when estimating long-term care needs and planning future facilities to serve the growing population of elderly ethnics.

HEALTH STATUS OF ETHNIC ELDERLY

In general, we know very little about the health status of a number of groups of ethnic elderly. Most reports from government agencies compare "white" and "non-white," or "white," "black," and "other." Small area studies focusing on specific ethnic groups, or studies of a more clinical nature, provide some insight into the health status of some of the larger ethnic groups. For other ethnic groups, such as white ethnics or Hispanic subgroups, we know very little.

Comparisons among these groups is somewhat problematic. Studies may focus only on one or two ethnic groups (e.g., white and black, or Hispanic and white), which makes comparing other ethnic groups difficult or impossible. In this section we will look briefly at the health status of the larger ethnic groups. Comparisons between these groups are made when possible.

Blacks

Blacks appear to have poorer health than whites, based on functional health indicators, and according to mortality rates (Greene & Sielger, 1984; Markides & Mindel, 1987). There is some evidence that blacks also have poorer health and greater limitations than Hispanic elderly (Markides & Mindel, 1987). Another study found that black elderly spent more days in the hospital and had more visits to the doctor than either whites or Hispanics (Stull, 1987). However, using several self-rated health and functional health indicators among white, black, and Hispanic elderly, this same study found that Hispanic elderly had more health problems and more severe health problems than either the white or black elderly. Blacks experience higher mortality rates than whites, particularly as a result of circulatory diseases, and average life expectancy is about six years less for blacks than for whites.

Hispanics

Information on health and functional status of Hispanic elderly is limited (Becerra & Shaw, 1984; Lacayo, 1984). What information is available provides some generally mixed findings. For example, Hispanics generally have poorer health, both self-rated and on functional indicators than whites (Becerra & Shaw, 1984; Lacayo, 1984; Markides & Mindel, 1987; Stull, 1987). However, as noted above, when comparing Hispanics and blacks, and such studies are limited in number, reported findings have been less consistent. Information from the National Health Interview Survey (National Center for Health Statistics, 1984) indicates that Hispanics are generally better off than blacks, but are similar to whites on a number of health indicators. Another study, however, found that Hispanics had poorer health (overall, self-reported, and functional health) then either blacks or whites, and blacks had poorer health than whites (Stull, 1987). Caution should be stressed regarding the findings of the latter study, due to the somewhat small sample of Hispanic elderly.

Asians

Available information on the health of Asian elderly is virtually nonexistent, though some research has been conducted on service utilization. What little information there is indicates that they are in somewhat poorer health than the general population. For example, Carp and Kataoka (1976) reported that nearly two-thirds of Chinese-American elderly living in San Francisco's Chinatown said they had fair or poor health compared with about one-third of white elderly. The Chinese elderly were also more likely to report that health limits their activities.

A critical factor in the health of Asian elderly appears to be language and cultural differences. Reliance on folk medicine as a consequence of both cultural experiences and lack of English language proficiency may lead to poorer health and hasten the health decline. In addition, there appears to be a sense of shame, especially among Japanese-American elderly, about using formal services. This seems to represent a sign of dependency and inability to care for themselves (Kii, 1984).

Native Americans

As with some of the other ethnic groups, information on the health status of Native American elderly is limited. Despite this limitation, it is clear that Native American elderly have poorer health, higher mortality, and shorter life expectancy than white elderly (National Indian Council on Aging, 1984). Several factors seem to contribute to their poorer health. For example, living conditions (such as housing) tend to be worse than those of their white counterparts. Diabetes and related complications exist to a greater extent in the Native American population, especially among elderly, than in the general population. An additional factor is the generally greater isolation of Native American communities. This isolation, coupled with a reliance on folk medicine, precludes regular visits to health care facilities.

Implications for Long-Term Care

Many of the contributors to this volume will provide current information on the health status of several of these ethnic groups, including white ethnics. The differential health status of these groups, and their respective "causes," has important implications for long-term care planning and programs. For example, physical or cultural isolation may preclude some groups from having access to or seeking primary care, thus putting them at greater risk for acute care involving serious illnesses. Additionally, they may be at greater risk for needing long-term care because of chronic conditions or when acute conditions left untreated deteriorate into chronic conditions. If, however, such long-term care is not available, or is not sensitive to the special needs or circumstances of these ethnic elderly, the elderly may not use the services. Consequently, mortality rates may not be improved, and in some cases as these elderly populations increase, we may see higher rates of mortality and no increase in life expectancy.

ETHNICITY AND LONG-TERM CARE UTILIZATION

Black, Hispanic, Asian, and Native American elderly tend to have lower incomes than white elderly. They are also less likely than white elderly to use services. Blacks and other minority groups are generally underrepresented in nursing homes. An important question is, Why do ethnic elderly use health, social, and long-term care services less than white elderly? We have alluded to some of the possible causes earlier. Such things as cultural isolation, including language barriers; physical isolation, such as long distances needed to travel to get to health care facilities; and the general lack of services available that are specifically oriented toward and operated by members of respective ethnic groups.

There is additional speculation that for some groups (e.g., blacks and some Asians), the family represents a kind of first and last line of defense for their elders. That is, strong kin ties and informal care mean that many ethnic elderly do not need formal care. However, the evidence for this hypothesis is not conclusive. It is believed that among Asian-Americans there are strong family ties and concern about "caring for one's own." This reduces the need for formal services. The problem with such a conclusion is that it is the result of looking at low utilization rates and concluding that families are caring for their elderly, a conclusion usually drawn by non-Asian-Americans (Kii, 1984). Such a conclusion will obviously lead to a lower concern about developing and implementing services for Asian-American elderly.

Conclusion

It should be clear from the discussion above that concern about the ethnic dimension of long-term care is an important one. With the elderly, especially ethnic elderly, being the fastest growing age group, it is important to understand the long-term care needs of these different ethnic groups. Planning, designing, implementing, and financing long-term care programs and services will have to take into account the varied histories, cultures, circumstances, and needs of each of these groups.

REFERENCES

American Association of Retired Persons and the Travelers Foundation. (1988). *A National Survey of Caregivers: Final Report.* Washington, DC: A.A.R.P.

Barresi, C. M. (1990). Ethnogerontology: Social aging in national, racial, and cultural groups. In K. F. Ferraro (Ed.). *Gerontology: Perspectives and issues.* New York: Springer Publishing Co.

Barresi, C. M., & Hunt, K. (1990). The unmarried elderly: Age, sex, and ethnicity. In T. H. Brubaker Ed.), *Family relationships in later life.* Beverly Hills, CA: Sage.

Becerra, R. M., & Shaw, D. (1984). *The Hispanic elderly: A reference guide.* New York: University Press of America.

Callahan, J. J. (1989). Play it again Sam—There is no impact. *The Gerontologist, 29,* 5-6.

Carp, F. M., & Kataoka, E. (1976). Health care problems of the elderly in San Francisco's Chinatown. *The Gerontologist, 16,* 30-38.

Coulton, C., & Frost, A. K. (1982). Use of social and health services by the elderly. *Journal of Health and Social Behavior, 23,* 330-339.

Cuellar, J. B., & Weeks, T. (1980). *Minority elderly Americans: The assessment of needs and equitable receipt of public benefits as a prototype for Area Agencies on Aging final report.* San Diego, CA: Allied Home Health Association.

Disman, M. (1987). Explorations in ethnic identity, oldness, and contnuity. In D. E. Gelfand & C. M. Barresi (Eds.), *Ethnic dimensions of aging.* New York: Springer Publishing Co.

Doty, P. (1986). Family care of the elderly: The role of public policy. *Millbank Memorial Fund Quarterly, 64,* 34-75.

Eisdorfer, C., Kessler, D. A., & Spector, A. N. (1989). *Caring for the elderly: Reshaping health policy.* Baltimore: Johns Hopkins University Press.

Gelfand, D. E. (1982). *Aging: The ethnic factor.* Boston: Little, Brown & Co.

Gelfand, D. E., & Barresi, C. M. (1987). Current perspectives in ethnicity and aging. In D. E. Gelfand & C. M. Barresi (Eds.), *Ethnic dimensions of aging.* New York: Springer Publishing Co.

Gelfand, D. E., & Kutzik, A. (1979). *Ethnicity and aging: Theory, research, and policy.* New York, Springer Publishing Co.

George, L. K., & Gwyther, L. P. (1986). Caregiver well-being: A multidimensional examination of family caregivers of demented adults. *The Gerontologist, 26,* 253-259.

Gordon, M. M. (1964). *Assimilation in American life.* New York: Oxford University Press.

Greene, R. L., & Sielger, I. C. (1984). Blacks. In E. B. Palmore Ed.), *Handbook of the aged in the United States.* Westport, CT: Greenwood.

Hayes, C. L., Kalish, R. A., & Guttmann, D. (Eds.). (1986). *European-American elderly.* New York: Springer Publishing Co.

Holzberg, C. S. (1982). Ethnicity and aging: Anthropological perspectives on more than just the minority elderly. *The Gerontologist, 22,* 249-257.

Horowitz, A. (1985). Family caregiving to the frail elderly. In C. Eisdorfer Ed.), *Annual review of gerontology and geriatrics* (Vol. 5). New York: Springer Publishing Co.

Jackson, J. J. (1980). *Minorities and aging.* Belmont, CA: Wadsworth.

Jackson, J. J. (1985). Race, national origin, ethnicity and aging. In R. Binstock & E. Shanas (Eds.), *Handbook of aging and the social sciences* (2nd ed.). New York: Van Nostrand Reinhold.

Kane, R. A., & Kane, R. L. (1987). *Long-term care: Principles, programs, and policies.* New York: Springer Publishing Co.

Kii, T. (1984). Asians. In E. B. Palmore Ed.), *Handbook of the aged in the United States.* Westport, CT: Greenwood.

Kovar, M. G. (1986). Expenditures for the medical care of elderly people living in the community in 1980. *The Millbank Quarterly, 64,* 100-132.

Krout, J. A. (1983). Correlates of senior center utilization. *Research on Aging, 5,* 339–352.

Lacayo, C. G. (1984). Hispanics. In E. B. Palmore Ed.), *Handbook of the aged in the United States.* Westport, CT: Greenwood.

Lawton, M. P., Brody, E. M., & Saperstein, A. R. (1989). A controlled study of respite service for caregivers of Alzheimer's patients. *The Gerontologist, 29,* 8–16.

Manuel, R. C. Ed.). (1982). *Minority aging: Sociological and social psychological issues.* Westport, CT: Greenwood Press.

Markides, K. S., & Mindel, C. H. (1987). *Aging and ethnicity.* Newbury Park: Sage.

McNeely, R., & Colen, J. (1983). *Aging in minority groups.* Beverly Hills, CA: Sage.

Moen, P., & Schorr, A. L. (1987). Families and social policy. In M.B. Sussman & S. K. Steinmetz (Eds.), *Handbook of marriage and the family.* New York: Plenum Press.

National Center for Health Statistics, R. Stone. (1987). Aging in the eighties, age 65 and over—Use of community services, preliminary data from the Supplement on Aging to the National Health Interview Survey: United States, January–June, 1984. *Advance Data from Vital and Health Statistics.* No. 133. Hyattsville, MD: Public Health Service.

National Center for Health Statistics. (1984). *Health indicators for Hispanic, black and white Americans.* Vital and Health Statistics, Series 10, No. 148. Washington, DC: Government Printing Office.

National Indian Council on Aging. (1984). Indian and Alaska Natives. In E. B. Palmore Ed.), *Handbook of the aged in the United States.* Westport, CT: Greenwood.

Rabin, D. L., & Stockton, P. (1987). *Long-term care for the elderly: A factbook.* New York: Oxford University Press.

Rivlin, A. M., & Wiener, J. M. (1988). *Caring for the disabled elderly: Who will pay?* Washington, DC: The Brookings Institution.

Rosenthal, C. J. (1986). Family supports in later life: Does ethnicity make a difference? *The Gerontologist, 26,* 19–24.

Sokolovsky, J. (1985). Ethnicity, culture, and aging: Do differences really make a difference? *Journal of Applied Gerontology, 4,* 6–17.

Stone, R., Cafferata, G. L., & Sangl, J. (1987). Caregivers of the frail elderly: A national profile. *The Gerontologist, 27,* 616–626.

Stull, D. E. (1987). *Long-term care service use among elderly in Greater Cleveland: Methods of payment, knowledge of Medicare, and interest in Social/HMOs.* Final report to the Federation for Community Planning, Cleveland, Ohio and the Fellowship Program in Applied Gerontology of the Gerontological Society of America.

Stull, D. E., Bowman, K., Cosbey, J., McNutt, W., & Drum, M. (1990). A family perspective of the institutionalization of frail elderly. Paper presented at the 43rd annual meeting of the Gerontological Society of America, Boston.

U. S. Bureau of the Census. (1982). *Ancestry and language in the United States: November 1979.* Current Population Reports, Series P-23, No. 116. Washington, DC: U. S. Government Printing Office.

U. S. Bureau of the Census. (1983). *1980 Census of population, general population characteristics, United States summary.* Vol. 1, PC 80-1-B1. Washington, DC: U. S. Government Printing Office.

U. S. Bureau of the Census. (1991a). *United States Department of Commerce News, Press Release CB91-216*. Washington, DC: Public Information Office.

U. S. Bureau of the Census. (1991b). Selected population tables provided by the Age and Sex Statistics Branch of the Population Division. Washington, DC: U. S. Department of Commerce.

U. S. Department of Health and Human Services. (1985). *Report of the Secretary's Task Force on Black and Minority Health, Vol I: Executive Summary*. Washington, DC: U. S. Government Printing Office.

U. S. Health Care Financing Administration. (1986). *Health Care Financing Review*, Summer. Washington, DC: U. S. Printing Office.

ENDNOTE

1. Some persons are beginning to use the term Afro-American to emphasize the ethnic and cultural roots of black Americans. It appears, however, that the majority of black scholars, including contributors to this volume, continue to use the term "black." To keep with current convention, we will use the term "black" throughout this volume.

2

Ethnic Variations in Measurement of Physical Health Status: Implications for Long-Term Care

Elena Bastida*
Genaro Gonzalez

Kane and Kane note, "measurement is essential to good geriatric care. . . . Any strategy for altering the health status of the elderly requires a technology for first assessing that health status and then detecting increments of progress" (1981, p. 1). Given their recommendations, it is surprising that issues of ethnicity and measurement across diverse aging populations are seldom investigated in long-term care assessment. This chapter attempts to respond to this gap in the study of ethnicity and long-term care by exploring the effect, if any, of ethnicity on measurements of health status and its implications for long-term care.

The measurement of health status through self-assessment has become an important component in the delivery of community-based long-term care.

*This author is especially indebted to Linda Redford, Ph.D., then Associate Director of The University of Kansas Center on Long-term Care. Her encouragement and expertise on the subject are appreciated.

Hence it is important to understand the effect of ethnicity on this measure. In particular, practitioners and researchers alike must consider variations that may result in the administration of a given assessment tool across an ethnically diverse group of elderly. Moreover, because health status is so important in determining the long-term care needs of elderly persons, and because community-based research relies heavily on selected indicators of health status in making policy recommendations and in implementing health and social services to diverse aging populations, it is critical to caution practitioners against making recommendations without duly considering the effect of ethnic diversity on their assessments.

The degree to which ethnicity affects the aging experience of minority populations has been extensively explored in the last two decades (Bastida, 1984, 1987; Becerra, 1983; Harel, 1985; Jackson, 1980; Jackson & Gibson, 1985; Kalish & Moriwaki, 1973; Manson & Callaway, 1985; Torres-Gil, 1982, 1986; Ujimoto, 1985). Articles that explore issues of measurement across diverse populations of ethnic/minority and nonminority elderly are less frequent in the gerontological literature.

Data presented and discussed in this chapter address the above considerations by examining selected measures of health status across three ethnic groups. Unlike most research on long-term care, emphasis is given to variations in response to selected indicators of health status rather than on listing and discussing the physical and social needs of the elderly studied.

The findings discussed below are used to illustrate cross-ethnic variations in response to perceived general health and other indicators of health status. Salient characteristics and recommendations on the general application of these measures are discussed within the context of cross-ethnic research.

THE DATA

Three data sets were combined in examining the questions addressed here. These data sets corresponded to three studies conducted by the authors during a four-year period. Data were gathered by administering the same set of questions to three different populations. Face-to-face structured interviews, each lasting two hours, were conducted with all respondents. A total of 401 elderly persons were interviewed. The study samples included 142 Anglos, 174 Mexican-Americans, and 85 Puerto Ricans, age 60 and over. None of the elderly was institutionalized at the time of the study. Data for the Anglo and Mexican-American populations were gathered as part of a statewide study designed to explore the need for a community-based long-term care program. Data for the Puerto Rican population were drawn from a much larger and comprehensive long-term care study conducted by the National Hispanic Council on Aging under the direction of Dr. Marta Sotomayor. This chapter reports only on the set of data obtained for the Puerto Rican population.

The findings presented below are based on a descriptive analysis of the data and are used throughout the chapter in substantiating and illustrating the major points raised by the discussion.

FINDINGS

It is important to describe, albeit briefly, some of the salient ethnic and socioeconomic characteristics of the studied populations. A total of 142 Anglo elderly were interviewed. Of those 48% were rural and 52% urban. The Mexican-American sample consisted of 174 respondents with 35% of those living in predominantly rural settings and 65% in large urban areas. Finally, the Puerto Rican sample consisted of 85 respondents, all of whom were drawn from a medium-sized Eastern city. At the time of the interview, all Puerto Rican respondents lived in a large urban area; however, over 50% ($n=52$) of those interviewed were from rural backgrounds.

Although the rural Anglo population was primarily of German background, only a few identified strongly with their ethnicity and none spoke German in spite the small number who acknowledged learning German before learning English. Among the urban Anglos, the sample was much more diverse, with few of these elderly identifying their ethnic backgrounds. In contrast, data obtained from the Mexican-American and Puerto Rican samples revealed a strong ethnic identification, with all respondents identifying their ethnic backgrounds and acknowledging speaking Spanish. Only a few of the Mexican-American respondents ($n=9$) chose to be interviewed in English, whereas all the Puerto Ricans chose Spanish.

Generally speaking, the term Hispanic is used when referring to the various Spanish-speaking subpopulations living in the United States. For our purposes, the term Hispanic is used when alluding to the joint Puerto Rican and Mexican-American samples. Specific ethnic identifiers, that is, Mexican-American and Puerto Rican, are used whenever referring to each of the two samples separately.

Controls were used in order to obtain some degree of comparability in socioeconomic condition among the three populations studied. Given the lower socioeconomic condition of the two Hispanic populations, only those Anglo elderly with low socioeconomic backgrounds were included in the study. Table 2.1 briefly lists the major characteristics of respondents by ethnicity. Moreover, the Mexican-American and Anglo samples were drawn from the same communities. Finally, it is emphasized that although the three subsamples are comprised of lower income elderly, the lower income Anglo elderly, as a group, were

TABLE 2.1 Major Characteristics by Ethnicity

Characteristics	Total	Anglo	MA	PR
Totals (%)	401 (100%)	142 (36%)	174 (43%)	85 (21%)
Gender				
Males (%)	128 (99%)	49 (38%)	49 (38%)	30 (23%)
Females (%)	273 (100%)	93 (34%)	125 (46%)	55 (20%)
Age				
Median		76	66	65
Marital Status				
Married (%)	143	54 (38%)	81 (47%)	8 (9%)
Residence				
Urban (%)	272	74 (52%)	113 (65%)	85 (100%)
Rural (%)	129	68 (48%)	61 (35%)	0 (0%)
Education (yrs.)				
Median		12	6	5
Income				
Median		7,200	5,000	4,800

in better socioeconomic condition, but older, than the minority elderly (Table 2.1).

SELF-ASSESSED GENERAL HEALTH

Given the overriding purpose of this chapter to examine cross-ethnic variations in measuring health status, general issues of reliability and validity relating to self-assessments of health status are not discussed here. In particular, it is recognized that self-ratings sometimes differ substantially from physician ratings and that gender and socioeconomic conditions are intervening factors. Our concern here, however, is to investigate the validity of selected indicators of general health across three populations of elderly.

Findings indicate that the two Hispanic populations rated their health poorer than the Anglo elderly in the study. All three populations were asked: "Would you say that your health in general is: Excellent, good, fair, poor?" Of particular interest is the pattern of variation obtained. Only 2% of Mexican-Americans and 1% of Puerto Ricans rated their general health status as excellent, while 21% of the Anglo elderly reported excellent health. It should be noted that as a group the Anglo elderly were, on the average, 10 years older than the ethnic elderly and thus one would expect the reverse results (Table 2.1). Moreover, only 23% of the Mexican-American and 27% of the Puerto Rican elderly, but 46% of the Anglo elderly, rated their health as good.

To further investigate cross-ethnic variations in self-assessments of physical

**TABLE 2.2 Percentage of Respondents with Specific Health
Problems by Ethnicity**

Health Problems	Anglo	MA	PA
High blood pressure	40	40	42
Heart problems	40	8	22
Diabetes	7	13	9
Arthritis	63	54	60
Circulatory problems	29	35	32
Vision impairment	68	41	48
Hearing impairment	29	25	23
Respiratory problems	21	14	20
Stomach problems	27	7	18
Cancer	16	4	5

health, a new variable was created, yielding only two groups—those who responded excellent or good were collapsed into one group (good health) and those who responded fair or poor were collapsed into the second group (poor health). The largest number of Hispanic respondents were in the second group, with 75% of Mexican-American respondents and 72% of the Puerto Rican elderly reporting poor health. In contrast only 33% of the Anglo elderly were in the poor health group.

A better understanding of ethnic patterns of variation in group response is obtained when the top five self reported leading illnesses are examined for each population under study (Table 2.2).

Given the large number of Hispanic respondents who self-assessed their health as poor and the large number of Anglo elderly who self-assessed their health as good, we would expect a much larger percentage of Hispanic respondents reporting serious and or disabling illnesses or conditions. However, this is not the case (Table 2.2). Only 56% of Hispanics, but 63% of the Anglo elderly, reported arthritis as a serious and or disabling illness. Proportionately, an equal number of respondents among all groups listed high blood pressure. Blindness and diseases of the eye were much more common among the Anglo elderly than among the Hispanic elderly. Finally, while 40% of the Anglo elderly reported heart disease, only 22% of the Puerto Rican and a minimal number of Mexican-American respondents (8%) listed this condition. In sum, when examining the number of illnesses for these population, the reverse finding is obtained. In fact, it is noted that the Hispanic population is "healthier"—if the measure used is number of reported illnesses and not a general self-assessment of health. The above finding is partly explained by the youthfulness of the Hispanic population. What remains to be explained, however, given the youthfulness and lower number of serious or disabling illnesses, is why the Hispanic population self-rated general health poorer than Anglos.

ILLNESSES/CONDITIONS

In order to further explore the question of poor self-ratings of general health among the Hispanic population, we examined the relationship between the number of illnesses reported and self-assessments of health. We found the relationship to be strongest among those Hispanic respondents who reported "poor" as their general health status. However, only minor differences were found between those who rated their health "good" and those who rated it "fair." Moreover, we found that collapsing the variable into good/poor confounded the results. It was only when the measure was used as originally coded that the usefulness of self-assessed general health status could be examined. In general, of course, a strong direct relationship was found between self-ratings of health and number of illnesses reported. However, the measure discriminates only toward the "poor" end of the scale.

When results for both populations were compared, the Anglo elderly rated their health better with the same number of illnesses and conditions than the Hispanic population. For example, 69% of the Anglo elderly who rated their health "excellent" reported two illnesses/conditions; and 20% reported three or more illnesses. Since only 3% of the Hispanic population rated their health "excellent," it is difficult to compare the two populations. However, it must be noted that the Hispanic respondents who were in this category did not report any major illnesses or conditions.

When the number of illnesses/conditions reported by the Hispanic population who self-assessed their health "good" was further examined, we found that 11% of those in this category reported no major illnesses or conditions; 66% reported one illness or condition and 23% reported two illnesses or conditions. It is only among those Hispanics who rated their health "fair" that we find the number of illnesses or conditions reported to be three or higher, whereas among the Anglo respondents, 47% of those who rated their health "good" also indicated three or more illnesses or conditions.

Obviously, the self-assessment measure of health status is discriminating within the populations studied. Caution, however, must be exercised when the same measure is applied to diverse ethnic groups without an understanding that cross-ethnic variations may be obtained.

USE OF MEDICATION

The use of medications also serves as an indicator of health status. Anglo elderly respondents indicated they took from zero to seven prescription medications on a regular basis. The number of medications was relatively low, with a mean of 2.3 prescription medications and 1.1 nonprescription medications. Still, 67% of the respondents indicated that they took one or more prescription medications and 57% indicated taking one or more over-the-counter drugs.

Among the Mexican-American population, the number of prescribed medications was lower, with a mean of 1.8 medications; however, the number of nonprescription medications was higher, with a mean of 2.4. Still, the percentage of respondents indicating that they took one or more prescription medications was slightly higher than for the Anglo population, with 69% indicating at least one prescription medication and 63% indicating taking one or more over-the-counter drugs. No comparable data were obtained for the Puerto Rican elderly.

When comparing the Mexican-American sample and the Anglo elderly sample, an important difference is found in the mean number of nonprescription medications. That is, Mexican-Americans are more likely to use over-the-counter drugs. Partly this may be explained by the lower cost and greater accessibility of the latter; however, it is noted that the major illness/condition reported by these elderly was arthritis. It is common to use aspirin to relieve the pain and discomfort caused by arthritis. It is also possible to suggest that Mexican-Americans were more likely to rely on folk remedies to relieve pain or discomfort; however, our data do not allow us to investigate this possibility. No significant differences were found in the number (percentages) of Mexican-American and Anglo elderly taking prescription medications and over-the-counter drugs. Hence, the two populations were fairly similar in this indicator of health status.

HOSPITALIZATION

Thirty six percent of the rural and 27% of the urban Anglo elderly had been hospitalized at least once in the year prior to this study. Further analysis of hospitalizations by age of the respondents indicated that respondents 80 years of age and older were responsible for only 12% of the hospitalizations in the sample group. The majority of hospitalizations occurred among individuals in their 60s and 70s. Among the Hispanic population 32% of the Mexican-American elderly had been hospitalized at least once in the year prior to this study, and respondents over the age of 80 accounted for 15% of the hospitalizations in the sample group. Thirty four percent of the Puerto Rican elderly indicated at least one hospitalization for the same time period, and respondents over 80 years old were responsible for 7% of the hospitalizations in the sample group. Of all three populations studied, however, Puerto Ricans were the youngest, with only seven octogenarians in the sample. As with the previous indicator, no major differences were found among the three subpopulations studied.

BED DISABILITY DAYS

Another measure of health status examined in this study was the number of days individuals were confined to bed at home. Eighteen percent of the Anglo respondents indicated being confined in bed one or more days during the previous year. The mean range for days in bed was between four and seven days. Only 4% of the respondents indicated that they were confined to bed for longer than a two-week period.

Similarly, 17% of the Puerto Rican elderly and 18% of the Mexican-American elderly indicated being confined in bed one or more days during the previous year. As noted earlier, arthritis was the top ranked illness among the Hispanic elderly, and many respondents indicated that very bad arthritic pain had been the major reason for a one- or two-day bed confinement.

DISCUSSION

In reviewing the above findings, the health indicator most affected by ethnicity is self-assessment of general health. Clearly, this is the single major difference between the two ethnic/minorities and the Anglo population studied. Other, more objective indicators of physical health (e.g., number of illnesses/conditions, number of prescribed medications, number of over-the-counter drugs, hospitalization, and bed disability days) appear to offer comparable data on health status across the three populations studied.

The question, however, remains as to why the Hispanic respondents in the study self-rated their health poorer than the Anglo elderly. A few plausible explanations are considered below.

Education

Cokerham, Sharp, and Wilcox (1983) show that education and number of illness symptoms experienced are especially important influences on self-assessments of health. Multivariate analysis of their data indicates that the more education a person has, the more likely health is perceived in a positive fashion. Cockerham (1991) suggests that perhaps those persons with more education consider themselves more healthy relative to others because they feel their social environment is more conducive to maintaining good health than members of less educated and, most likely, less affluent groups.

Clearly, both Hispanic subpopulations are less educated than the Anglo population in this study. As Table 2.1 indicates, the median number of years of school completed is 6 years for Mexican-Americans, 5 years for Puerto Ricans, and 12 years for the Anglo elderly—the latter indicating an advantage, on the average, of 6 years of education over the Hispanic populations studied. Although the number of Hispanic elderly with 12 years of education is very small, with only 5% of the Mexican-Americans and 2% of the Puerto Ricans in this category, their self-ratings, controlling for number of illnesses, are compared with those of the Anglo elderly. Still, there are differences between the groups, the Hispanic elderly rating their health poorer than the Anglo elderly, with a mean of 2.4, for the Hispanic population (on a scale ranging from 1 = poor to 4 = excellent) and a mean of 3.1 for the Anglo elderly. These results are used only to illustrate the situation discussed here, given the small number of Hispanics in this category. Thus, while education is obviously one major factor mediating results, it does not fully respond to the question raised here.

Age

David Mechanic and Ronald Angel (1987) suggest that the elderly appear to adjust their perceptions of their health as they modify their expectations with age. Cockerham observes that when younger people are asked to compare their health with others their age, the evaluation is likely to be "about the same." Elderly people appear more likely to rate their health higher than that of their peers. Cockerham (1991) has noted that health differences between people become more obvious as they grow older. Stoller (1984) explains that comparisons with peers is of major importance, and it may be that such a comparison is a primary factor in influencing relatively high self-ratings.

Since the Hispanic elderly were, on the average, 10 years younger than the Anglo elderly in the study, the need for optimizing self-health ratings may be less. Cokerham and his colleagues (1983) in a statewide sample of persons over the age of 18 found that the proportion of people who feel their health is much better than others their age is almost twice as high among people age 60 and over than for those under 60. Hence, it is possible to assume that the Hispanic elderly, being younger, were more likely to have younger "peers" as a reference group and less likely to have begun to modify their health expectations with age.

Minority Status

The degree to which the health of members of ethnic/minority groups is affected by occupying a minority status in our society is of paramount importance and cannot be overlooked in explaining variations in self-assessments of health among these populations. Much has been written on the "double jeopardy" suffered by the minority aged, and it is not our purpose to discuss this subject at length here. Suffice it to say that by now it is widespread knowledge that elderly minorities are socioeconomically disadvantaged. Thus, they are less likely to receive adequate and quality medical care. Moreover, they are more likely to have been deprived of the benefits of health care in their earlier years, which directly affects their current health conditions.

Many of our Puerto Rican and Mexican-American respondents alluded to major economic and physical hardships experienced during their childhood and early adult years. Many of these have had a cumulative deteriorating effect on their current health. In fact, the lower educational achievement of the Hispanic elderly in the study, which was offered among the plausible explanations for poor self-assessments of health above, is very much a product of the overriding significance of minority status on their lives.

A finding that needs to be highlighted within this context is that the two minority populations studied, although younger, reported similar number of illnesses, use of prescribed medications, use of over-the-counter drugs, hospitalizations, and bed disability days as did the Anglo elderly, who were considerably older. Hence, the younger advantage of the minority population does not contribute to a health advantage. It is presumed that minority status, as a structural characteristic, has had a strong influence on this result and partly explains the deterioration of their health at a younger age.

Cultural Orientation

As suggested by Mechanic (1979) and Twaddle and Hessler (1977), the interpretation of symptoms and the assumption of illness behavior and sick role are influenced by one's social interaction and cultural tradition. Cultural differences among the populations studied were expected to influence patterns of response to the question on general health. The frame of reference employed by the Hispanic populations in the study, a product of both social interaction and cultural tradition, is different from that of the Anglo elderly in the study. However, it is underscored that both Hispanic and Anglo populations were employing cultural and social expectations of quality of health. To a certain extent these are also culturally defined since they are reinforced by peers. Since both Hispanic populations self-assessed their general health much poorer than did the Anglo elderly (although younger and with about the same health problems), it could be presumed, as has been done with other measures (e.g., life satisfaction), that one population, or its culture, has a more "optimistic" approach. We refrain from that assumption because we find it highly subjective. Rather, it is suggested that the cultural parameters employed in determining quality of health and health expectations vary for each of the populations studied and that such parameters need to be further explored before attempting causal explanations.

CONCLUSION

Throughout our years of research on ethnic/minority populations, we have observed that when cultural variations in patterns of response are discussed, researchers and practitioners respond despairingly and with frustration. They frequently note that if all of the possible methodological and measurement nuances involved in cross-ethnic research are to be considered, much-needed cross-cultural comparisons, particularly necessary for policymakers, would never be accomplished. The purpose of this chapter is not to discourage investigators from conducting cross-cultural research. Rather, it is to sensitize researchers to the source of variations so that the overall quality of cross-ethnic research is improved by generating more comparable data. Obviously, much remains to be investigated in cross-cultural research that will contribute to the overall understanding of the social aspects of aging and long-term care.

A question that arises whenever research findings are discussed is how they are applicable to the more practical concerns of providers and policymakers. In responding to this concern, it is important to realize that both levels, the study *and* the practice of long-term care, require some process of data collection. The objectives guiding the data collection process may be highly theoretical or highly practical, for example, individual functional assessments or program evaluations. In either situation, however, the investigator, must be cautioned about possible sources of variations in response patterns when administering the same instrument to a cross-ethnic population. Otherwise, an inadequate interpretation of findings may result in harmful consequences for the populations at risk.

Let us briefly illustrate this problem. For example, let us assume that, as indicated by the findings discussed, the Hispanic population is considered to be in poorer health than the Anglo population. Yet other findings indicate that they may be underutilizing the formal network of aging services, specifically those targeted to prevent institutionalization. The response, as has been frequently the case, may be to assume that these elderly are receiving informal supports from family and kin. Yet it may be that although the self-assessments of health status are, in general, "poor," their level of functional ability is still "fair." In this case, formal services are not required. This is the case not necessarily because they are receiving supports from other sources, but simply because their functional incapacity has not yet reached the stage where those services are necessary.

A wrong assessment of the population's health status may lead toward ignoring their situation altogether rather than planning ahead for a time, probably rather near, when, indeed those services may become necessary. The opposite interpretation is equally dangerous. Let us suppose that the same findings are interpreted as assuming that Hispanics tend to overreact about their illnesses and/or their functionality. That is, they are not as "stoic" as their Anglo elderly counterpart. How will this assumption, based on a rather subjective interpretation of the findings, affect long-term care policymaking and provision of services at the local level? We find that this should be a critical concern of those involved in the direct provision of services and policymaking locally and statewide, for it directly affects the well-being of the Hispanic elderly population who may be in need of long-term care.

This situation has become critical as society moves in the direction of more functional assessments in order to justify the delivery of community-based long-term care services. This is particularly salient for those impoverished elderly receiving Supplemental Security Income and Medicaid. Moreover, as state policies increasingly require standardization of instruments employed in evaluating clients, a greater risk of wrongly evaluating Hispanic clients seeking those services exists. Unless we understand possible response variations in the application of standardized instruments, we run the risk of incorrectly evaluating and interpreting the long-term care needs of the Hispanic population.

The consequences of such erroneous evaluations and interpretation of data will be detrimental to the needs of Hispanics seeking those services. It is important to note that Hispanics, in general, but particularly Hispanic women, are much more dependent on Supplemental Security Income than Anglos. Hence, an awareness of the "problem of measurement" discussed in this chapter is more critical for the practitioner in terms of direct human cost than for the basic researcher.

We could, of course, also expand on our findings to alert practitioners and policymakers of the fact that Hispanics report the same number of impairments, illnesses, bed disability days, and hospitalization days as Anglos but at a younger age. For the purposes of the findings reported here, this younger age means, on the average, a 10-year difference. We may then ask, How is this finding translated in practice? How can practitioners and policymakers respond to this finding?

We suggest that functional impairment at a younger age usually means that it will be necessary to work with couples, rather than the individual, and, in some cases, with family members. Given that Hispanic women bear children at a later age, they may still have late adolescent children at home at the onset of their own chronic illnesses. It is important for practitioners and policymakers to recognize the spouses and children in reaching out for these elderly in need of community-based long-term care. The fact that they have family support does not necessarily mean that they are not in need of professional services.

In closing and to summarize, we must emphasize that it remains critical for practitioners and policymakers to understand how a given response to a closed-ended questionnaire item may be affected by that respondent's cultural orientation and membership within a group. This is particularly relevant for those researchers involved in community-based long-term care since many rely on self-assessed indicators of health status to gauge the extent to which community-based programs are needed. We would like to discourage those researchers from using self-perceived general health comparatively across diverse ethnic groups, unless extensive effort is taken to understand the underlying factors contributing to cultural/minority variations in patterns of response. Other measures of self-assessed health status are recommended, such as illness/condition, hospitalizations, bed disability days, and number of prescribed and over-the-counter medications. Given the dramatic changes in the ethnic composition of the American population and the substantial growth in the number of ethnic minority aged in this and future decades, an awareness of patterns of response variation and an understanding of the source of these variations is of paramount importance to the quality of care offered all elderly in our society.

REFERENCES

Bastida, E. (1984). Reconstructing the social world at 60: Older Cubans in the United States. *The Gerontologist, 24,* 465–470.

Bastida, E. (1987). Sex-typed age norms among older Hispanics. *The Gerontologist, 27,* 59–65.

Becerra, R. (1983). The Mexican-American: Aging in a changing culture. In R. McNeely & J. Colen (Eds.), *Aging in minority groups.* Beverly Hills, CA: Sage.

Cockerham, W. C. (1991). *The aging society.* Englewood Cliffs, NJ: Prentice-Hall.

Cockerham, W. C., Sharp, K., & Wilcox, J. (1983). Aging and perceived health status. *Journal of Gerontology, 38,* 349–355.

Harel, Z. (1985). Nutrition site service users: Does racial background make a difference? *The Gerontologist, 25,* 286–291.

Jackson, J. J. (1980). *Minorities and aging.* Belmont, CA: Wadsworth.

Jackson, J. S., & Gibson, R. C. (1985). Work and retirement among the black elderly. In Z. Blau (Ed.), *Current perspectives on aging and the life cycle.* Greenwich, CT: JAI Press.

Kalish, R. A., & Moriwaki, S. (1973). The world of the elderly Asian American. In J. Hendricks & C. D. Hendricks (Eds.), *Dimensions of aging.* Cambridge, MA: Winthrop Publishers.

Kane, R., & Kane, R. L. (1981). *Assessing the elderly: A practical guide to measurement.* Lexington, MA: Lexington Books.

Manson, S., & Callaway, D. (1985). Health and aging among American Indians: Issues and change for the biobehavioral sciences. Unpublished monograph.

Mechanic, D. (1979). Correlations of physician utilization: Why do major multivariate studies of physician utilization find trivial psychological and organizational effects? *Journal of Health and Social Behavior, 20,* 387–396.

Mechanic, D., & Angel, R. J. (1987). Some factors associated with the report and evaluation of back pain. *Journal of Health and Social Behavior, 28,* 131–139.

Stoller, E. P. (1984). Self-assessments of health by the elderly: The impact of informal assistance. *Journal of Health and Social Behavior, 25,* 260–270.

Torres-Gil, F. (1982). *The politics of aging among elder Hispanics.* Washington, DC: University Press of America.

Torres-Gil, F. (1986). An examination of factors affecting future cohorts of elderly Hispanics. *The Gerontologist, 26,* 140–146.

Twaddle, A. C., & Hessler, R. M. (1977). *A sociology of health.* St. Louis, MO: C. V. Mosby.

Ujimoto, K. V. (1985). The allocation of time to social and leisure activities as social indicators for the integration of aged ethnic minorities. *Social Indicators Research*, *16*, 253–266.

PART II

Home Based Long-Term Care: Caregiver Issues

When elderly persons begin to experience problems with health and activities of daily living, they generally turn to informal care sources. These include family, friends, and neighbors. This is especially true among ethnic groups. The difficulties that aged ethnic elders may have with the language and culture of the host society can cause them to become isolated and withdrawn from formal sources of help, or may make it more difficult for them to contact formal sources for help. Consequently, they depend more on the familiar and often less threatening help from persons who are close either in distance or in social and cultural practices.

The chapters in this section deal with the caregiving behaviors of family and other informal sources. They remind us that these services are the first line of defense against a life of dependency for many elders. Not only do they receive instrumental help—that which provides for their physical needs—but they turn to these sources for emotional help as well. As other authors have stated, without this level of care, the formal sources of care for the elderly would be overwhelmed with demands for help.

The first chapter, by Wood and Wan, is on a topic that has received scant attention in the past: family caregiving to rural black elders. They point out that the rate of black elderly in institutions is much less than that of whites. This causes the black elders to depend more on informal services. The lack of transportation that affects many elderly is magnified for these rural residents. They point out that there are special strains that rural caregivers experience in providing care to cognitively impaired rural black elders. One of the main difficulties comes from the traditional view of medicine held by blacks. Folk beliefs may view illness as having a spiritual as well as a physical dimension. Both sick elderly and their caregivers are likely to turn to coping strategies that are more compatible with their belief systems such as prayer or dependence on superstitions to manipulate the unknown.

The other chapter in this section, by Cox and Monk, also deals with family caregiving but focuses on both black and Hispanic dementia victims in urban settings. They remind us that because these caregivers are effective in providing care for their relatives there is often a belief that they do not require formal assistance. They find some differences between the black and Hispanic caregivers in their sample, particularly in their dependence on formal support sources. Hispanic respondents depended more on these private and government sources of assistance than did blacks. Also, it was noted that in the black sample more informal assistance related to more formal support. The reverse was found for Hispanic caregivers. An important finding from their research points out that for both groups, turning to formal sources of support may pose a potential risk to their own emotional well-being as they cope with their emotions and cultural values.

3

Ethnicity and Minority Issues in Family Caregiving to Rural Black Elders

Joan B. Wood
Thomas T. H. Wan

INTRODUCTION/OVERVIEW OF FAMILY CAREGIVING

The purpose of this chapter is to discuss ethnicity, minority status, and rurality as correlates of family caregiving for rural black elders. Recent research relating to these issues will be reviewed, and results of an exploratory study (Wood & Parham, 1990) indicating significant cultural influences in the coping strategies employed by family caregivers for frail black elders will be presented. Methodological issues raised by this research will also be discussed. A better understanding of ethnic families and the cultural meanings attached to caregiving can assist policymakers, program developers, and formal service providers to enhance and support the family as an effective caregiving unit.

As the editors of this volume have acknowledged in the introductory chapter, families are the mainstay of long-term care for older adults. The National Survey of Caregivers (American Association of Retired Persons and The Travelers Foundation, 1988) estimated that approximately four out of five older Americans whose ability to function is impaired by physical and/or mental dis-

39

abilities have avoided institutionalization because of the availability of personal care and financial assistance provided by informal networks. Professional health care providers are sometimes jolted by estimates that 80 to 90% of all health care to older adults is provided from informal sources, chiefly family members.

Family caregiving behaviors are usually conceptualized in two broad categories: instrumental and expressive. Instrumental caregiving behaviors include: (1) assistance with personal care functions (activities of daily living) such as dressing, feeding, or bathing, and/or (2) assistance with instrumental activities of daily living such as managing finances, assisting with shopping or housework, or administering medications. Expressive caregiving behaviors include sharing in social activities, providing emotional support, and the elusive but important characteristic of "being there" when the older family member needs someone.

Both the National Survey of Caregivers (AARP and The Travelers Foundation, 1988) and the Informal Caregivers Survey (see Stone, Cafferata, & Sangl, 1987), which was a component of the 1982 National Long-Term Care Survey, provide information on instrumental caregiving activities. The domain of expressive caregiving, which is difficult to articulate and quantify, remains largely unexplored. The social and emotional support provided by families likely enables a still larger percentage of frail elders to remain independent. Surely, support from family affects their quality of life.

A major caregiving task in helping the older family member remain independent involves serving as the family liaison with the formal service network. Family caregivers who have access to and are able to utilize formal supports such as respite, day care, or in-home services report them to be beneficial in maintaining their own well-being as well as that of their care recipient (Burdz, Eaton, & Bond, 1988; Lawton, Brody, & Saperstein, 1989; Miller & Goldman, 1989; Scharlach & Frenzel, 1986).

Involvement of the family caregivers in providing care does not end with institutionalization. Studies show that not only is the family likely to remain involved with the institutionalized elder, but that the level of caregiver burden is not significantly different from that of caregivers whose patients are not institutionalized (George, 1984; Pagel, Becker, & Coppel, 1985; Pratt, Schmall, Cleland, & Wright, 1985; Wood, 1987). Family caregivers continue to assist with personal care of institutionalized elders and to provide social and emotional support (Bowers, 1988). They continue to serve as advocates and brokers of services and, with training, can serve as effective members of the health care team (Eyde & Rich, 1983; Hanson, Patterson, & Wilson, 1988; Seltzer, Ivry, & Litchfield, 1987; Stoller & Pugliesi, 1989).

Thus, family caregivers of frail or impaired elders play important roles along the entire continuum of long-term care. Among no population subgroup are the roles and functions of family caregivers more important than among rural blacks in the southeastern United States, where 59% of the nation's black elderly live (Watson, 1984).

A FRAMEWORK FOR STUDYING FAMILY CAREGIVING FOR RURAL BLACK ELDERS

There are numerous complex issues relating to family caregiving for frail rural black elders. A schematic diagram that specifies the complex relationships among multiple factors will help to explicate the intricacy of the correlates and consequences of family caregiving for black elders in rural communities.

Figure 3.1 shows that institutionalization is positively influenced by inaccessibility to formal community-based care and concomitant reliance on informal support networks. Three factors (characteristics of rural living, disadvantaged minority status, and ethnic/cultural identity) predispose black elders to have poor access to formal care and to rely on informal support networks for caregiving.

Only 3% of black elders over the age of 65 are institutionalized, in comparison with 5% of white elderly. This trend is accentuated among the oldest-old (85 and over), who are generally more likely to be frail and in need of more intensive levels of care. Among this population, only 12% of blacks live in nursing homes or other institutional facilities, compared to 23% of whites. (American Association of Retired Persons, 1986). Data from the National Long-Term

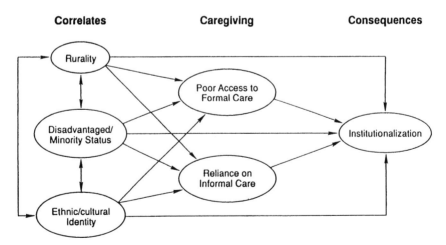

FIGURE 3.1 A schematic diagram portraying the correlates and consequences of family caregiving for frail black elders in a rural community.

Care Channeling Demonstration show that blacks have less than half (45%) the odds of admissions to nursing home of whites (Greene & Ondrich, 1990). In most instances, long-term institutional care is considered the last resort when both formal and informal caregiving networks are absent in the community or when family resources are strained beyond endurance.

Effects of Rurality: Limited Availability of Formal Services

Objective needs of the rural elderly are known to be higher than those of their urban counterparts (Coward, 1983; Coward & Smith, 1982; Nelson, 1983). Generally, in addition to the informal care provided by friends and families, formal community-based long-term care services include: (1) in-home services such as skilled nursing, physical therapy, home health aide services, and homemaker services; (2) geriatric day care and other support services such as home-delivered meals, adults foster care, and transportation; and (3) respite care, emergency lodging, or community housing options. In rural areas, many of these services are not available. Institutional care, in the form of nursing homes or homes for adults, is often the only alternative to home care for family members. In-home services, such as homemaker/home health aides or companion services, may be available through the area agency on aging or the local department of social services or public health. Limited transportation and home maintenance services may also be available. Few support services for family caregivers are available. Respite and adult day care services are almost nonexistent in rural areas. Caregiver support groups are usually available on a limited basis.

Disadvantaged/Minority Status

The major challenge to rural black families in providing care to frail elders is the lack of socioeconomic resources. Older blacks are generally disadvantaged with regard to education, income, health, transportation, and housing (Wan, 1977). This is particularly true in rural areas, where nearly 50% of all black elders live in poverty. More than two-thirds (68%) of rural black women over the age of 75 are in or near poverty levels (American Association of Retired Persons, 1986).

Rural blacks, especially older adults, are less likely to own and drive a personal car. In rural areas where public transportation is less frequently available, persons without automobiles are more isolated by physical distance (Krout, 1983). Thus the low socioeconomic status of older blacks is compounded with the financial and physical realities of rural living that place black elders at a double disadvantage with regard to transportation.

Diminishing resources for service programs in a climate of fiscal austerity also impact differentially on minority families with dependent elders. In many instances, means tests limit the availability of services to the most financially needy, and decreased federal allocations have resulted in waiting lists for many who are eligible. This poses an added disadvantage to black caregivers, proportionately more of whom are likely to be in poverty and near-poverty categories.

Service eligibility criteria that discourage large households may also discriminate against the living patterns of rural blacks. The size of many minority households is determined more by economic necessity than by cultural preference. These are likely to include extended or fictive kin in need of shared housing. Indeed, any number of dependent or financially independent younger individuals are likely to share the household of an older black family member in the reverse of the living pattern in majority families, where the older relative is more likely to move in with an adult child or younger sibling. Service eligibility criteria that require the reporting of pooled household incomes may present a distorted view of the resources available to an older adult.

Ethnic/Cultural Identity

In discussing the special caregiving challenges for black families in rural areas, race itself is not a sufficient explanation for the differences. It is important to note the conceptual difficulties that may be encountered if the distinctions between ethnic identity and minority status are not clarified (see comments on this point by the editors in the introductory chapter of this volume). George (1988) posits that racial differences may be explained as resulting from deprivation relative to whites (i.e., attributable to minority status) or from subgroup preference deriving from a unique collective history and intragroup commitment (i.e., ethnic culture). Thus, minority status and ethnic identity may be distinguished conceptually on the basis of involuntary factors (e.g., socioeconomic variables) and voluntary factors (e.g., cultural patterns of behavior).Service delivery systems are, in general, insensitive to the values of minority culture. Policy is usually developed in response to needs of majority elders. Cross-cultural differences are largely ignored in both the development and implementation of models of care. For example, the first line of response to the needs of family caregivers of frail elders in rural and urban communities alike has been to establish caregiver support groups. The support group model is oriented to and usually supported by caregivers from majority culture. Minority caregivers do not frequently attend.

Rural service delivery systems not only ignore minority cultural issues; they are typically based on urban models, which are not well suited to a rural environment. Eligibility criteria based on means tests discriminate against rural elders, who are more likely to own their own homes and additional property. As Groger (1983) pointed out in her study of land ownership by black and white elders in a southern rural community, the information that an individual owns a large acreage says nothing about the quality of the land, or about the low return on the investment. Older rural blacks who may, with difficulty, have acquired property in addition to their homes will be loathe to risk their control over these economic resources in exchange for services of questionable benefit.

Another cultural issue relates to the absence of truly community-based services, according to rural definition of community. Life in rural areas is still shaped by the scattered nature of settlement. Communities that cover a large geographic area may be quite small in numbers of people. The social life of the community is usually centered around a general store, post office, or church. Patterns of interaction are informal and based on face-to-face contact. Much value is placed on knowing community residents personally. Health services are usually provided by a general practitioner who knows his/her patients individually. The chief providers of mental health services, especially to the aged, are likely the same general practitioner and the local minister (McAuley, Arling, Nutty, & Bowling, 1980). Therefore, mental health, health, and social services located at the county courthouse office complex are not community-based given this perspective. The lack of facilities in respondents' area of reference is often a major reason for nonutilization of services (Cuellar & Weeks, 1980).

Access to Formal Services

A number of problems related to access to formal services pose special challenges to rural, black elders and their families. Some are related to the physical and cultural characteristics of rural living; others are related to minority status, still others are rooted in African-American ethnic culture. Disentangling the effects of these characteristics on access to formal care is often difficult, if not impossible. A major barrier to access services involves lack of information about existing services. Not only are fewer services available in rural areas, rural elders are typically not well-informed about services that are available (Krout, 1983; Wan, Odell, & Lewis, 1982). Many public service delivery agencies, with scant resources to support existing programs, do not advertise the availability of services. When service availability is promoted, the methods used to communicate affect those who respond. Announcements through large daily newspapers and television stations in urban centers miles away have less impact than notices in local newspapers and on local radio stations. The printed word also presents a problem for many older blacks, who are more likely to have low literacy levels.

Issues relating to racial discrimination in service delivery constitute another factor affecting access to formal services. Although overtly racist practices have been legally disallowed and have become socially unpopular, practices reflecting categorical stereotyping continue to exist on both an institutional and an individual level. Older blacks who do have access to services are often offended by service providers' use of first names or excessive eye contact, both of which are seen as disrespectful.

Reliance on Informal Care

The most salient characteristics of long-term care arrangements among rural black families is the continued reliance on traditional informal supports. But this situation is far more complex than the stereotypical belief that ethnic families "take care of their own," (see Wright & Mindel in this volume). This simplistic view is largely a traditional ideal and is unsupported by research (Jackson, 1977; Jackson & Walls, 1979; Rosenthal, 1986). However, ethnic culture may be a resource in family caregiving to impaired elders.

Before discussing this issue at length in the next section, a word of warning regarding research issues is in order. First, while it may be assumed that there are cultural distinctions in norms of filial responsibility, empirical research on this issue has yielded conflicting results (Hanson, Sauer, & Seelbach, 1983; Schorr, 1960; Schneider & Smith, 1973). In investigations of ethnic or cultural effects on caregiving patterns in black families, behaviors must be kept distinct from cultural norms. Ethnic group differences in expressed norms of familial obligation may not be matched by actual behaviors (Hanson et al., 1983; Tate, 1983). Structural aspects of family life, for example, socioeconomic status, area of residence, should also be controlled to ensure that findings associated with minority status are not inappropriately attributed to cultural differences (Cantor, 1979; George, 1988; Mitchell & Register, 1984).

Ethnic differences in the structure and quality of informal support networks of the black elderly have been well documented (Cantor, 1975; Conway, 1985; Jackson & Walls, 1979; Sokolovsky, 1985; Tate, 1983; Taylor, 1982; Wood & Parham, 1990). Size of the network and frequency of contact do not appear to be significant distinguishing variables. Blacks seem to have available and to utilize a significantly broader range of informal supports, not just larger numbers of individuals willing to provide supports. Informal support systems among aged blacks appear to generate a greater variety and more depth in instrumental and emotional types of support (Sokolovsky, 1985; Wood & Parham, 1990).

Older blacks in the rural South have reported more support from non-kin (neighbors, friends) (Chatters, Taylor, & Jackson, 1986; Wood & Parham, 1990). The reasons for this are not readily apparent. Unique regional cultural values relating to helping and/or regional effects of black migration patterns may be reflected (Chatters et al., 1986).

In any case, black families seem to demonstrate a flexibility in kinship boundaries, which may have arisen from their Afro-American heritage (Jackson & Walls, 1979; Tate, 1983; Taylor, 1982). These kinship links (i.e., unrelated persons regarded in terms of kinship) are based upon functional expectations within the context of cultural norms and existing interpersonal relationships

(Chatters et al., 1986; Tate, 1983; Taylor, 1982). Extended kin, friends, and neighbors appear to perform functions that only close relatives perform in white families.

The black church also plays a special role in the support networks of older rural blacks. The church remains a significant provider of tangible services, as well as emotional and social support, in black communities. Ministers and parishioners are often involved in providing both instrumental and expressive care on a long-term basis for frail elders (Wood & Parham, 1990).

These kinds of informal services are often seen as filling the void where formal services are not available or where utilization of formal services are not seen as culturally appropriate. Informal transportation networks function in much the same manner. Individuals who have automobiles and who have the time to provide transportation services often do so. However, such services are not always inexpensive. In many instances, these individuals may be retirees or persons who are otherwise unemployed. Even family members may charge considerable fees for transporting frail elders to doctors' appointments or to do regular shopping. Individuals who provide transportation services may support themselves financially or enhance otherwise meager income in this manner over periods of many years.

While older adults, and others who have need of such services, may feel that the charges are exorbitant, they continue to utilize them, when other choices seem unavailable. The provision of transportation and other informal services may be interpreted within the context of a system of exchange. Norms of reciprocity are usually quite strong in black communities, having evolved from the cooperative lifestyle that served as a survival mechanism in earlier times and that continues to serve as a source of support, especially among families of low socioeconomic status. Even frail elders may provide child care, shared housing, or financial assistance to younger family members in need of aid. In return, health care and transportation services are provided informally in order to allow the older individual to live out his/her life within the context of home and community.

Institutionalization: Caregiving Consequence of Last Resort

Formal services, particularly institutional services, are sought among older rural blacks, as among members of majority culture, as a resource of last resort. Little outcome research on health care decision making among minority families has been done. Significant predictors of decisions to institutionalize a frail elder are unknown. One might suppose that, as among majority families, the availability of an informal caregiver, whether family or extended kin, is likely to be the best predictor (Arling & McAuley, 1983; Palmore, 1983; Scott & Roberto, 1985).

Morycz (1985) found, in a small sample ($N = 18$) of black caregivers to relatives with Alzheimer's disease, that decisions to institutionalize were predicted most often by conflicts with the patient. In general, however, caregiver strain did not play a significant role in predicting desire to institutionalize (Morycz, 1985).

Although empirical data are inadequate to fully support our theoretical model (see Figure 3.1), research reviewed in this chapter indicates that limited access to formal services places rural black elders at special risk for institutionalization when family resources for care are unavailable. Greene and Ondrich (1990) found that blacks who are admitted to nursing homes are less likely to leave. This may reflect a propensity for black families to delay admission until resources are unable to support continued care. When informal resources are exhausted, few alternatives to institutionalization are available. Thus, attention to the special concerns of rural black caregivers is warranted.

SPECIAL STRAINS FOR RURAL BLACK CAREGIVERS IN PROVIDING CARE TO COGNITIVELY IMPAIRED ELDERS

As noted earlier, rural minority caregivers function in a context that presents special challenges (i.e., disadvantages with regard to socioeconomic status, health, transportation, access to services). However, studies comparing caregivers of different racial/ethnic backgrounds have not found significant differences in the amount of strain/burden experienced by black or rural caregivers to frail elders (Cantor, 1983; Morycz, 1985; Wood & Parham, 1990). Although these studies have compared *racial* differences (i.e., used race as an independent variable) in the *amount* of caregiver strain/burden, cultural/ethnic differences in *sources* of strain have not been investigated. In other words, no effort has been made to determine whether there are unique sources of strain for black caregivers that may be attributable to cultural behavior patterns. The philosophical orientation of the African-American world view may indeed be a unique source of strain/burden for black caregivers.

African-American View of Illness

In black folk medicine, diseases are seen as arising from natural, that is, physical, causes. However, "natural" illnesses may also be spiritual in nature, for example, the result of sin or the willful violation of sacred beliefs (Watson, 1984). Natural illnesses may also be seen as divine punishment; thus, the fear of illness may function as an instrument of social control (Snow, 1983). Unnatural or occult illnesses are believed to be the works of evil spirits or conjurers and re-

flect conflict in the social network (Snow, 1983; Watson, 1984). (See Davis &
McGadney in this volume for additional insight into this issue.)

In traditional African systems of thought, the power of God is believed to be
present in humans as in all other forms of matter. For this reason, it is considered important not only for one's spiritual well-being but for one's physical
health as well to live in harmony with all of nature. Good health is seen as indication that one's life is in harmony, and disharmony is reflected in illness
(Watson, 1984). Thus, African-Americans, especially those from rural areas and
lower socioeconomic status, who likely continue to be influenced by traditional
folk beliefs, may conceive of illness as having a spiritual dimension. This culture-specific view of disease may be an especially troubling one for relatives providing care for frail elders.

Anecdotal evidence from research with rural black caregivers of Alzheimer's
patients supports this hypothesis (Wood, 1987). One caregiver commented to a
researcher that "we have just learned to accept cancer as a physical illness. This
Alzheimer's disease is something else." Another rural black caregiver sought
the help of a "conjure woman," believing that his wife's cognitive impairment
was the result of a hex or "sign" put on her by someone who wished her harm.
These folk views of illness are not mere exotic and rare occurrences, but are
common among a significant number of black Americans (Carter, 1988).
Eighty percent of the black elderly participants in a Michigan home health
study reported the practice of folk remedies, without the knowledge of their
physicians (Boyd, Shimp, & Hackney, 1984).

A few researchers have begun to explore cultural differences in coping strategies relative to the stress of health concerns. Conway (1985) found significant
differences in the mechanisms utilized by elderly whites and blacks in coping
with medical problems. Blacks reported more frequent use of prayer as a coping
mechanism and more use of nonprescription drugs.

Cultural differences in beliefs about the nature of specific illnesses may also
be a factor in differing sources of stress related to self-perceived health. Krause
(1987) found that chronic financial strain was related to the perceived health
status of older whites, but not older blacks. Crises within support networks affected health perceptions of older blacks, but not older whites. Presumably,
blacks had learned to cope with the reality of inadequate financial resources
but saw support network crises as threatening to self-perceived health. This
perception of stress is understandable from the perspective of a world view in
which some diseases are seen as resulting from conflict in the social network.

Awareness of the importance of harmony in the African world view also provides a framework for understanding Morycz's (1985) findings that conflict
with the patient-predicted caregiver willingness to institutionalize. This conflict
may represent such a threat to the caregiver's well-being that he or she is unable to continue the caregiving relationship.

CULTURAL VARIATIONS IN COPING STRATEGIES: RESULTS FROM AN EXPLORATORY STUDY

In an exploratory study of cultural differences in coping strategies employed by family caregivers of Alzheimer's patients, blacks reported more frequent use of prayer as a coping strategy (Wood & Parham, 1990). While white caregivers in this study reported more behavioral coping strategies, such as attendance at Alzheimer's support groups meetings, black caregivers reported more use of a number of internal cognitive strategies for coping. These included reliance on religious belief systems and more frequent cognitive reframing of the situation in positive terms. Many of these cognitions (e.g., I have to get through this. I've been through a lot before; I'll get through this, too) reflect determination to survive the caregiving experience. Similarly, Segall and Wykle (1988–89) found that black caregivers of dementia patients selected two dominant styles of coping in caring for their confused relative: (1) prayer and faith in God and (2) accommodating oneself to the situation. The use of these coping strategies likely reflect an ethnic heritage evolved from status as a racial minority. Varghese and Medinger (1979) point out that passive appraisals of difficult situations may be adaptive responses for minority group members. They may also function as secondary control techniques, that is, represent a way of gaining perceived control in situations where efforts to manipulate the environment have limited success. These types of coping strategies would seem to be adaptive for Alzheimer's caregivers who may be powerless to change the external and objective stressors in the caregiving situations.

Black caregivers in the Wood and Parham (1990) study had available and utilized a significantly broader range of informal social supports than did whites. These included family, friends, and members of the clergy, who were actively involved in providing instrumental support to the caregiver (e.g., assistance in providing physical care for the patient, financial assistance, assistance with running errands for the caregiver). Conway (1985) also found that black ministers were more likely than whites to provide support in illness-related situations.

Wood and Parham (1990) found that there is a very strong indication that black caregivers considered God as a part of their support system. Blacks reported the receipt of instrumental support and respite from God. This is distinct from the use of cognitive coping strategies reflecting a religious mind set and a personal conception of the divinity, reported also by Wood and Parham (1990) and earlier by Taylor (1982) and Conway (1985). The implication of this finding supports a culturally based distinction between a moral belief and a personal relationship. From the perspective of black caregivers in this sample, God is perceived in a very personal way and is considered as much a part of the informal support system as family, friends, or neighbors.

While exploratory, this study suggests ethnic/cultural variations in coping strategies that may be impacted by minority status and/or conditions of rural living. Clearly, the effectiveness of culturally distinct coping strategies would affect caregivers' ability to continue to provide care. The theoretical model presented in Figure 3.1 posits that a number of variables (minority group membership, ethnic culture, and rural living) interact in a complex configuration to predict the nature and type of services utilized. Caregivers' coping strategies may be posited in the model as a significant mediator between use of formal/informal care and institutionalization. Empirical validation of this model remains an important research agenda.

DIFFICULTIES IN STUDYING RURAL BLACK CAREGIVERS

Smaller population bases and scattered patterns of settlement in rural communities create special problems in doing research. The physical distances between subjects require a larger time investment and more financial resources in order to have access to subjects. Consequently, rural studies are more expensive and are less frequently undertaken.

Additional pragmatic issues warrant attention in conducting studies among minority groups. Primary among these is the need for support from informal community leaders (Burton & Bengtson, 1982; Cox, 1987). At best, minority communities, especially African-American communities in the rural South, are not likely to be oriented to research. At worst, community leaders are likely to be sensitive or possibly hostile to potential exploitation of minority individuals and groups by researchers. In any case, researchers will do well to seek community support before attempting to recruit subjects.Researchers and others working within minority populations should realize that community leaders do not occupy the same positions in all ethnic groups. Rural minority communities often coexist with majority communities, sharing the same geographic area, but with each having its own community name and identity. If the focal point of the white community is the post office, the social center of the black community may be a church. The community leader from whom sanction must be sought is likely not the minister, for many rural black churches are pastored by ministers who may live an hour's drive or more away. Instead, the person to consult to about the proposed research may be a local hairdresser, funeral director, retired teacher, or other individual whose family has been influential in the church for many years. The involvement of these informal community leaders can be crucial to the success of a research project. They legitimize the study within the ethnic community and can facilitate access to participants. A number of researchers (Burton & Bengtson, 1982; Cox, 1987; Gelfand & Tow,

1978; Jackson, 1988) have documented the value of involving community leaders very early in the planning stages of ethnic research.

Findings from the exploratory study presented in this chapter point up the importance of utilizing what Ramon Valle (1989) has referred to as "culturally fair" research methodologies. In order to collect accurate data relating to ethnic and cultural variables, we must make use of both quantitative and ethnographic methods. Continued use of standardized, culturally biased research instruments will deprive us of richness in ethnic data. Jackson (1989) has argued that all scientific research in aging should be conducted within an "ethnogerontological model."

Operationalization of variables, selection of instruments, and the wording of questions can be important factors in research with black elders. Lack of attention to racially sensitive issues may lead to collection of inaccurate data. Jackson (1988) reported that, in the National Survey of Black Americans (NSBA), many older blacks preferred a racial designation of colored or negro, reflecting an age-by-race interaction issue. Limitation of choices to more current terms of racial designation (e.g., black, African-American) might have produced negative attitudes or lack of cooperation with the survey. In the NSBA, researchers also found that respondents' cultural interpretation of scale items affected their responses (Jackson, 1988). Effort must be directed to developing research methodologies that are culturally fair.

An important instrumentation issue involves the use of minority staff in data collection. This is not to suggest that only indigenous researchers who know the minority community and its residents should be utilized. Minority researchers may have fewer problems than majority researchers in attempting to conduct studies in a minority community. However, maintenance of scientific objectivity in the face of one's own ethnic loyalty and expectations from the community for support and advocacy can place conflicting demands on the minority researcher (Maykovich, 1977). As Jacqueline Jackson (1967) has pointed out, the important criteria for conducting effective research in minority aging are methodological expertise in gerontology, a solid interdisciplinary foundation in the content area, and understanding of the subject population. Sensitivity to ethnic and cultural issues, awareness of one's own ethnocentrism, and respect for cultural differences are more important than the racial background of the researcher.

Nonetheless, if the project is to have credibility in the minority community, the research staff must include more than token representation of the minority group(s) being studied. Inclusion of minority researchers on the staff will do much to promote acceptance for the project. Projects that are staffed by white researchers only are likely to be met with suspicion, if not hostility. The likely perception in the black community is that white researchers cannot possibly understand the black experience. Indigenous/minority researchers can provide vital insight into the social structure and mores of the community, including attitudes toward the aged. For example, Jackson (1988) reported that black respondents' responses were influenced by their perception of the interviewer's race.

POLICY AND PRACTICE IMPLICATIONS

Given the paucity of research in ethnic and minority issues in family caregiving to frail elders, and given the significance of family caregivers in the spectrum of long-term care, an obvious need exists for continued study of this population. Existing studies of rural black caregivers point to a number of barriers and service needs. Several recommendations can be made based on current data.

First, more community-based and in-home services are needed for older adults in rural areas. Proper assessment of service needs should be made so that funding formulas can consider their unique needs and special characteristics of life in rural areas.

Second, existing and newly developed services should be culturally compatible. Vestiges of overt and covert racism must be removed. Bastida (1983) found that community context, (i.e., accessibility to and control of power resources) was a major mediating factor predicting service utilization by minority elders. In instances where culturally compatible services have been developed, the utilization rate of minority clients is comparable to the rate of nonmonorities.

Third, culturally sensitive intervention strategies should be developed to support minority caregivers. Since black caregivers typically do not participate in caregiver support groups, there is a need to develop an acceptable ethnic alternative. Black caregivers have expressed the need for peer support (Wood & Parham, 1990). Perhaps caregiver peer support could be added to the growing list of social services offered through black churches.

Finally, education about aging, the chronic illnesses that frequently accompany advancing years, and available community resources is a critical need in black communities. Specific educational initiatives could focus on teaching caregivers about behavioral management techniques and family care management strategies. Resource guides are needed to identify available community services. Again, the church may serve as a medium to provide caregiver information and education services.

In conclusion, culturally compatible counseling services are needed to assist family caregivers in building on the culturally specific coping styles that have been identified (Conway, 1985; Segall & Wykle, 1988–89; Wood & Parham, 1990). Additionally, more frequent use of problem-focused, behavioral coping strategies such as seeking information about the problem or the resources available to deal with it (Segall & Wykle, 1988–89; Wood & Parham, 1990) may help alleviate some of the barriers to care for the minority family. Finally, the resources of the ethnic family should be strengthened so that continued care for the frail elderly may be provided within the family context.

REFERENCES

American Association of Retired Persons. (1986). *A Portrait of Older Minorities.* Washington, DC: American Association of Retired Persons.

American Association of Retired Persons and The Travelers Foundation. (1988). *A National Survey of Caregivers: Final Report.* Washington, DC: American Association of Retired Persons.

Arling, G., & McAuley, W. J. (1983). The feasibility of public payments for family caregiving. *The Gerontologist, 23,* 300–306.

Bastida, E. M. (1983). Minority decision-making accessibility, and resource utilization in the provision of services: Urban–rural differences. In R. L. McNeely & J. L. Colen (Eds.), *Aging in minority groups.* Beverly Hills, CA: Sage.

Bowers, B. J. (1988). Family perceptions of nursing home care: A grounded theory study of family work in a nursing home. *The Gerontologist, 28,* 361–368.

Boyd, E., Shimp, L. A., & Hackney, M. J. (1984). *Home remedies and the black elderly.* Ann Arbor, MI: University of Michigan.

Burdz, M. P., Eaton, W. O., & Bond, J. B., Jr. (1988). Effect of respite care on dementia and nondementia patients and their caregivers. *Psychology and Aging, 3,* 38–42.

Burton, L. & Bengtson, V. L. (1982). Research in elderly minority communities: Problems and potentials. In R. C. Manuel (Ed.), *Minority aging.* Westport, CT: Greenwood Press.

Cantor, M. (1975). Life space and social support system of the inner city elderly of New York *The Gerontologist, 15,* 23–27.

Cantor, M. H. (1979). The informal support system of New York's inner city elderly: Is ethnicity a factor? In D. Gelfand & A. Kutzik (Eds.), *Ethnicity and aging.* New York; Springer Publishing Co.

Cantor, M. H. (1983). Strain among caregivers: A study of experience in the United States. *The Gerontologist, 23,* 597–604.

Carter, J. H. (1988). Health attitudes/promotions/preventions: The black elderly. In J. S. Jackson, (Ed.), *The black American elderly: Research on physical and psychosocial health.* New York: Springer Publishing Co.

Chatters, L. M., Taylor, R. J., & Jackson, J. S. (1986). Aged blacks' choices for an informal helper network. *Journal of Gerontology, 41,* 91–100.

Conway, K. (1985). Coping with the stress of medical problems among black and white elderly. *International Journal of Aging and Human Development, 21,* 39–47.

Coward, R. T. (1983). Serving families in contemporary rural America: Definitions, importance, and future. In R. T. Coward & W. M. Smith (Eds.), *Family services: Issues and opportunities in contemporary rural America.* Lincoln: University of Nebraska Press.

Coward, R. T. & Smith, W. M. (1982). Families in rural society. In D. A. Dillman & D. J. Hobbs (Eds.), *Rural society in the U.S.: Issues for the 1980s.* Boulder, CO: Westview Press.

Cox, C. (1987). Overcoming access problems in ethnic communities. In D. E. Gelfand & C. M. Barresi, (Eds.), *Ethnic dimensions of aging*. New York: Springer Publishing Co.

Cuellar, J. B., & Weeks, J. R. (1980). *Minority elderly Americans: A prototype for area agencies on aging*. Executive Summary, Administration on Aging, Grant No. 90-A-1667 (01). San Diego, CA: Allied Home Health Association.

Eyde, D. R., & Rich, J. A. (1983). *Psychological distress in aging: A family management model*. Rockville, MD: Aspens Systems Corporation.

Gelfand, D., & Tow, M. (1978). Theoretical and applied inputs in mental health center research. *American Journal of Community Psychology, 6*, 81–89.

George, L. K. (1984). *The dynamics of caregiver burden*. Final report submitted to the AARP Andrus Foundation.

George, L. K. (1988). Social participation in later life: Black–white differences. In J. S. Jackson (Ed.), *The black American elderly: Research on physical and psychosocial health*. New York: Springer Publishing Co.

Greene, V. L., & Ondrich, J. I. (1990). Risk factors for nursing home admissions and exits: A discrete-time hazard function approach. *Journal of Gerontology Social Sciences, 45*, S250–258.

Groger, B. L. (1983). Growing old with or without it: The meaning of land in a southern rural community. *Research on Aging, 5*, 511–526.

Hanson, S. S., Patterson, M. A., & Wilson, R. W. (1988). Family involvement on a dementia unit: The resident enrichment and activity program. *The Gerontologist, 28*, 508–510.

Hanson, S. L., Sauer, W. J., & Seelbach, W. C., (1983). Racial and cohort variations in filial responsibility norms. *The Gerontologist, 23*, 626–631.

Jackson, J. J. (1967). Social gerontology and the Negro: A review. *The Gerontologist, 7*, 168–178.

Jackson, J. J. (1977). The black aging: A demographic overview. In R. Kalish (Ed.), *The later years: Social applications of gerontology*. Monterey, CA: Brooks-Cole.

Jackson, J. J., & Walls, B. E. (1979). Aging patterns in black families. In A. J. Lichtman & J. R. Challinor (Eds.), *Kin and communities*. Washington, DC: Smithsonian Institution.

Jackson, J. S. (1988) Survey research on aging black populations. In J. S. Jackson (Ed.), *The black American elderly: Research on physical and psychosocial health*. (pp. 327–346). New York: Springer Publishing Co.

Jackson, J. S. (1989). Race, ethnicity and psychological theory and research. *Journal of Gerontology, 44*, 1–2.

Krause, N. (1987). Stress in racial differences in self-reported health among the elderly. *The Gerontologist, 27*, 72–76.

Krout, J. A. (1983). Correlates of service utilization among the rural elderly. *The Gerontologist, 23*, 500–504.

Lawton, M. P., Brody, E. M., & Saperstein, A. R. (1989). A controlled study of respite service for caregivers of Alzheimer's patients. *The Gerontologist, 29*, 8–16.

Maykovich, M. K. (1977). The difficulties of a minority researcher in minority communities. *Journal of Social Issues, 33*, 108–119.

McAuley, W.J., Arling, G., Nutty, C., & Bowling, C. (1980). *Statewide survey of older*

Virginians, Final Report, *Vol. II Findings*. Richmond, VA: Virginia Center on Aging.

Miller, D. B., & Goldman L. (1989). Perceptions of caregivers about special respite services for the elderly. *The Gerontologist, 29*, 408–410.

Mitchell, J., & Register, J. C. (1984). An exploration of family interaction with the elderly by race, socioeconomic status, and residence. *The Gerontologist, 24*, 48–53.

Morycz, R. K. (1985). Caregiving strain and the desire to institutionalize family members with Alzheimer's disease. *Research on Aging, 7*, 329–361.

Nelson, G. M. (1983). A comparison of Title XX services to the urban and rural elderly. *Journal of Gerontological Social Work, 6*, 2–23.

Pagel, M. D., Becker, J., & Coppel, D. B. (1985). Loss of control, self-blame, and depression: An investigation of spouse caregivers of Alzheimer's disease patients. *Journal of Abnormal Psychology, 94*, 169–182.

Palmore, E. (1983). Health care needs of the rural elderly. *International Journal of Aging and Human Development, 18*, 39–45.

Pratt, C. C., Schmall, V.L., Cleland, M., & Wright, S. (1985). Burden and coping strategies of caregivers to Alzheimer's patients. *Family Relations, 34*, 27–33.

Rosenthal, C. J. (1986). Family supports in later life. Does ethnicity make a difference? *The Gerontologist, 26*, 19–24.

Scharlach, A., & Frenzel, C. (1986). An evaluation of institution-based respite care. *The Gerongologist, 26*, 77–82.

Schorr, A. L. (1960). *Filial responsibility in the modern American family*. Washington, DC: U. S. Department of Health, Education and Welfare.

Schneider, D. M., & Smith, R. T. (1973). *Class differences and sex roles in American kinship and family structure*. Englewood Cliffs, NJ: Prentice-Hall.

Scott, J. P. & Roberto, K. A. (1985). Use of informal and formal support networks by rural elderly poor. *The Gerontologist, 25*, 624–630.

Segall, M., & Wykle, M. (1988–89, Fall/Winter). The black family's experience with dementia. *Journal of Applied Social Sciences, 13*, 170–191.

Seltzer, M. M., Ivry, J., & Litchfield, L. C. (1987). Family members as case managers: Partnership between the formal and informal support networks. *The Gerontologist, 27*, 722–728.

Snow, L. F. (1983). Traditional health beliefs and practices among lower class black Americans. *Western Journal of Medicine, 139*, 820–828.

Sokolovsky, J. (1985). Ethnicity, culture, and aging: Do differences really make a difference? *Journal of Applied Gerontology, 4*, 6–17.

Stoller, E. P., & Pugliesi, K. L. (1989). The transition to the caregiving role: A panel study of helpers of elderly people. *Research on Aging, 11*, 312–330.

Stone, R., Cafferata, G. L., & Sangl, J. (1987). Caregivers of the frail elderly: A national profile. *The Gerontologist, 27*, 616–626.

Tate, N. (1983). The black aging experience. In R. L. McNeely & J. L. Colen (Eds.), *Aging in minority groups* (pp. 95–107). Beverly Hills, CA: Sage.

Taylor, S. P. (1982). Mental health and successful coping among aged black women. In R. C. Manuel (Ed.), *Minority aging* (pp. 95–100). Westport, CT: Greenwood Press.

Valle, R. (1989). Cultural and ethnic issues in Alzheimer's disease family research. In E.

Light & B. Lebowitz (Eds.), *Alzheimer's disease treatment and family stress: Directions for research* (pp. 122–154). Rockville, MD: National Institute of Mental Health.

Varghese, R., & Medinger, F. (1979). Fatalism in response to stress among the minority aged. In D. E. Gelfand & A. J. Kutzik (Eds.), *Ethnicity and aging*. New York: Springer Publishing Co.

Wan, T. T. H. (1977). The differential use of health services. A minority perspective. *Urban Health*, 16, 47–49.

Wan, T. T. H., Odell, B., & Lewis, D. (1982). *Well-being for the elderly: A community diagnosis*. New York: Haworth Press.

Watson, W. H. (Ed.). (1984). *Black folk medicine* New Brunswick, NJ: Transaction Books.

Wood, J. B. (1987). *Coping with the absence of perceived control: Ethnic and cultural issues in family caregiving for patients with Alzheimer's disease*. Unpublished doctoral dissertation.

Wood, J. B, & Parham, I. A. (1990). Coping with perceived burden: Ethnic and cultural issues in Alzheimer's family caregiving. *Journal of Applied Gerontology*, 9, 325–339.

4

Black and Hispanic Caregivers of Dementia Victims: Their Needs and Implications for Services

Carole Cox
Abraham Monk

Family caretaking of dementia victims can impose substantial burdens and demands on both emotional and physical resources, affecting many spheres of the caregiver's life. Extensive literature has documented the common occurrence of chronic fatigue, anger, depression, and increased mental problems associated with the caregiving activity (Chenoweth & Spencer, 1986; George & Gwyther, 1986; Rabins, Mace, & Lucas, 1982). Yet the majority of these persons continue to provide needed care at home, usually without the assistance of formal services (Caserta, Lund, Wright, & Redburn, 1987; Mace, 1984; Zarit, Todd, & Zarit, 1986).

Several factors, including a lack of knowledge or access, attitudes, poor link-

This project was supported by a grant from AARP Andrus Foundation.

57

age between services, financial restrictions, and strong informal networks, may affect this utilization of services. Among minority caregivers, whose use of formal support services is consistently less than their white counterparts, comparatively less is known about their patterns of service utilization. There is, in fact, an underlying premise that the families manage effectively through the informal network and, thus, do not require formal assistance. The aim of the study described here is to examine the use of both informal and formal services by black and Hispanic families in order to further our understanding of their caregiving experiences and needs.

BLACK AND HISPANIC FAMILIES

Family Supports

Both black and Hispanic families have been characterized as having extensive and very involved support networks (Billingsley, 1970; Mindel, Wright, & Starrett, 1986). However, research also suggests that these networks may be influenced by social and demographic factors. Black elderly of lower socioeconomic status appear to have more supportive relationships with their children than those in higher economic groups (Cantor, 1979). Elderly blacks living in the South seem to possess more consistent support than those in the Northeast and to have a larger reservoir of informal helpers (Chatters, Taylor, & Jackson, 1985; Taylor, 1985). At the same time, adherence to norms of filial responsibility have been found to be less strongly supported among middle-aged and older blacks living in the Midwest, perhaps due to financial and family pressures (Hanson, Saueer, & Seelbach, 1983). These findings imply that many characteristics need to be considered if accurate profiles of caregiving relationships within the black community are to be made.

Within the Hispanic culture, the children have traditionally acted as the main providers of assistance (Maldonado, 1975). Among Hispanics, reciprocal caregiving between the generations has been the basis for a natural helping network as well as for providing links with the formal system (Valle & Martinez, 1981). It is not clear, however, the extent to which filial supports persist or change in their functions over time. Some studies indicate that family structures tend to weaken as a function of generational succession and that elderly Hispanics are becoming more isolated in the community (Newton, 1980; Solis, 1975). Due to increasing participation in the labor force and geographic mobility, children are no longer readily available to provide customary services and assistance to their parents. Contrasting research has found that filial assistance remains strong and intact (Torres-Gil, 1983). Older Hispanics continue to expect, receive, and be satisfied with the help provided by their adult children and to feel that their support needs are being adequately met (Cox & Gelfand,

1987; Lopez & Pearson, 1985). These conflicting findings suggest that, as within the black community, generalizations regarding the nature of caregiving activities and relationships may be difficult to substantiate.

SAMPLE SELECTION AND DESIGN

The research reported on here attempted to assess the use of both informal and formal supports by black and Hispanic family caregivers caring for a relative suffering from Alzheimer's disease or a related dementia. Interviews were conducted with 76 black and 86 Hispanic persons in New York City and Baltimore, Maryland. Respondents were located through hospital clinics, senior centers, community organizations, family support groups, and the waiting lists of day care centers.

Data were collected on these persons' utilization of informal and formal services and their attitudes toward caregiving. In addition, measures were also made of patient functioning (Memory/Behavior Checklist, Zarit, Reever, & Bach-Peterson, 1980), caregiver depression through the CES-D Scale (Radloff, 1977), and caregiver sense of burden (Zarit et al., 1986).

RESULTS

Description of Caregivers

Most caregivers and the dementia patients were female, with a median age of 60 years for the black caregivers and for the Hispanics, 54 years. Only a minority of each group were spouses of the patients, 25% of the black and 23% of the Hispanic. In most cases care was being provided to a mother or mother-in-law and had been for a median duration of 4 years. The median ages of the patients were 77 years for the black group and 75 years for the Hispanics.

Almost all of the black caregivers and their relatives were born in the United States. The majority were Protestant (81%) and felt that religion was important in their lives, although they did not attend religious services regularly. For many, it was their religious faith that seemed to be a primary support. "I know Jesus won't give me more than I can bear," was often heard in the interviews. However, it is important to note that only a minority of respondents, 40%, had actually discussed their relative with their clergyman.

In contrast to the black respondents, the majority of the Hispanic group were born in Puerto Rico. Indicative of their maintenance of close ties with the traditional ethnic culture, most spoke Spanish at home and with their friends. The majority were Catholic and, similar to the black group, religion was important in their lives. But, as found among the black respondents, only a minority, 47%, had consulted a clergyman regarding their relative.

The caregivers had a median education of 12 (black) and 11 (Hispanic) years. Slightly more blacks (47%) than Hispanics (40%) were employed. Of those no longer working, very few in either group had stopped working in order to provide full-time care. Both groups were within the lower socioeconomic strata, with the median income between $6,000 and $10,000 per year.

In each sample, the first noticeable symptom of dementia was forgetfulness. As other symptoms such as confusion, wandering, and hallucinations developed, caregivers sought advice. For the majority of both groups of caregivers, persons first turned to relatives for consultation and then to physicians. Overall, the most important source for obtaining information on Alzheimer's disease was the media, including newspapers, radio, and magazines.

In describing their own physical health, caregivers in both groups, 54% of the blacks and 60% of the Hispanics, felt their health had not altered within the past year and that it was not affected by their caregiving responsibilities. But more black caregivers (60%) than Hispanic (49%) felt their own health interfered with their ability to provide assistance. Respondents tended to rate their health positively in comparison to that of others in their age groups. However, within each group, the majority of persons were under a physician's care for at least one medical condition.

Although both sets of caregivers measured within the moderate range on the Burden scale, the Hispanics had a significantly higher score ($p < .001$) than did the blacks. At the same time, the Hispanic sample appeared to be clinically depressed. Their scores on the CES-D scale were elevated (18.5) and significantly higher than those of the black caregivers ($p < .001$), whose scores were within the normal range. Scores on the scale range from 0 to 60, with a score of 16 or more indicating high levels of depressive symptomatology. Although the validity of the CES-D instrument with ethnic groups has been questioned (Aneshensel, Clark, & Freichs, 1983; Sagetta & Johnson, 1980), the findings among the Hispanics are replicative of those of a comparable population of elderly Puerto Ricans in New York (Mahard, 1988). In Mahard's study, the elevated scores were found to accurately discriminate between psychiatric patients and nonpatients in the community.

Use of Informal and Formal Supports

Isolation can be devastating to caregivers since it can have both emotional and practical consequences. Within these groups, caregivers did not appear to suffer the same sense of seclusion often experienced by their white counterparts. Respondents reported that they had close confidants with whom they talked frequently, discussing their worries and concerns so that their needs for nurturance and support were being met. However, more blacks (50%) than Hispanics (33%) saw these supportive others on a daily basis. It is, thus, not surprising that the black caregivers received more instrumental assistance with caregiving tasks from the informal network than did the Hispanics.

Although their needs for emotional support were met through the informal network, the Hispanic respondents depended more upon the formal services for caregiving assistance than did the blacks. A further difference between the two groups of caregivers was the relationship of the informal to the formal network. Within the black sample, the use of informal assistance was positively related to the use of formal services. This was not true within the Hispanic group, where increased formal assistance was associated with less informal support.

In both samples, the use of formal assistance was negatively related to income. Since persons are entitled to home care and home help assistance under state Medicaid programs in both New York and Maryland, many of the respondents were eligible for these benefits. Higher income persons were most likely unable to afford private caregiving services. Other formal services such as day care, support groups, and respite care were infrequently used due to either a lack of access or long waiting lists.

Both groups expressed needs for more assistance. The black respondents desired significantly ($p < .05$) more help than Hispanics with the activities of daily living, dressing, shaving, medicating, and walking the patient. Blacks also expressed the need for more relief assistance so that they could do errands and have more time for themselves. Hispanics expressed a significantly greater need ($p < .05$) in help with paying bills, appearing to be satisfied with the other types of assistance.

An important factor provided by informal supports, aside from the emotional and instrumental assistance they may offer, is their practical availability to completely take over caregiving responsibilities. But only a minority of caregivers, 34% of the blacks and 43% of the Hispanics, had someone who could assume this role. Thus, for the majority of all caregivers, there were no persons who could provide alternative total or respite support in their networks. The effects of this absence are illustrated in the following two examples.

In the first, a schoolteacher who had her mother with severe Alzheimer's disease living with her, with four siblings in the local area, found they offered only occasional assistance and money. Total responsibility for care rested with her as the primary caregiver, with her requests for more tangible involvement in the form of temporary care by her family generally going unheeded. As a result, her own marriage was beginning to suffer under the dual strain of continual caregiving and professional demands.

Another example of the burden of relentless caregiving is provided by that of a university professor caring for her mother-in-law. She intricately juggled her caregiving and professional responsibilities. Leaving her home at 6:30 A.M. daily, she drove her mother-in-law to her mother, who provided care until her husband collected her in the afternoon. Before leaving the house in the morning she had to feed, dress, and often redress her mother-in-law, frequently arriving at the university exhausted. Moreover, her own health was beginning to suffer, with her hypertension becoming worse. As in the case described above, there was no one else in the family who could provide even occasional respite care.

Caregivers were familiar with a variety of formal service providers but infrequently used them. For both the black and Hispanic respondents the most frequently used services were social workers, home attendants, and visiting nurses. The frequency of the use of social workers and home attendants may be accounted for by the fact that, as stated above, home care services are available to Medicaid eligible families in New York City; social workers are the primary source of referrals for this service. It is interesting to note that when asked what service they most needed, the largest proportion in each sample, 44% of the blacks and 41% of the Hispanics, responded that they needed home care.

Both black and Hispanic caregivers adhered to norms expecting that children should provide care for their parents. However, the Hispanic group felt significantly ($p < .05$) more strongly that children should live close to their parents in order to assist them and that children should be expected to do tasks for them ($p < .01$). Both sets of respondents favored familial over professional assistance, but neither felt that a person should give up work to provide care.

Assistance and Impairment Levels

In describing the impairment of the patient, the Hispanics felt their relative to be significantly more mentally and physically impaired ($p < .001$) than did the blacks. Furthermore, interesting differences were found between the blacks and Hispanics in the relationship of the condition of the relative to the use of informal and formal assistance. Within the black sample, increased impairment on the ADL scores was related to the more intensive use of formal supports ($p < .01$) while mental impairment was positively related ($p < .05$) to the use of more informal supports. At the same time, there was a positive relationship between the use of both types of supports ($p < .05$), indicating that they may complement each other and that persons may use them interchangeably.

Within the Hispanic sample, caregivers utilized less informal support ($p < .05$) and more formal supports ($p < .01$) in relation to the relative's degree of physical impairment. As with the black families, this suggests that caregivers and their supportive others are better able to cope with the mental problems associated with the illness than with the physical. But contrary to the experiences of the black sample, the two types of support services were negatively related ($p < .001$). This finding suggests that as the patient's functioning deteriorates, the caregiver relies more on professional help, with the informal network gradually dissipating.

As discussed earlier, one of the most frequently used formal services in both samples was the home attendant, with 39% of the blacks and 47% of the Hispanics utilizing this help at a minimum of 3 times a week. It is important to note, however, that in neither group was the use of the attendant associated with either the degree of impairment of the patient or the health status, sense of burden, or feelings of depression of the caregiver. Other undefined and intervening factors appear to influence the caregivers' use of these supports.

The relationship of the burden and depression scores to the attitudes of the caregivers merits special attention. Among the blacks, a greater sense of burden ($p < .05$) was experienced by those reluctant to use professional assistance and by those feeling that one should not give up employment to provide care. Persons experiencing the greatest sense of burden may therefore be those attempting to balance multiple roles. At the same time, those caregivers preferring professional to informal assistance were more likely to be depressed ($p < .05$).

Among Hispanics, those preferring professional assistance to that of a relative experienced greater feelings of burden ($p < .05$). Those more firmly adhering to norms of filial support that state that children should care for their parents and not use professional help manifested more depression ($p < .01$). These findings for both groups indicate that although caregivers may turn to the formal network for assistance, the utilization in itself may pose a potential risk to their emotional well-being.

DISCUSSION

The findings of this study reinforce those of other researchers that stress the significant role that cultural values and norms continue to play within ethnic groups. Consistent with the results of previous research, the study confirms that both black and Hispanic caregivers continue to express strong feelings of filial obligation that may influence their internalization of the caregiving role as well as the involvement of other informal supports in the network. This involvement, however, is limited in that there is an apparent lack of any alternative full-time caregiver. Thus, although persons do not experience a sense of emotional isolation and do receive emotional support, the primary responsibility for care rests with one person.

Both groups were knowledgeable about formal services and willing to use them. However, the factors associated with utilization among the two populations vary, suggesting that ethnicity may, in fact, be related to the coping skills of the caregivers and their supports. The Hispanics used less informal and more formal assistance as the patient's physical condition deteriorated. Although the blacks also used more formal services with increased physical impairment, they did not relinquish the use of the informal, utilizing both simultaneously. It may be that within the black community, relatives act as a link with the formal system, pooling their expertise and knowledge to obtain services. Within the Hispanic group, the decision to turn to formal services may only occur when the family is already overwhelmed. This may partially account for the fact that the Hispanic caregivers feel generally more burdened and depressed than their black counterparts, even when using formal supports. It is also important to note that within both groups the use of services contradicted cultural norms of responsibility. It is thus not surprising that such use could be associated with depression among the caregivers. Rather than relieving these feelings, the use of services may be experienced as a failure to live up to one's expected role. Service providers must be aware that reaching out for assistance may be traumatic for persons who have been raised to believe caregiving should be provided by the family. Counseling and reassurance to relieve caregiver guilt need to be incorporated into the service package.

Persons were knowledgeable about programs and ways to gain access to them. To a certain extent, this may be explained by the wide use of the media, which in New York City particularly, through the Spanish radio stations and television, have been very successful in targeting information on programs and services to the Hispanic community. This finding is noteworthy, as it underscores the prominent role the media can play in reaching and informing minority groups.

Although the physical health of the caregivers did not seem to be unduly threatened, there appears to be some risk to the mental well-being of the Hispanic sample, who did have elevated scores for depression. Watching the gradual decline of their relatives with a sense of helplessness, coupled with the ambivalence they may feel about using formal services, may contribute to this depression. Although the respondents felt satisfied with their informal supports, it is possible that they do not provide as much help or emotional assistance as needed. Indicative of this is the fact that the respondents, both black and Hispanic, often told the interviewers how much the interviews helped and that they were the first persons with whom they could really discuss their problems.

IMPLICATIONS

Due to its limited scope, this study does not lend itself to sweeping generalizations regarding minority caregivers nor to definitive conclusions on their experiences. The findings, however, do suggest that ethnicity continues to play a significant role in the maintenance of support networks. The results corroborate those of other studies that show the presence of strong informal networks among black and Hispanic families and continued adherence to norms of filial support toward the elderly. These norms do not inhibit the use of formal services, although in some cases they may conflict with other values and affect caregiver well-being. The norms also do not guarantee that there is necessarily a large reservoir of available caregivers within the informal network. Taking these factors into account, several recommendations for planners and service providers within the long-term care system can be made.

Services should be designed that strengthen the natural support systems found in black and Hispanic families. There is ample evidence that caregivers feel primarily responsible for their relative and do not want to turn this care over to someone else. However, few persons used support groups, day care, or respite programs, services that could enhance their ability to cope. At the same time, caregivers, particularly the Hispanics, are greatly in need of mental health counseling to relieve the sense of burden and depression they experience. This counseling must be sensitive to their cultural experience and values and understanding of the conflicts that may relate to the use of the formal system.

Neither black nor Hispanic caregivers had a reliable substitute who could provide care for any prolonged period of time. Training community volunteers who could provide some relief, particularly in times of emergency, could assist in providing this type of support. Moreover, developing support groups within the ethnic community where persons could feel comfortable discussing their problems while learning from each other could further enhance the strengths of the caregivers.

The findings also suggest that religion continues to play an important part in these persons' lives. With this in mind, the clergy should be further educated and encouraged to reach out to these families. Educating these religious leaders about the nature of dementia and the needs of the families could thus be an important means of assistance. Churches should also be encouraged to provide volunteer and support groups to these families as well as respite services. Programs such as these, offered through the traditionally respected institution, could play extremely meaningful roles in supporting these caregivers.

Finally, it must be accepted that minority families do reach out into the community for assistance. Although informal supports are present and do appear to provide some emotional and instrumental relief, they cannot be relied upon to meet all of the caregivers' needs. As with their nonminority peers, the primary responsibility for care generally rests with one person. In order to effectively support and sustain these persons, services and interventions must be developed that reflect knowledge about ethnic differences, cultural values, and norms.

REFERENCES

Aneshensel, C., Clark, V., & Freichs, R. (1983). Ethnicity and depression: A confirmatory analysis. *Journal of Personality and Social Psychology, 44*, 385–398.

Billingsley, A. (1970). Black families and white social sciences. *Journal of Social Issues, 26*, 127–142.

Cantor, M. (1979). The informal support network of New York inner city elderly. In D.

Gelfand & A. Kutzik (Eds.), *Ethnicity and aging*. New York: Springer Publishing Co.

Caserta, M., Lund, D., Wright, S., & Redburn, D. (1987). Caregivers to dementia patients: The utility of community services. *The Gerontologist, 27*, 209–213.

Chatters, L., Taylor, R., & Jackson, J. (1985). Size and composition of the informal helper networks of elderly blacks. *Journal of Gerontology, 40*, 605–614.

Chenoweth, B., & Spencer, B. (1986). The experience of family caretakers. *The Gerontologist, 26*, 267–172.

Cox, C., & Gelfand, D. (1987). Patterns of family assistance, exchange and satisfaction among Hispanics, Portuguese, and Vietnamese elderly. *Journal of Cross-Cultural Gerontology, 2*, 241–255.

George, L., & Gwyther, L. (1986). Caregiver well-being: A multi-dimensional examination of family caregivers of demented adults. *The Gerontologist, 26*, 253–259.

Hanson, S., Sauer, W., & Seelbach, W. (1983). Racial and cohort variations in filial responsibility norms. *The Gerontologist, 23*, 626–631.

Lopez, M., & Pearson, R. (1985). The support needs of Puerto Rican elderly. *The Gerontologist, 25*, 483–487.

Mace, N. (1984). Self help for the family. In W. Kelly (Ed.), *Alzheimer's disease and related disorders*.Springfield, IL: Ch. C. Thomas.

Mahard, R. (1988). The CES-D as a measure of depressive mood in the elderly Puerto Rican population. *Journal of Gerontology, 43*, 24–25.

Maldonado, D. (1975). The Chicano aged. *Social Work, 20*, 213–216.

Mindel, C., Wright, R. & Starrett, R. (1986). Informal and formal health and social support systems of the black and white elderly: A comparative cost approach. *The Gerontologist, 26*, 279–285.

Newton, F. (1980). Issues in research and service delivery among Mexican-American elderly, a concise statement with recommendations. *The Gerontologist, 20*, 208–213.

Rabins, P., Mace, N., & Lucas, M. (1982). The impact of dementia on the family. *Journal of the American Medical Association, 248*, 333–338.

Radloff, L. (1977). The CES-D Scale: A self report depression scale for research in the general population. *Applied Psychological Measurement, 1*, 385–410.

Sagetta, R., & Johnson, D. (1980). *Basic data on depressive symptomatology, United States, 1974–1975*. Vital and Health Statistics, Series 11, 216, DHEW Publication No. 80-1666. Washington, DC.

Solis, R. (1975). Cultural factors in programming of services for the Spanish speaking elderly. In A. Hernandez & J. Mendoza (Eds.), *National conference for the Spanish speaking elderly*. Kansas City, MO: National Chicano Social Planning Council.

Taylor, R. (1985). The extended family as a source of support to elderly blacks. *The Gerontologist, 25*, 488–496.

Torres-Gil, F. (1983). Dismantlement of assumptions in Hispanic gerontology: Assessment of the rehabilitative, physical, and mental health status of elderly Hispanics. Paper presented at the 36th Annual Meeting of the Gerontology Society of America, San Francisco.

Valle, R., & Martinez, C. (1981). National networks of elderly Latinos of Mexican heritage: Implications for mental health. In M. Miranda & R. Reiz (Eds.), *Chicago aging and mental health*. Washington, D.C.: National Institute of Mental Health.

Zarit, S. H., Reever, K. E., & Bach-Peterson, J. (1980). Relatives of the impaired elderly: Correlates of feelings of burden. *The Gerontologist, 20,* 649–655.

Zarit, S. H., Todd, P., & Zarit, J., (1986). Subjective burden of husbands and wives as caregivers: A longitudinal study. *The Gerontologist, 26,* 260–266.

PART III

Long-Term Care Practices in Ethnic Communities

There are two central points on which this book is organized: (1) there are many types of long-term care, and (2) long-term care practices vary both within and between ethnic communities. Long-term care can include not only the formal level of care such as nursing homes and day care centers, but also the informal level as found in family care and neighbors offering needed services. Variations in long-term care practices and beliefs follow from the differences in cultural norms regarding family relationships as well as views of health, religion, and other relevant areas. Not only do these beliefs vary between ethnic groups, but heterogeneity within groups leads to further differences.

The first chapter in this section deals with self-care, a seldom discussed type of long-term care. Davis and McGadney define self-care as lay persons initiating and performing health activities on their own behalf to promote life, health, and well-being. They contend that the self-care practices of black elders differ from those of other groups because of their cultural history and continuing social and economic inequalities. They also note that because of heterogeneity among black elderly, these practices vary within the group. A cornerstone on which self-care practices are based is the belief that good health is an individual responsibility. African traditions blended with Southern roots form the foundation used to maintain health and treat illnesses. In summarizing, Davis and McGadney discuss self-care in the context of an illness model that takes into account the intersection of client and practitioner perspectives. They conclude with the suggestion that self-care practices and the underlying belief system may impact formal medical treatment and long-term care.

The next chapter in this section deals with the type of long-term care that is found in congregate housing for the elderly. Yu, Kim, Lin, and Wong present data from a study of Chinese and Korean elders, in congregate housing in Chicago. They focus on the level of functioning among these elderly in order to appraise the long-term care needs of the residents. They call attention to the complexity of these cultures and the long-term care expectations of Asian elderly. By focusing on congregate housing for elders these authors highlight two major points. The first is that as a resident population ages, there is need for more and more assistance, both formal and informal. The second point is the need for long-term care facilities that can provide the secure feeling that ethnic elderly have in a facility that is culturally relevant. They also discuss the differences in cultural beliefs between the Chinese and Korean elders in regard to the use of long-term care and their expectations regarding support from their children. Again we are reminded of the heterogeneity within racial and ethnic groups. Yu and her colleagues end by stating that long-term care issues of the Asian elderly are viewed within these communities as an individual family matter and not a social issue. They hold that these beliefs may lead to further benign neglect by the host society of the problems faced by Asian elders.

The last chapter in this section reviews the current state of knowledge regarding the relationship between elderly Hispanics and long-term care. Espino also presents data from a study of nursing homes in the Southwest in order to present a profile of the typical Mexican American nursing home patient. He points out that the family, especially the extended family, provides the greatest source of support for the Hispanic elder. In addition, community networks may provide a "safety net" in the event that the family cannot meet the needs of the elder and aid in the prevention of institutionalization. This helps to meet the cultural preferences of elderly Hispanics to avoid entrance into a nursing home until all other means of support have ben exhausted. This may account for the fact that Espino found that elderly Mexican-Americans were more physically and functionally impaired than non-Hispanics in the same nursing home settings. He argues that the tendency toward delayed entry into the nursing home among Hispanic elderly requires planning now for future needs. The failure to do so may lead to greater problems in meeting the future long-term care requirements of Hispanic elderly.

5

Self-Care Practices of Black Elders

Lucille H. Davis
Brenda F. McGadney

The purpose of this chapter is to examine self-care practices within the context of long-term care. The historical, social, and economic factors that affect the life situations of black elders and their health beliefs and self-care practices will be discussed. Definitions of self-care vary and many times they are used interchangeably with informal supports such as family and community, or with terms like self-help, self-maintenance, self-management, and self-surveillance (Chappell, 1987). Self-care is distinguished by the fact that it is autonomous, voluntary, and self-directed. In contrast to the medical model, self-care stresses individuals' participation in the care process and focuses on their roles as decision makers (Connelly, 1987). Katz (1986) and Orem (1980), in defining self-care, emphasize that it is a process where laypersons initiate and perform health activities on their own behalf to promote life, health, and well-being. Thus, self-care is a multidimensional concept and a component of a complex network involving various degrees of assistance from formal and informal networks.

Self-care encompasses the whole range of health-related behaviors, including illness behaviors. Illness behaviors are those that involve the perception and evaluation of symptoms and consequent actions taken (Mechanic, 1982). Health behaviors include actions that are taken to promote health, prevent disease, or restore health. They refer to actions taken when bodily symptoms are not out of the ordinary or when persons define themselves as healthy (Chappell, Strain, & Badger, 1988).

UTILIZATION OF SERVICES

Utilization of formal health services and informal practices, such as self-care, are strongly influenced by socio-economic and sociocultural factors. The incidence of chronic diseases has been estimated to be twice as high among blacks as among whites, and blacks perceive themselves as being in poorer health than their white counterparts. However, blacks utilize health services less than whites. Hooyman and Kiyak (1988) note that only 3% of blacks age 65 and older were institutionalized in 1980. They suggest that these data may reflect a lack of nursing homes in black communities, lack of economic resources, and acts of racism by providers and nursing home staffs. Understandably, economics may explain much of the variance in the underutilization of health services by black elders, since they are disproportionately represented at the lower end of the socioeconomic scale. Also, a lack of economic resources plays a large role in the use and support of an extended family system in caring for black elders, since in many cases, intergenerational housing arrangements may develop out of economic necessity rather than by choice (Jackson, 1977).

In relation to sociocultural factors, black elders, as ethnic minorities of color, experience environments significantly different from nonminority elders and are at greater risk of being poor, unhealthy, alone, and inadequately housed (Hooyman & Kiyak, 1988). Although there are black elders who have resources such as education and finances, they have also experienced collective discrimination by virtue of their social class and race (Jackson, 1981). Therefore, regardless of social class, black elders have had a lifetime to integrate the beliefs and values of their cultural heritage into their everyday behavior. Based on their unique history, black elders have developed methods of coping with life crises resulting in both vulnerabilities and strengths in the ways in which they age physically, psychologically, and socially. The extent to which black elders use formal and/or informal care, including self-care, is influenced by the structural variables of accessibility and affordability. Other influences include the definition of illness and treatment responses used by the black ethnic group.

Data about health attitudes and behaviors of black elders and their use of formal and informal systems of care is scant and inconclusive (Jackson, 1981). Furthermore, there is little information on how informal and formal health systems interface among black elders. There is evidence that the boundaries between the two systems are fluid and, as Watson (1984, p. 11) states, "remedies that have been developed by scientific medicine may become the parmacopoeia of folk medicine." In fact, in many cases, black elders use formal and informal systems in a complementary fashion. That is, self-care is used as a substitute, a supplement, or a stimulus to seek formal medical services (Fleming, Giachell, Anderson, & Andrade, 1984). Since black elders use health systems in a complementary fashion, educational materials that integrate culturally based self-care practices with health information are more likely to be used by this population (Davis, McGadney, & Perri, 1990).

The initiation of Medicare in 1965 has increased the use of formal medical services by black elders; however, they have not abandoned self-care practices, and in many situations such practices are used as adjuncts to formal medical care (Jackson, 1981).

SELF-CARE AND BLACK ELDERS

Although the scope of self-care is undetermined, all disciplines agree on selected characteristics (Gantz, 1990). As a concept, self-care: (1) is specific and culture specific; (2) involves the capacity to act and make choices; (3) is influenced by knowledge, skills, values, motivation, locus of control, and efficacy; and (4) focuses on aspects of individual health care control rather than on social policy or legislation (Gantz, 1990, p. 2).

Many self-care behaviors and practices of black elders may be the same as those of other minority groups and white elders; however, there are differences because of blacks' cultural history and continuing social and economic inequalities. Recently, a variety of self-care studies have been reported in the literature (Chappell, 1987; Dean, 1986, Kart & Dunkle, 1989). However, these studies have not included representative samples of black elders; therefore, it is not known how black and white elders differ in their self-care practices. Furthermore, the range of self-care responses used by black or white elders, such as home remedies, lay consultations, and other lay strategies, are not known. More importantly, as noted in other chapters in this book, black elders are not a homogeneous group and there is a need for studies which compare self-care practices within the group itself.

In order to understand attitudes and beliefs that underlie self-care practices of black elders, one must appreciate the social and cultural roots of blacks in this country. African-Americans are unique immigrants in the United States because, unlike other immigrants, they were brought here involuntarily. Due to the economics of slavery, slaves usually received better medical care than free blacks (Jackson, 1981). After slavery, blacks generally became responsible for their own health care. The persistence of self-care and underutilization of modern medicine by many blacks today is related to continued economic poverty of the masses and to institutional racism.

Generally, black elders believe that good health is an individual responsibility and its absence can be attributed to failure to take care of oneself (Jackson, 1981). Blacks hold beliefs about health maintenance that are similar to historical Hippocratic medicine in that both emphasize harmony, balance, and moderation. Adequate care can include specifics, such as wearing an undershirt in the winter, not washing one's hair during menstruation, or never going to bed on a full stomach. As stated in a black newspaper,

> In general, African Americans traditionally have had a high regard for the value of health and life. That fact is easily realized when one considers the countless herbs, ointments, toddies and other home remedies that our forefathers used to fight illnesses and to improve the quality of their lives during and after 1619 (when the first slave ship landed on American shores). (*Chicago Defender*, April 2, 1990, p. 11)

African traditions, blended with Southern traditions, form the foundation for practices that black elders use to maintain health and treat illnesses. No matter where they live, most black elders have Southern roots that affect all aspects of their lives, including life-style. Health practices learned in the South, in many cases, have been maintained and blended with mainstream medicine. Health practices based on Southern traditions, including self-care, vary according to group orientation and income and are found not only in the rural South but also in the North in "well-to-do" homes (White, 1977).

If black elders live in situations where they do not have access to modern medical resources, and if there are socioeconomic constraints, they will rely or depend on informal resources; and health beliefs and practices that have Southern origins will be dominant. In the authors' ethnographic interviews (Davis & McGadney, 1990) with urban black elders about their health practices, the black elders described how they frequently sent relatives home (after consulting the black doctor in the community) if the person did not get better because "people at home [rural South] know how to take care of the sick—they feed you good food and you get fresh air." Although blacks may not articulate their self-care practice as such, their self-care practices are nonetheless influenced by lay theories or explanatory models of health and illness. Such theories provide a framework for determining ways to maintain health, as well as how to label, explain, and respond to illnesses.

Snow's (1974) research on lower-class, Southern blacks illustrates the significance of beliefs about illnesses. For example, beliefs about a physical illness such as hypertension led to a specific type of self-treatment. Hypertension, called "high blood," was based on the idea of the autoregulatory function of blood and the notion that high pressure opens the skin pores and allows excess blood to be sweated out. Treatment consisted of the use of astringent substances such as vinegar, lemon juice, pickles, and epsom salts. Consistent with this belief, some individuals with high blood pressure would drink brine from pickles or olives in the belief that it would help the "blood go down."

Black elders engage in self-care for a variety of reasons. Reasons include: (1)

fragmentation of the health care system; (2) the use of lay consultation; (3) beliefs about efficacy of treatment; and (4) perceived cause of illness. Some of these reasons are discussed and illustrated in the vignettes below:

(1) Fragmentation of the health care system. Elders experience their health problems holistically; however, the health system is highly specialized and therefore treats elders in a fragmented manner.

> Mrs. Ida Mae Smith, a 70-year-old black female, was recently diagnosed as having glaucoma and hypertension and was assigned to the glaucoma and hypertension clinics. On her clinic date, she attended the glaucoma clinic in the morning and the hypertension clinic in the afternoon. In the morning, the doctor in the glaucoma clinic told her that her pressure was "excellent" and in the afternoon at the hypertension clinic the doctor told her that her pressure was "up." She decided not to come back because the doctors didn't know anything—"one doctor says my pressure is ok and the other one says it's up"; she decided that she would be better off taking care of herself.

(2) Use of lay consultation. Ideas and attitudes about illness do not take place in a vacuum. If the illness is not perceived as serious, family and friends may be consulted first, followed by the use of a home remedy and then a patent medicine; finally, if there is no relief, as evidenced by symptom abatement, a doctor may be consulted.

> Mr. George Washington Black, a 72-year-old black male, had a persistent cough for several weeks. He and his wife consulted with two of his neighbors who lived in the senior housing unit where they resided and each person they consulted recommended a toddie made of "lemon, honey and a shot of whiskey." After a week, he did not experience any relief so his wife suggested that he ask the pharmacist for a suggestion. He subsequently purchased a cough syrup from the drug store and only consulted his doctor two weeks later when the cough increased to the extent that he could not sleep at night.

Educated black elders who are knowledgeable about health and medicine tend to attribute their symptoms to psychosocial stress as noted by terms such as "burnout" or "stress"; therefore, self-care may consist of advice obtained through the media.

> Mr. David Anthony, a 65-year-old black male, made an appointment to see the doctor at his HMO due to complaints of tiredness and nervousness. Upon questioning, he stated, "My eyes have almost become like slits and I really have to hold them open to see. Sometimes I'm so tired I can hardly walk. Is this just nerves? I read in a magazine that stress can cause this." The doctor told him, "It sounds like you have a well-known neurological illness that responds to treatment (myasthenia gravis)." Because the man believed that he was just tired and under stress, he had been treating himself for "tired blood."

(3) Beliefs about efficacy of treatment.   In some cases, elders believe that one only goes to a doctor and takes medication if one is ill, and then stops the treatment and medication when one "feels better." This presents a problem when the condition is chronic and the person may be asymptomatic, as in the case of hypertension, or when the person has to take a course of antibiotics after the acute infection is over.

> Mrs. Addie Mae Jones, a 65-year-old black female, told the nurse that she only took her medicine for high blood pressure when she "really needed it." She stated, "I know when my pressure is up." The nurse asked her how she knew and she stated, "I get spots in front of my eyes and a heavy feeling in my chest, and when that happens I take my garlic water and lemon juice first and then I take my pills if I don't feel better—that is, if I haven't run out."

(4) Perceived cause of illness.   Perceived cause of illness and its consequences can also influence self-care practices. For example, some illnesses are seen as a normal part of aging and this attitude is reinforced by family members.

> Mrs. Blondie Jones, a 74-year-old black female, told the nurse, "I can put up with the pain because arthritis runs in the family and all of us get it when we reach our fifties."

In addition, a perception of the seriousness of the illness can influence the extent of self-care and compliance with medical advice. For example, life-style changes and compliance are more likely to occur with a diagnosis of cancer than in hypertension because the latter is perceived as more benign and non-life-threatening.

The current highly technological, biomedical model of disease views independent self-care-initiated activities as inherently dangerous because they can cause delays in medical care. Historically, however, self-care was basic to blacks' survival and served to strengthen informal support systems. (Wood and Wan report similar findings in their chapter on rural black elderly in this volume.)

Watson (1984) speaks to the positive aspects of self-care and the significance of informal support systems blacks used during the years they were isolated from mainstream medicine. "Of particular importance among the proactive responses of Afro-Americans was the emergence of strong family bonds, churches and neighborhood self-help groups and practitioners of folk medicine" (Watson, 1984, p. 53). The importance of home remedies in relation to survival is described by Watson (1984, p. 55) in an interview with a black elder:

> "Colored folks was brought up on these home remedies. Like I tell you 'bout this fever grass-hump [laughing]. You know when folks in the community—lots of em would make that fever grass the same day or night and give it to em. You know we stayed up too, with the chillun; didn't have no doctors. These old remedies; that's all I ever took. Right now you know I ain't never been [to] a doctor."

PERSPECTIVES ON SELF-CARE

Self-care activities exist in all cultures and are a significant component of health care systems around the world (Kart & Dunkle, 1989). According to Dean (1986), self-care is important in health maintenance and restoration after the onset of illness and disease. Historically, most people received their health and medical care from family, friends, and neighbor's wives; all of whom have largely depended on traditional remedies (Elliott-Binns, 1973). In fact, it can be argued that healing was originally a familial activity, and self-diagnosis and self-treatment appear to be an integral part of the American tradition, as noted by Roebuck and Quan's discussion of Jones et al. (1976, p. 143):

> As the country was being settled, doctors were very few and transportation was very poor, so self-treatment was a necessity. Even today, most physicians are very busy, appointments are difficult to get, and for many people, the cost of proper medical care is discouraging. For many residents of rural areas and ethnic ghetto areas of large cities, transportation to medical facilities remains a problem. In addition to these factors, there is the continuing barrage of advertisements for self-treatment products for ailments of every description.

The current self-care phenomenon emerged out of the consumer movement about two decades ago. Changing disease patterns and the development of sophisticated consumer groups in relation to information and technology have resulted in a rise in public expectations and in the practice of exercising more control over one's health destiny (Levin & Idler, 1983).

Despite a sophisticated health system, the majority of symptoms experienced by individuals are not presented for medical attention. The decision to seek treatment is but one option in a complex process, grounded in personal biographies, culture, attitudes, and knowledge of traditional and nontraditional systems of care and access to each. The ambiguity of symptoms and the associated costs and benefits of entering the sick role also influence whether one privities illness or makes it known to the health professional (Ford, 1986). Even today, the majority of people having illness experiences take care of themselves without the assistance of professionals (Chappell, 1987). Known as the "illness iceberg" (Last, 1963), nonconsultation and delay are the norm rather than the exception (Zola, 1966; 1973).

MODELS OF SELF-CARE

There are two models, by Jackson (1981) and by Tripp-Reimer (1984), that are especially useful for conceptualizing how black elders perceive and define symptoms and decide on treatment, including self-care modalities. Jackson's (1981) model (Figure 5.1) illustrates factors that influence perception and interpreta-

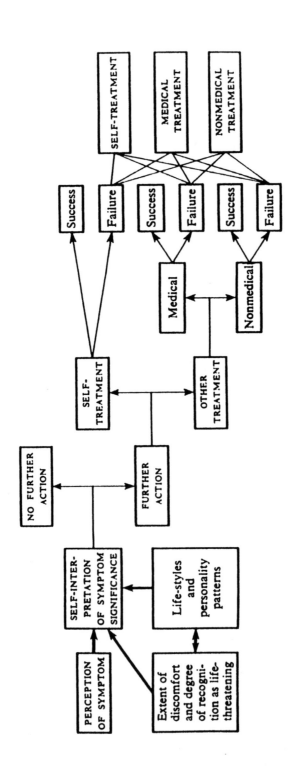

FIGURE 5.1 Process of system management.

Source: Jackson, J. (1981). Urban black Americans. In A. Harwood (Ed.), *Ethnicity in health care*, p. 82. Cambridge, MA: Harvard University Press. Reprinted with permission.

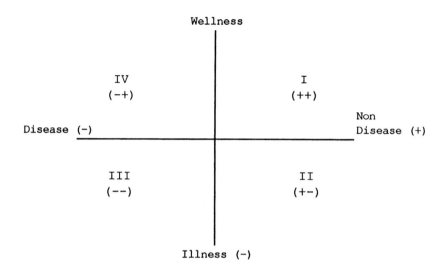

FIGURE 5.2 Th emic-etic health grid: Quadrants specifying areas of congruence or incongruence resulting from the intersection of client and practitioner perspectives.

Source: Tripp-Reimer, T. (1984). Reconceptualizing the construct of health: Integrating emic and etic perspectives. *Research in Nursing and Health, 7,* 101–109. Reprinted with permission.

tion of symptoms, such as extent of discomfort and life-threatening nature of the symptoms. Other variables influencing responses include personality, life-style, and prior history of symptoms. In order to relieve symptoms, the person may engage in self-treatment or treatment by others using either the medical or the nonmedical system. As suggested by Snow (1974), if the illness is determined to be of natural or environmental etiology, then medical intervention is used and if there is successful resolution, then the process is completed. However, if treatment is unsuccessful, self-care and/or nonmedical sources are consulted. In some situations, there may be vacillation between medical and nonmedical systems or they may be used simultaneously.

Tripp-Reimer's (1984) model (Figure 5.2) uses a holistic approach and takes into account perspectives of both the client and the professional. This model is important because it highlights the cultural incongruencies common in a stratified society such as the United States. This model differentiates between illness and disease. As Kleinmann (1978, p. 252) indicates, "disease is malfunctioning or maladaptation of biologic and psychophysiologic processes in the individual; whereas illness represents personal, interpersonal and cultural expectations to disease or conflict."

The Tripp-Reimer model contains two dimensions; the etic (objective) and the emic (subjective). The vertical (emic) axis ranges from illness at the bottom to wellness at the top. The horizontal (etic) axis consists of the disease and nondisease continuum. There are quadrants that specify congruence and incongruence between client and professional perspectives.

The quadrants of congruence (I and III) are not problematic because both client and professional agree that there is or is not disease and illness. In quadrant I the black elder feels well and there is no objective pathology. This quadrant emphasizes self-care activities that promote health or prevent illness. For example, many black elders stress the importance of "acting right and eating right" or taking good care of oneself when one is young in order to have a long, healthy life. As one 92-year-old black female stated, "I learned a long time ago that everyone has to learn to weed his own garden."

In quadrant III, there is congruence because the individual feels ill and there is objective pathology.

> Mrs. Ruby Jewel Robinson, a 65-year-old black female, goes to the doctor because she has been losing weight and feeling tired for the last two months. The doctor, through a series of tests, determines that she is diabetic. In this case the woman has determined that the symptoms are serious and that the medical system can help her.

In quadrants II and IV, there is incongruence. In quadrant II there is no objective pathology, but the elder, as in the following example, defines herself as ill. This quadrant also includes categories of illnesses designated as unnatural illnesses, which lie outside the biomedical domain.

> Geraldine Sams, a 68-year-old black female, was sitting in church in a revival service. The church was very full and the heat was turned on high because it was a cold winter day. The woman was sitting with the nursing board and she was clapping her hands and singing with the choir and started to feel dizzy; when she was helped by one of the members, she mentioned that she had become dizzy last Sunday also. Once of the ladies told her that it was probably her "pressure" because she had the same problem and her doctor told her that she had high blood pressure. Concerned, the lady decided that she would make an appointment to see her physician. When she visited the doctor, she had her blood pressure checked by the nurse and the doctor and both determined that her pressure was *not* elevated. She was given another appointment so that it could be checked again. On the next appointment, her blood pressure was once again determined to be normal. The doctor explained to her that her original dizziness may have been due to the hot, overcrowded church; however, the woman was not convinced that she was not hypertensive.

In quadrant IV there is obvious pathology, which can be identified by a health professional, but the elder does not define him/herself as ill. These illnesses may be asymptomatic (e.g., hypertension) and remain undetected or the illness may be considered normal among the reference group. For example, "all of my family members are fat" or "all old people have bad kidneys." Or, in some cases, the doctor may use terminology that gives the elder a false sense of security, as illustrated in the following.

> The doctor told Mrs. Daisy Blockman, 69-year-old black female, that she was a "borderline diabetic." The doctor told her that she did not have to take insulin but needed to lose weight and watch her diet. The elder defined a diabetic as someone who was on "the needle" and therefore thought that she was not a "real diabetic." In this situation, despite objective pathology and symptoms, this lady did not define herself as ill and believed she could treat herself without professional assistance.

In summary, self-care of black elders is influenced by beliefs and practices that are rooted in culture and shaped by social and economic factors. Folk systems of care, including self-care practices, overlap with the biomedical system and the two are frequently blended together. The two systems are complementary, coexisting with one another, and fulfilling different functions. Self-care can be used as a substitute, supplement, or a stimulus for medical services (Fleming et al., 1984). In a pluralistic, aging society, both systems need to be understood and strengthened so that health care can be maximized during the later years for all black elders.

SIGNIFICANCE FOR LONG-TERM CARE

Long-term care refers to the need for ongoing assistance, which is required for elders with chronic illnesses or conditions (Haber, 1989). The long-term care needs of black elders within community and institutional settings should enhance their capacity to cope successfully with chronic health problems and prevent complications associated with chronicity. Elders can enhance and maintain their health if the environment is flexible and nonrestrictive. To this end, health professionals must be prepared to actively negotiate with the elder as a "therapeutic ally" (Kleiman, Eisenberg, Good, 1978). Negotiation is important in relation to treatment, expectations, and outcomes.

Unfortunately, self-care behaviors, especially those defined as folk medicine, have been seen as nonnegotiable by health professionals. However, folk practices and beliefs that underlie many self-care behaviors constitute an organized system grounded in elders' experiences and experientially tested by the elders and perceived as useful or "therapeutic." Health professionals tend to view some self-care behaviors as "folk practices" or as deviant and dangerous when, in fact, some of them may be similar to professional interventions. Ferguson's (1991) study on health-promoting behaviors of black elders found that their self-care behaviors include health practices (e.g. diet, exercise) and over-the-counter medicines that are part of the scientific medical community. However, if self-care practices are not congruent with the health professional's beliefs or values, then they may not be seen as having any value. Hautman (1987, p. 234) suggests that "one way of minimizing ethnocentric tendencies is to reconceptualize what has been traditionally termed 'folk practices' to the less culturally biased term 'self-care practices.'"

In a pluralistic, aging society, regardless of where care is provided, self-care beliefs and practices of black elders are important because these practices are rooted in a black cultural heritage and tradition. Integration of cultural beliefs and values that underlie self-care practices into long-term care systems can be an important step in promoting elders' trust of health professionals and in improving compliance. For example, an elder's belief in a home remedy such as lemon and garlic water for high blood pressure may not be harmful if taken along with prescribed medications; on the other hand, in some situations this type of home remedy may be harmful and discussions of substitutions may be necessary. At any rate, attempting to persuade elders of the incorrectness of their beliefs or to change beliefs is a difficult task (Kleinman, 1978). Furthermore, understanding and appreciating elders' perspectives and belief systems can help them maintain a sense of control in an environment that is usually becoming restrictive because of declining resources such as health and finances. Fewer choices in life have been available to black elders compared with their white counterparts because of racism and discrimination. With advancing age, there is the likelihood that even fewer decision-making opportunities may be available to them.

Control is a potent factor in increasing life satisfaction and quality of life for elders (Palmore & Luikart, 1972). It is widely recognized that many institutional long-term care settings, such as nursing homes, do not provide an environment that promotes choices within a cultural context. Some community settings, like day care centers, can also become too institutional and can again take away individual choices. Regardless of the dependency level of elders, they have the potential to participate and collaborate in their health care (Vogel & Palmer, 1983). Feelings of personal efficacy are a significant factor in life satisfaction in elders. Therefore, it is essential that health professionals and planners integrate cultural and ethnic values, beliefs, and practices into long-term care systems.

REFERENCES

Chappell, N. L. (1987). The interface among three systems of care: Self, informal, and formal. In R. A. Ward & S. S. Tobin (Eds.), *Health in aging: Sociological issues and policy directions.* New York: Springer Publishing Co.

Chappell, N. L., Strain, L. A., & Badger, M. (1988). Self-care in health and in illness. *Comprehensive Gerontology, 2,* 92–101.

Connelly, C. E. (1987). Self-care and the chronically ill patient. *Nursing Clinics of North America, 22,* 621–629.

Davis, L., McGadney, B. (1990). *Social factors in the health of black urban elders.* Final report (NIA 1R21G07169) Chicago: Northwestern University.

Davis, L., McGadney, B., & Perri, P. K. (1990). *Living with diabetes: A self-care guide for black elders; Living with hypertension: A self-care guide for black elders; Living with arthritis: A self-care guide for black elders.* Lisle, IL: Tucker Publishing Co.

Dean, K. (1986). Self-care behavior: Implications for aging. In K. Dean, T. Hickey, & B. E. Holstein (Eds.), *Self-care and health in old age: Health behavior implications for policy and practice.* London: Croom Helm Ltd.

Elliot-Binns, C. P. (1973). An analysis of lay medicine. *Journal of the Royal College of General Practitioners, 23,* 225.

Ferguson, D. B. (1991). *Health promoting behaviors of African American elderly living in high rise apartments.* Chicago: University of Illinois at Chicago.

Fleming, G., Giachell, A. L., Anderson, R. M., & Andrade, P. (1984). Self-care: Substitute, supplement or stimulus for formal medical care services? *Medical Care, 22,* 950–966.

Ford, G. (1986). Illness behavior in the elderly. In K. Dean, T. Hickey & B. E. Holstein (Eds.), *Self-care and health in old age: Health behavior implications for policy and practice.* London: Croom Helm, Ltd.

Gantz, S. B. (1990). Self-care: Perspectives from six disciplines. *Holistic Nursing Practice, 4,* 1–12.

Haber, D. (1989). *Health care for an aging society: Cost conscious community care and self-care approaches.* New York: Hemisphere Publishing Co.

Hautman, M. A. (1987). Self-care responses to respiratory illness among Vietnamese. *Western Journal of Nursing Research, 9,* 223–236.

Hooyman, N. R. & Kiyak, H. A. (1988). *Social gerontology: A multi-disciplinary perspective.* Boston: Allyn and Bacon.

Jackson, J. (1977). The black aged: A demographic overview. In R. Kalish (Ed.), *The later years.* Monterey, CA: Brooks/Cole.

Jackson, J. (1981). Urban black Americans. In A. Harwood (Ed.), *Ethnicity and medical care.* Cambridge, MA: Harvard University Press.

Kart, C. S., & Dunkle, R. E. (1989). Assessing capacity for self-care among the aged. *Journal of Aging and Health, 1,* 430–450.

Katz, A. H. (1986). Self-care and self-help programmes for elders. In K. Dean, T. Hickey, & B. E. Holstein (Eds.), *Self-care and health in old age: Health behavior implications for policy and practice.* London: Croom Helm, Ltd.

Kleinman, A. (1978). Concepts and a model for the comparison of medical systems as cultural systems. *Social Science and Medicine, 12,* 85–93.

Kleinman, A., Eisenberg, L., & Good, B. (1978). Culture, illness and care: Clinical lessons from anthropological and cross-cultural research. *Annals of Internal Medicine, 88,* 251–293.

Last, J. (1963). The iceberg—Completing the clinical picture in general practice. *Lancet, 2,* 28–31.

Levin, S. L., & Idler, E. (1983). Self-care in health. *Annual Review of Public Health, 4,* 181–201.

Mechanic, D. (Ed.). (1982). *Symptoms, illness behavior, and help seeking.* New York: Prodist Press.

Orem, D. E. (1980). *Nursing concepts of practice* (2nd ed.). New York: McGraw-Hill.

Orem, D. E. (1985). *Nursing concepts of practice* (3rd ed.). New York: McGraw-Hill.

Palmore, E., & Luikart, C. (1972). Health and social factors related to life satisfaction. *Journal of Health and Social Behavior, 13,* 68–80.

Roebuck, J., & Quan, R. (1976). Health care practices in the Deep South. In R. Wallis & P. Morley (Eds.), *Marginal medicine.* London: Peter Owen.

Snow, L. F. (1974). Folk medical beliefs and their implications for care of patients: Review based on studies among black Americans. *Annals of Internal Medicine, 81,* 82–96.

Tripp-Reimer, T. (1984). Reconceptualizing the construct of health: Integrating emic and etic perspectives. *Research in Nursing and Health, 7,* 101–109.

Vogel, R. J., & Palmer, H. (Eds.). *Long-term care: Perspectives from research and demonstrations.* Washington, DC: U. S. Department of Health and Human Services.

Watson, W. (Ed.). (1984). *Black folk medicine: The therapeutic significance of faith and trust.* New Brunswick, NJ: Transaction Books.

White, E. H. (1977). Giving health care to minority patients. *Nursing Clinics of North America, 12,* 27–40.

Zola, I. K., (1966). Culture and symptoms: An analysis of patients presenting complaints. *American Sociological Review, 31,* 615–630.

Zola, I. K. (1973). Pathways to the doctor—From person to patient. *Social Science and Medicine, 7,* 677–689.

6

Functional Abilities of Chinese and Korean Elders in Congregate Housing

Elena S. H. Yu
Katherine Kim
William T. Liu
Siu-Chi Wong

INTRODUCTION

To write about the long-term care of Asian-American elderly is a difficult, if not an impossible task, given the current state-of-the-art research on long-term care in the United States and the failure of federal and state statistical reporting agencies to recognize the diversity within Asian-Americans or, for that matter, "Asian/Pacific Islanders." Indeed, in several important surveys conducted by the federal government—such as the 1982 National Long-Term Care Survey

The authors gratefully acknowledge the National Institute on Aging for its funding award (1 R21 AG07022-01 & -01S1) to the Pacific/Asian American Mental Health Research Center with William T. Liu as the P. I., which made possible the collection of data presented in this paper. The encouragement from Shirley Bagley and Katrina Johnson to do the study is very much appreciated. Thanks are also due to G. H. Wang, Angela Yuan, Sue Kang, and other members of the Chinese and Korean community for the roles they played in facilitating our access to the congregate housing units whose residents we studied as part of this NIA grant.

(NLTCS) and the 1977 National Nursing Home Surveys—Asians were not identified separately. They were classified as "Other"—a term denoting a mixture of persons who are neither "black," "white," nor "Hispanic."

Research into long-term care is also in a state of flux insofar as concepts and measurements are concerned. What sorts of care consitutes *long-term* care? For measurement purposes, how does one decompose care and distinguish it from social visits and informal contacts? Since long-term care refers to "a set of health, personal care, and social services delivered over a sustained period of time to persons who have lost or never acquired some degree of functional capacity" (Kane & Kane, 1987, p. 4), how is functioning best measured? How does one estimate the need for long-term care when researchers are agreed that current use of long-term care is a most imprecise predictor of future need, and nonuse of services does not necessarily mean the absence of need for assistance? If these issues are as yet unresolved in studies of the mainstream population, they are even more problematic when one adds the dimensions of "culture" or "ethnicity" to the assessment of the need for long term care of Asian-American elderly.

For these reasons, the objective of this chapter is not to present a global view of the informal and formal sources of long term care for the Asian elderly. Rather, we wish only to report our findings on the *functioning* of persons 60 years or older from the most recent study of four congregate housing units for the elderly in Chicago. The study was one of only four developmental research projects funded by a special program under the Social and Behavioral Sciences Branch of NIA and the only one focused on Asian-Americans. To our knowledge, this is the first study of Asian elders in congregate housing units that collected data on cognitive impairment, physical functioning, 24-hour dietary intake, and anthropometric measurements, combined with psychosocial variables on acculturation and social support. Due to space limitation, data on nutrition and anthropometric measurements are not reported here.

We will begin by describing the characteristics of the Asian-American elderly population, followed by a report of our findings on the level of *functioning* among Chinese and Korean elders,[1] in order to be apprised of their long-term care needs. In the discussion section, we call attention to the complexity of understanding culture and long-term care expectations of the Asian elderly. Hopefully, the issues raised in this chapter will give the reader a flavor of the nature of the crisis that is imminent in the long term care needs of the Asian elderly in America.

RECORD ASIAN IMMIGRATION

Compared to other ethnic groups, the graying of Asian America is occurring at the fastest rate—with the population 65 years and older increasing by 109% between 1970 and 1980, vis-à-vis 25.2% and 40.3%, respectively, for white and African-Americans in the same age groups (Manuel & Reid, 1982). Bureau of the Census publications in 1988 show detailed information for several ethnic subpopulations included under the rubric, "Asian-Americans and Pacific Islanders." One notes that the percentage of persons 65 years or older in each Asian group varies considerably. If the cut-off age of 60 years or older as the definition of "elderly" is used, then three Asian immigrant groups had reached or were approaching the 10% mark a decade ago: Japanese (12.1%), Chinese (10.3%), and Filipinos (9.6%). The comparable figure for white Americans is 16.9% and for African Americans, 11.2%. These statistics must be understood in the context of a widely recognized, but thus far unestimated, *gross undercount* of the minority populations, especially the elderly Asians. Already, immigrants from Asia on average form between 40% and 45% of all immigrants entering the United States annually since the 1980s. Many of these are parents sponsored by their immigrant children. Barring swift and sudden changes in future U. S. immigration policies toward persons born in the Pacific Rim countries, this growth is expected to show no appreciable abatement over the next several decades. On the contrary, it is expected to continue its upward trend.

There is considerable variability within the Asian-American subgroup, not only in the percentage of persons 65 years and older, but also in the percentage of foreign-born within that age group. Of the older immigrant groups (i.e., Chinese, Japanese, and Filipinos), the Filipino elderly have the highest percentage of foreign-born persons (95.9%), followed by Chinese (80.9%), and Japanese (43.1%) (U. S. Department of Commerce, 1988). Among the new immigrants (such as Koreans and Thais) or refugees (such as the Vietnamese, Laotians, or Cambodians), the percentage of foreign born is even higher. These statistics suggest the importance of taking *non-English language, culture,* and *nativity* into account in all research on the Asian elderly in the United States They are also helpful in understanding the findings reported from our studies of Chinese and Korean elderly living in Chicago's congregate housing units.

CHINESE AND KOREAN ELDERLY IN CHICAGO

Precisely how many Chinese or Korean elderly there are in Chicago is impossible to determine. Available tabulations from the U. S. Census data indicate that some 13,638 Chinese, 8,307 Japanese, and 10,165 Koreans of all ages were enumerated in 1980. Together, they made up only 1.07% of Chicago's 3,005,072 population—a city composed of 43.25% non-Spanish white, 39.53% non-Spanish black, 6.34% Spanish white, and 0.30% Spanish black.

The arrival of distinct waves of Asian immigrants has changed the urban ecology of Chicago. The "old" Chinatown which had its beginnings during the last decade of the nineteenth century and was originally located just south of the loop on Clark Street, was reconstructed around Cermak and Wentworth in 1912. It is now undergoing rapid change as Chinatown expands to include the area once owned by the Santa Fe Railway Company. A congregate housing unit for Chinese elderly, located just one block away from Wentworth Street, is in the heart of this "old" Chinatown. Meanwhile, a suburban shopping center called the Diho International Plaza, financed largely by Taiwanese capital, was developed in this decade in a suburb due west of Chicago called Westmont. The second congregate housing unit for Chinese elderly is located about five minutes' drive away from this plaza.

The growth of the Chinese population is overshadowed by the influx of other immigrants, particularly Koreans, Filipinos, and Southeast Asians. These latter groups began to increase significantly after the 1965 amendments to the U. S. Immigration and Naturalization laws were passed. Korea, in particular, re-sponded to changes in the U. S. immigration laws by relaxing its restrictions against travels abroad. The first visible Korean community emerged in Uptown Chicago during the mid-1970s, later expanding to the northwest side of the city bounded on the east by Western Avenue, on the north by Lawrence Ave-nue, on the west by Pulaski, and on the south by Montrose. During the 1980s, large concentrations of Korean residents began to form in the suburbs of Sko-kie, Niles, Morton Grove, and Lincolnwood. Today, Koreans may be found in newer suburbs such as Vernon Hills and Libertyville. A "new" Koreantown is also emerging in the suburb of Schaumburg. During the 1980s, only a decade after Chicago felt the presence of Koreans among its growing populations, the cohesive Korean community built two residential facilities for predominantly Korean elderly.

THE NIA-FUNDED EXPLORATORY STUDY

Residents of the two Chinese and two Korean congregate housing units for the elderly were targeted for an NIA-funded exploratory study. Despite ethnic dif-ferences, these populations share some interesting characteristics. They are el-derly living apart from their children. Given the deep roots of Confucianism in Chinese and Korean cultures, and the thick layers of traditional family values that shape their personality and social structure, such a living arrangement is culturally inconsistent with the concept of filial piety. In this study we wanted to understand these groups of elderly—their sociodemographic characteristics, cognitive and physical functioning, health and nutrition status, acculturation level, and depression symptom scores. In light of the paucity of previous empiri-cal studies on the Asian elderly, an inductive approach was preferred over a de-ductive one. The data collection began in midsummer of 1988 and was com-pleted in 1989.[2] In this chapter, only the data pertinent to physical functioning and long-term care issues are presented.

TABLE 6.1 Sociodemographic Characteristics of Asian-American Elderly in Chicago's Congregate Housing Units

Total	Chinese (N = 169)		Korean (N = 90)	
	%	(n)	%	(n)
Age				
< 75 yrs	52.1	(88)	66.7	(60)
75 yrs +	47.9	(81)	33.3	(30)
Sex				
Male	34.9	(59)	33.3	(30)
Female	65.1	(110)	66.7	(60)
Marital Status				
Married	52.1	(88)	40.0	(36)
Non-married	47.9	(81)	60.0	(54)
Percent with no				
children nearby	13.7	(23)	7.8	(7)
Nativity				
Foreign-born	99.4	(168)	100.0	(90)
Most of Childhood				
Rural	58.6	(99)	22.2	(20)
Age of arrival				
45–64	58.6	(99)	66.7	(60)
65 +	23.1	(39)	33.3	(30)
Years lived in Chicago				
< 2	3.6	(6)	1.1	(1)
2–5	19.6	(33)	14.4	(13)
6–10	19.1	(32)	50.0	(45)
> 10	57.7	(97)	34.4	(31)
Formal Education				
None	25.4	(43)	25.6	(23)
Elementary	29.0	(49)	38.9	(35)
High School +	45.6	(77)	35.6	(32)
Speak English				
Well	2.4	(4)	1.1	(1)
So-so	18.3	(31)	17.8	(16)
Poorly/not at all	79.3	(134)	81.1	(78)
Read in Native Language				
Well	47.3	(80)	73.3	(66)
So-so	21.9	(37)	14.4	(13)
Poorly/not at all	30.8	(52)	12.2	(11)

Sociodemographic Profile of the Residents

About two thirds of the respondents in our exploratory study are females (Table 6.1). Sixty-seven percent of the Korean residents are less than 75 years of age, compared to 52% of the Chinese. This statistically significant age difference is consistent with the recency of Korean immigration in Chicago. In terms of marital status, only two out of five Koreans were married at the time of interview, compared to more than half (52%) among the Chinese. In both ethnic groups, more males living in the congregate housing units were married than females. This cohort of Asian elderly residents in Chicago's congregate housing is characterized by a preponderance of foreign-born persons. Indeed, all the females in our sample were of foreign birth. One out of four Chinese and Koreans had had no formal education. A larger percentage of males had high school or more education than females. (Tables by sex not shown due to space limitation.)

Language Barriers

Table 6.1 also shows that about four out of five Asian elderly (79% of Chinese and 81% of Koreans) speak English poorly or not at all. Some 31% of Chinese and 12% of Korean elderly may be considered functionally illiterate even in their own native language—that is, they read either poorly or not at all. Despite their language handicaps, a slight majority of the elderly (57% of Chinese and 51% of Koreans) did not think that doctors of the same nationality treat them better than health providers who were different from them. (Table not shown due to space limitation.) Nonetheless, language barriers remain an important issue in *access* to health care, as evidenced by the fact that, for Koreans, as large as 97% spoke directly in their native language with health providers during the past year, and for Chinese the figure is 70%, with some additional 13% communicating through an interpreter.

ASSESSING FUNCTIONING

Rather than inventing new instruments without prior evidence of the inapplicability of existing instruments, we assessed the mental and physical functioning of the elderly, as well as their nutritional status, using existing ones that we adapted culturally and translated into Chinese and Korean. Briefly, the ascertainment of cognitive impairment using the Mini-Mental State Examination developed by Folstein, Folstein, and McHugh (1975) was used to provide an indication of the mental functioning of the Asian elderly. Physical functioning was determined using Katz's ADL Scale (Katz, Ford, Moskowitz, Jackson, & Jaffe, 1963) with some minor modifications. Finally, long-term care needs were evaluated by asking a number of questions concerning expectations for the most suitable living arrangement when a person becomes old.

Cognitive Functioning

The Mini-Mental Status Examination (MMSE) is designed to assess, among other things, a person's orientation to time and place, instantaneous recall, short-term memory, and ability to do reverse spelling. Its validity and reliability have been documented in several clinical studies (Anthony, LeResche, Niaz, Von Korff, & Folstein, 1982; Folstein & McHugh, 1979; Folstein et al., 1975) and community surveys (Zhang et al., 1990). Based on findings obtained from previous studies, a cut-off score of 17 or less[3] was used to define "cognitive impairment." Persons who scored below the cut-off point were *not* asked the rest of the questions in our interview schedule. The rationale is that recall errors may be rather problematic for persons who score below 17 out of a total of 30 points on the MMSE.

Among the 176 Chinese who were interviewed, some seven persons (4%) scored below the cut-off point in the Mini-Mental Status Examination (MMSE). Five of the seven persons were females. Among the 95 Koreans who were interviewed, five persons scored below the cut-off point. For the Chinese sample as a whole, regardless of sociodemographic factors, about 34% were showing signs of *mild* cognitive impairment at the time of interview, while 4% evidenced symptoms that would be considered *severe*. For the Korean sample, the figure for mild cognitive impairment is about 36%, and for severe cases, exactly 2.2%. Six cases of severe cognitive impairment were found among the Chinese women interviewed, and two cases of equally severe impairment found among the Korean women, compared to zero cases among males—Chinese or Korean.

Consistent with the findings reported by other investigators using non-Asian populations, age is a risk factor for cognitive impairment or dementia. Moreover, in the age group most at risk of dementia (i.e., persons 75 years and older), lack of education just about doubles the rate of cognitive impairment for men as well as for women in the Chinese sample. Such differences also exist among the Koreans, but they are not as great as those found in the Chinese sample. A plausible explanation for this ethnic difference in memory problems is that the Korean elderly in our sample are slightly younger than the Chinese elderly (the mean age for the Korean sample is 72.1 years, compared with 74.6 years for the Chinese). Consistent with the literature on dementia in general, the old and illiterate females are particularly at high risk of suffering from cognitive impairment. Questions arise as to where the immigrant Asians with little or no English-speaking ability can go when they lose their capacity for independent living.

Physical Functioning

The ability of older individuals to perform activities of daily living (ADLs) is commonly used as a measure of functional health and as a key indicator of the ability to remain independent in the community (Wolinski, 1978). Hence, measurements of ADLs are important to the issue of community service delivery as well as to family decisions to institutionalize. To help in summarizing the data on activities of daily living, a common practice is to regroup the ADLs into basic and instrumental ADLs. Basic ADLs refer to a list of activities that satisfy the basic needs of the individual and include the following items: eating, dressing, grooming, walking, climbing, transferring, bathing, and using the toilet.[4] Instrumental ADLs (or IADLs) represent more advanced and complex behaviors for independent living, namely: managing money, shopping, light housework, meal preparations, making a phone call, and taking medications.

Respondents were questioned regarding the extent to which they are limited in their ability to carry out each basic and instrumental activity of daily living. Limitation exists when the respondent reports that he/she either "cannot do the task at all," or "can do it only with assistance," or "with great difficulty." We note that age is an important factor in IADL, except for Korean females. Within the Chinese sample, more males are limited in IADL than females. Insofar as ADL is concerned, no Chinese or Korean reported being limited in five or more activities; very few reported having three or more limitations. But we note with interest the large differences between Chinese and Koreans in the percentage claiming to have mild disabilities.

Controlling for sex and age, the percentage with ADL limitation among Koreans is at least twice that found among Chinese. The ethnic difference is greatest among females. Of the many activities of daily living, climbing stairs is the activity with the highest percentage of Koreans reporting having difficulty or needing assistance. Just why this may be so is far from clear. However, we are aware that residences in Chinatown consist mostly of either two-flat townhouses or three-flat single family dwelling units, which may or may not be partitioned into separate apartments, while the housing structures in uptown (where the Koreans live) consist of numerous high-rise and mid-rise apartments with five or more floors.

Given the location of the specific housing units where we conducted the interviews, it is conceivable that more Korean elderly than Chinese visit with friends and relatives who are living in high-rise housing units without functioning elevators and, therefore, more Korean women are forced to use the stairs and would have actually experienced limitations in daily activities associated with this particular activity. An alternative explanation is cultural differences in the concept of aging and response styles. Chinese women may underreport difficulty climbing stairs because they see it as part of normal aging. Suffice to say that this area of research is only beginning. Much remains to be understood as to what the findings really *mean*, and the task of cross-cultural researchers in the area of aging is not necessarily to construct *new* questions, but to understand what identical questions mean to different ethnic groups. Bastida and Gonzalez, in this volume, also discuss this issue. Findings such as these underlie the importance of an exploratory study before planning a large-scale community survey.

Utilization of Health Services

Data on the utilization of health services among the Asian elderly in congregate housing units are consistent with the data on limitations of activity in the sense that, compared to Chinese elderly of the same age groups, Koreans appear to have had more medical visits for preventive purposes, more contacts with traditional health practitioners (called *Han Yi*), more frequently used the emergency room services in the past year, and spent more days in a hospital overnight. Without further investigations, it is not clear if this finding reflects a true ethnic difference in disease prevalence and/or incidence.

During the interviews, for instance, we were aware that Korea-trained physicians made regular rounds of visits at the Korean housing units for the elderly as part of a volunteer service, whereas few Chinese-speaking physicians offered a similar service free of charge to residents of the Chinese housing for senior citizens. But even if this were an important factor explaining the ethnic differences in the utilization of physician services for preventive health purposes, it is not sufficient to explain the higher use of emergency room services or more days of hospital stay found among the Koreans. Much remains to be understood about the health care needs of the different Asian ethnic elderly.

CULTURE AND LONG-TERM CARE

Traditionally, nursing home services have been the largest component of long-term care. Given the fact that most of the Asian elderly originate from countries with no previous history of a developed social service program outside of kinship, what is their attitude toward the most suitable long-term care for the elderly in the United States? This is not an easy question to ask our respondents, many of whom came to the United States in order to be reunited with their children. The possibility that someday they may be in a nursing home was the farthest thought from their mind. As a roundabout way of examining their expectations for long-term care and informed by knowledge of their reluctance to voice their thoughts, we did not pose our questions on long-term care directly. Rather, we presented our questions in a culturally acceptable format—by seeking their advice and opinion as to what is the best living arrangement when a person becomes old, in general and under four varying health conditions—if healthy, chronically ill, disabled, and incontinent.

Analysis of the answers we obtained from the Chinese and Korean senior residents in Chicago's congregate housing units reveals some interesting results. Of immediate interest is that the percentage of Chinese who recommended a "nursing home" as the best living arrangement becomes smaller as the condition of the elder changes from being healthy to being incontinent. While initially some 90% of the respondents thought that *in general* a nursing home is the best living arrangement when a person becomes old, that percentage drops to 84% if the elder is chronically ill, down to 76% if disabled, and finally to 60% if incontinent—or a total decrease of 30 percentage points. At the same time, the percentage endorsing "living in the home of one's children" and "other living arrangements" increased gradually as the health condition of the elder declined. The latter include living alone in one's own place, with relatives, or even with non-relatives—anything outside of an *institutionalized setting*. Under the worst condition, when the elder is totally incapable of caring for self and yet does not wish to be a burden to one's children, close to one-fourth of the Chinese (about 23%) expressed a preference for "other" living arrangements, compared to about 18% who would still rather be taken care of by their children.

Implicit in the Chinese response pattern is the expectation that the **nursing home is a place for the healthy or to become healthy, but it is *not* for the sick and incapacitated, or those with deteriorating health.** There is fear of losing control over the situation should one be placed in a nursing home under the worst health condition. How, then, do public policy makers plan for the long-term care needs of Asian elderly? Before we venture any recommendations, it is important to realize that not all Asian elderly are alike.

The Korean response pattern offered an interesting contrast to that of the Chinese. Only about 6% would advise an elderly person who has children living in the same city to live in a nursing home. The desire for independence is strongly indicated by the large percentage of respondents (71%) who voiced a preference to live on their own apart from their children, all the more so if the elder is healthy (81%). But once the elder becomes chronically ill, as much as 31% of the respondents felt that a nursing home is the best living arrangement, with 41% still stating a preference to live in one's own home, and some 28% believing that living in one's children's home would provide the best long-term care. These percentage distributions do not change as we varied the hypothetical elderly's condition from being chronically ill to being disabled. But under the worst possible scenario of incontinence, the majority of Koreans (70%) believe that nursing homes are the best living arrangements. Only 12% would insist on living in their own home still and, like the Chinese, some 18% wanted to live in their children's home.

Close to two-thirds of all the Chinese we interviewed (63.3%), compared to 46% of Koreans, believed that children *should* support their parents, even when the parents are financially self-supportive. Hence, the Chinese dependency on children as a source of long-term care goes beyond issues of economics. It lies in the realm of cultural beliefs as to what *should be* even when reality forces the parents to realize that what should be cannot be fulfilled.

It is reassuring to note that, in general, about three-quarters of the Chinese (75.9%)—compared to four-fifths (81%) of the Koreans—believe that if they ever got to the point where they could not care for themselves, they think their own children would take care of them. However, as shown in Table 6.1, some

14% of the total number of Chinese and 8% of the Koreans have no children who live nearby at all—defined as within 1–2 hours' drive from where they now live. Nonetheless, it appears at this time that the Chinese and Koreans do not differ in terms of their estimation of the availability of informal social support for short-term care, or for long-term care.

About 93% in each ethnic group felt certain that if they were sick or disabled, there is someone who would care for them for a short time, and about 79% of the Chinese and 76% of the Koreans believed that they have someone who would care for them as long as needed. Who would that be? Besides the care they expect to receive from their own children, some expressed the wish that their children would hire a personal nurse or caregiver to attend to their physical health and social services; others thought that a relative could be found or brought to this country if necessary in order to provide long-term care.

How do they feel about using the services of an Adult Day Care Center? The concept is a new one to many of these respondents, and the interviewers had to explain what an Adult Day Care Center was before the respondents could give their answer. Only 36.5% of the Chinese and 23.3% of the Koreans would be willing to use the services of an Adult Day Care Center.

DISCUSSION

The waves of new immigrants who have arrived on our shores during the last two decades have accelerated the graying of Asian America. Most Asians who sponsored their parents to come to the United States did so out of a desire to complete their family formation pattern and to care for the elderly in their country of adoption. They have not given much thought as yet to the long-term care problems of their parents. Yet given the large numbers of foreign-born persons among the Asian elderly—the Japanese excepted—lack of fluency in the English language is a major obstacle to access to existing health care and social services. Besides language, culture and nativity are important issues to take into consideration in planning the long-term care of Asian-American elderly. These issues set the Asians apart from mainstream Americans.

The ethnic community, under the leadership of citizens with a social conscience, has been extremely resourceful in taking care of its elderly. But there are limits to what an individual or an ethnic community can do to assist in the care of non-English-speaking older persons without additional support from the city, state, or federal government. It is painful and unethical to ask an old person who cannot speak English and who cannot care for himself/herself to move out of a congregate housing setting when there are no alternative sources of nursing care other than those for the English-speaking mainstream population.

The basic dilemma of ethnic elderly care in congregate housing units may be articulated as follows. Although all the congregate housing units included in the present study were, and are, intended to house only persons capable of independent living at admission, once an elderly resides in the housing unit it becomes very difficult to enforce the "capacity-for-independent-living" rule for continued residency. The reasons are: (1) the burden of proof of incapacity rests with the housing management; (2) none of the housing units were intended to provide nursing care, nor required to have neurological testing apparatus or medical service personnel who were trained to identify signs of neurological problems or symptoms of dementia, much less provide psychiatric or other medical diagnoses; (3) when family members are notified by the management about the problematic behavior of their elderly relative, they often request a "grace" period during which they can search elsewhere for alternative care. Since there are no other places in Chicago that can accommodate non-English speaking Asian elderly in need of nursing home care, such a search inevitably causes some delay in transferring the mentally or cognitively impaired elderly out of the congregate housing unit. Family members of the elderly have to be convinced through their own search efforts that there are indeed no places to go other than nursing homes for the mainstream population before agreeing to place the elderly in an English-speaking facility. Comparison of costs between nursing homes causes further delays. Obviously, the need for nursing home care of the Asian elderly remains unmet.

The temptation to treat all Asian elderly *as if* they are alike should be resisted. Our data indicate that strong differences exist between Chinese and Korean elderly in their expectation for long term care and in their psychological "preparedness" for nursing home care. The foreign-born Chinese elderly currently living in Chicago's congregate housing for senior citizens view nursing homes as the place to go in order to "become healthier"—not as a place for long-term care of deteriorating health. Their cultural expectations are that, when faced with progressive incapacitation, long-term care should be provided by their own children or kinsmen. The latter have an obligation to support their parents even if their parents are financially able to support themselves. Such culturally rooted expectations and demands—if unfulfilled—are bound to create deep feelings of obligation and sense of inadequacy on the part of the Chinese children. They will certainly foster untold intergenerational tensions that have as yet remained undocumented in the literature on Asian-American aging.

The Korean elderly, on the other hand, though only two years younger on average than the Chinese elderly whom we interviewed, seem to hold a more "modern" view of long-term care. At least verbally and outwardly, they expect relatively less from their children than the Chinese parents, and they see nursing homes as the appropriate place to go if a person experiences rapidly progressive deterioration in physical health. They express less willingness to be a "burden" to their children and more readiness for solitary independent living than the Chinese elderly.

In both the Chinese and Korean ethnic communities, there has been relatively little public awareness of the forthcoming problems associated with aging Asian-Americans. The long-term care issues of the Asian elderly is viewed as an "individual" family matter, not as a "social" problem for which group actions are required—a situation that can lead to further benign neglect of the Asian aging problem by the mainstream society.

ENDNOTES

1. As funded by NIA, data were collected on Chinese, Japanese, and Korean elderly living in five Asian congregate housing units for the elderly. However, because the total number of completed interviews for the Japanese elderly was very small compared to that of Chinese and Koreans, findings from the Japanese data are not reported here.

2. In the proposal submitted to NIA for funding, we had planned to interview only 80 respondents per ethnic group. In conducting the exploratory study, we actually exceeded our proposed sampling size and completed more than 80 interviews for both Chinese and Koreans. Exactly 176 Chinese residents (69.6%) out of a combined total of 253 residents from two housing units were interviewed in this study. The reason for not interviewing 77 of the 253 Chinese residents are as follows: 24 were not home during the data-collection period, 18 refused to be interviewed, 14 were physically ill, 11 were mentally or cognitively impaired, 4 were deaf, 3 died, and 3 had moved between initial contact and the time the interviewers contacted them. The cognitive functioning of each of the 176 residents (61 males and 115 females) was first determined before proceeding with the rest of the interviews. Data collection was preceded by a time-consuming process of literature review, instrument selection, translation, revisions, back translations, and several modifications and pretest.

3. This cut-off score is a convention used in most studies conducted in the United States. Its universal applicability across groups is still being evaluated. In a separate collaborative study in Shanghai, China (Katzman et al., 1988; Yu et al., 1989), where the reliability and validity of the MMSE is compared against actual clinical diagnoses of dementia, we are exploring the utility of using education-dependent cut-off scores. Until these investigations are completed and a definitive conclusion is presented, we thought it best at this time to use the U. S. convention, so as to provide a baseline for comparing the present findings with others reported in the literature.

4. This definition of ADL is identical to the one presented in Katz et al., The Index of ADL (1963), except for the inclusion of *walking* and *climbing* in our construct and measurement of basic ADL.

REFERENCES

Anthony, J. C., LeResche, L., Niaz, U., Von Korff, M. R., & Folstein, M. F. (1982). Limits of the "Mini-Mental State" as a screening test for dementia and delirium among hospital patients. *Psychological Medicine* 12:397–408.

Folstein, M. F., Folstein, S. E., & McHughm, P. R. (1975). A practical method for grading the cognitive state of patients for the clinician. *Journal of Psychiatric Research* 12:189–198.

Folstein, M. F., & McHugh, P. R. (1979). Psychopathology of Dementia: Implications for Neuropathology. In R. Katzman (Ed.), *Congenital and acquired cognitive disorders*. New York: Raven Press.

Kane, R. A. & Kane, R. L. (1987). *Long-term care. Principles, programs, and policies*. New York: Springer Publishing Co.

Katz, S., Ford, A. B., Moskowitz, R. W., Jackson, B. A., & Jaffe, M. W. (1963). "The Index of ADL: A standardized measure of biological and psychosocial function." *Journal of the American Medical Association, 185*:914–919.

Katzman, R., Zhary, Y., Wang, Z., Liu, W. T., Yu, E., Wong, S.C., Salmon, D., & Grant, I. (1988). A Chinese version of the mini-mental state examination: Inpact of illiteracy in a Shanghai dementia survey. *Journal of Clinical Epidemiology, 41*, 971–978.

Manuel, R. C. & Reid, J. (1982). A comparative demographic profile of the minority and nonminority aged. In R. C. Manuel (Ed.), *Minority Aging: Sociological and social psychological issues*. Westport, CT: Greenwood Press.

U. S. Department of Commerce. (1988). 1980 Census of Population (Vol. 3): Subject Reports, Asian and Pacific Islander Population in the United States: 1980: PC80-2-1E, Tables 18, 24, 36, 42, 54, 60, 66, 72, 78, 84, 90, 96, 102, 108, 114, 120, 126, 132. Washington, DC: U. S. Government Printing Office.

Wolinsky, F. D. (1978). Assessing the effects of predisposing, enabling, and illness-morbidity characteristics on health service utilization. *Journal of Health and Social Behavior, 19*:384–396.

Yu, E. S., Liu, W. T., Levy, P., Zhang, M. Y., Katzman, R., Lung, C. T., Wong, S. C., Wang, Z. Y., & Qu, G. T. (1989). Cognitive impairment among elderly adults in Shanghai, China. *Journal of Gerontology, 44*:97–106.

Zhang, M. Y., Cai, G. J., Wang, Z. Y., Qu, G. Y., Katzman, R., Grant, I., Yu, E., Levy, P., & Liu, W. T. (1990). The prevalence of dementia and Alzheimer's disease (AD) in Shanghai, China. *Annals of Neurology, 27*: 428–437.

7

Hispanic Elderly and Long-Term Care: Implications for Ethnically Sensitive Services

David V. Espino

INTRODUCTION

The Hispanic elderly are a heterogeneous group made up of distinct subgroups, each with their own customs and mores. The Mexican-American, Cuban-American, mainland Puerto Rican and Central/South American elders come from diverse pasts but, in many ways, share a common future. The majority of Hispanics over the age of 65 are of Mexican-American descent (U.S. Census, 1985). This elderly group also continues to grow at a rate exceeding that of the Hispanic population "boom" in general (Metropolitan Life, 1988). As such, it is expected that many of the long-term care problems confronting the non-Hispanic white population will, in turn, be faced more commonly by the Hispanic population within the next 30 years. There continues to be a paucity of data, however, on Hispanics residing in extended care facilities. Those investigations done to date have been hampered by low numbers of subjects and limited generalizability.

The purpose of this chapter is to provide an overview of the current state of knowledge regarding the relationship between elderly Hispanics and long-term care. Furthermore, the results of an expanded community project will be presented in order to better profile the "typical" Mexican-American nursing home patient. Finally, there will be a discussion on the implications of these results for long-term care planning and policy development.

There are various caveats associated with the interpretation of study results in elderly Hispanics. As noted by the editors in the introductory chapter of this volume, most research has been hampered by difficulties in data gathering due to language barriers, lack of documentation, and/or mistrust of formal caregiving systems. In addition, a majority of the work has been derived independently, and consequently there has been a paucity of testing of previously derived hypotheses (Newton, 1980). Nonetheless, the work done to date does provide a glimpse into the problems associated with long-term care in this population.

The Hispanic elder, in general, is thought to have poorer health than the general population. Diseases most often mentioned are diabetes, hypertension, heart disease, and arthritis (Lopez-Aqueres, Kemp, Plopper, Staples, & Brummel-Smith, 1985). The Hispanic elder is also felt to be more functionally disabled, with reports of problems related to toileting, bathing, and others (O'Donnell 1989; Sotomayor & Randolph, 1988). The Commonwealth Fund Commission also indicated that Hispanic elderly have greater disability in instrumental activities of daily living as well (Westat, 1989). There is a lack of data on the profile of the "typical" Hispanic long-term care patient. The data from our retrospective pilot study limited to one New York City nursing facility indicates that the predominantly mainland Puerto Rican group studied was younger and more functionally impaired that their non-Hispanic white counterparts residing in the extended care facility (Espino, Neufeld, Mulvihill, & Libow 1988).

A similar retrospective pilot study was completed in institutionalized Mexican-American population in San Antonio (Espino & Burge, 1989). The Hispanic elders were somewhat younger than their non-Hispanic white (NHW) counterparts. They were less likely to be English-speaking (40.7% vs. 96.7% for NHW) and less likely to have been born in the United States (64.8% vs. 93.3% NHW). The Mexican-American elderly sample also demonstrated significantly higher degrees of mental and functional impairment when compared to the NHW population (Table 7.1).

Data available on social functioning indicates that older Hispanics face unique obstacles, such as language and culture, in adjusting to institutionalization, leading to a "double jeopardy" situation, that is being old and Hispanic. In addition to the common losses experienced by older persons in the institutionalization process, such as loss of home, social network, and autonomy, Hispanics also lose the social context for expression and reinforcement of cultural values (Brens-Jette & Remien, 1988). The family appears to be the greatest

TABLE 7.1 Comparing Functional and Mental Status Utilizing Student's *t* Tests

Category	Mexican-American		Anglo		
	Mean	s.d.	Mean	s.d.	*p* Value
Mental status:	3.2	2.0	2.3	1.6	.04
Functional status:					
Total	22.18	3.10	19.96	3.70	.005
Mobility	3.75	0.50	3.40	0.70	.017
Eating	3.26	1.17	2.80	1.00	ns
Transferring	3.71	0.66	3.40	0.67	.04
Toileting	3.75	0.58	3.43	0.72	.031
Bathing	3.86	0.34	3.40	0.72	.001
Grooming	3.83	0.42	3.46	0.62	.002

Source: Espinosa, D. V., & Burge, S. K. (1989). A comparison of aged Mexican-American and non-Hispanic white nursing home patients. *Family Medicine* (1989) 21(3), 191–194. Reprinted with permission.

source of support for the Hispanic elder. Markides and his associates have demonstrated increased intergenerational support between elderly Mexican-Americans and their children (Markides, Boldt, & Ray, 1986). There is no reason to believe that this support ends at the doors of the long-term care facility. Indeed, it has been hypothesized that extended family caregivers help to keep elderly Hispanics in the community longer until higher degrees of disability are reached (Espino et al., 1988; Mendoza, 1981).

Community networks may provide the elderly Hispanic with a "safety net," in the event that the extended family cannot meet the needs of the elder, and aid in prevention of institutionalization. Although no objective measures of support for institutionalized Hispanics exist, the current literature available indicates that the Hispanic community resources function in a variety of capacities such as providing information pertaining to community issues, socialization opportunities, financial credit for services and folk medicines (Torres-Gil & Negm, 1980; Zambrana, Merino, & Santana, 1979; Delgado, 1982). In this way the Hispanic community may provide resources that the extended family may not be capable of providing.

The most visible of the informal community support networks is that of religious organizations. Religious support, at its most basic level, consists of non-church related spiritual support derived from well-known media religious figures (Cruz-Lopez & Pearson, 1985). The church also provides the additional benefits of socialization and social support, which may help the most disabled Hispanic elders reside in the community longer (Gallego, 1989). Finally, the church begins to provide formalized services to Hispanic elders in the form of adult day care and other long-term noninstitutionalized services (Cubillos,

Prieto, & Paz, 1988; Donaldson & Martinez, 1981). Together, the range of informal caregiving provides information and helps to buffer disabilities that might lead to premature institutionalization.

Therefore, in spite of increased disability, Hispanic elderly prefer to remain in a more comfortable cultural setting and, consequently, use long-term care only when all other avenues of support have been exhausted. Current literature appears to bear this out as elderly Hispanics, though more impaired, use significantly less long-term care services (Eribes & Bradley-Rawls, 1978; Fellin & Powell, 1988; Greene & Monahan, 1984).

THE EXPANDED STUDY

The purpose of the expanded study was twofold: (1) to determine whether our original pilot study results were limited to the specific nursing home population originally studied (Espino et al., 1988) and (2) to determine whether elderly Mexican-Americans were younger, were more mentally and functionally impaired, and suffered from cerebrovascular accident effects to a greater extent than their non-Hispanic counterparts. This study further builds on the limited data available on elderly Mexican-Americans in the nursing home.

Methods

The subjects for this study of disability and chronic disease were drawn from the nursing facilities in predominantly Mexican-American neighborhoods in the San Antonio metropolitan area. The nursing care facilities are located in three distinct areas of metropolitan San Antonio. One facility is located in the Northwest section, one is located in the North Central section, and one was located in the South Central area of the city. The facility located in the South Central area has since closed. The financial case-mix of the three facilities was primarily Medicaid-pay with 10% or less private-pay population at each facility. Medical records from the facilities were reviewed for this expanded study. Subjects were selected using the following criteria:

1. Only current or past residents of the skilled nursing facility or the intermediate care facility of each nursing home were considered. Patients in the rehabilitation services section were excluded because of high patient turnover associated with the units.
2. Only patients who had resided in the facility for at least three months were included in the study to allow for comprehensive collection of data regarding functional and mental status.
3. Records for all Mexican-American residents, who were defined as having either Spanish maiden names (women) or Spanish surnames (men), who

were born in the United States, or who had immigrated from Mexico were considered to be Mexican-Americans. Non-Hispanic residents were identified as patients with non-Spanish surnames in the case of male residents and non-Spanish maiden surnames in the female residents. Residents who had immigrated from Latin American countries other than Mexico were excluded from the study.

Non-Hispanic whites have generally been used as a standard of comparison in Western geriatric literature. Therefore, African-Americans and other Hispanics were excluded from the control group. Variables coded for chart review collected from admission data included age, gender, marital status, living arrangements, years in the United States, and primary language.

Scores for the measure of mental and functional status (ADL) were derived using the Texas Department of Human Resources Level of Care assessment, which is described elsewhere (Espino & Burge, 1989). This is the standardized evaluation tool used with residents entering long-term care facilities in the state of Texas. Mental status assessment was divided into categories of consciousness, mood, and orientation/memory; the total score was computed as a sum of all category scores. To assess functional status, residents were scored in the categories for mobility/ambulation, transferring, bathing, dressing, grooming, and toileting. Again, the total functional score reflects the sum of all the categories. Items in both the mental and functional assessment were scaled from 0 to 4, with increasing numbers representing greater degrees of impairment. These instruments were completed by social workers at the respective facilities, post-admission, for all residents included in the survey.

Admission diagnoses were divided into the primary diagnosis, which was given by the admitting physician, and secondary diagnosis, which was also listed in the admission data. For the purpose of our study, both one major admission diagnosis and one secondary diagnosis were recorded.

For dichotomous or categorical variables, comparisons were made between Mexican-Americans and non-Hispanic whites using standardized scores to test the differences among independent proportions. For ordinal and interval data, comparisons were made utilizing Student's t-tests.

Results

Of the 300 residents selected, 136 were classified as Mexican-Americans, 140 were classified as non-Hispanic white, and 24 were classified as other, which included either African-American, Asian, or other Hispanic.

The study results are based on comparisons between 136 Mexican-Americans and 140 non-Hispanic white residents. A total of 93 residents were from the Northwest facility, 89 were from the North Central facility, and 94 were from the South Central facility. Demographic data on the Mexican-American and the

TABLE 7.2 Demographic Data on Expanded Survey

	Mexican-American	Non-Hispanic White
Age on admission[a]	72.9 ± 8.0	82.3 ± 6.3
Female gender	68.3% (93)	73.6% (103)
Married on admission[a]	38.2% (52)	69.7% (97)
Primary Language:		
Spanish/other[a]	62.5% (85)	0.71% (1)
English[a]	37.5% (51)	99.2% (139)
Living alone on admission[a]	50% (68)	13.6% (19)
Living in U.S. more than 30 years	95.5% (130)	97.8% (137)
Born in U.S.[a]	68.3% (93)	98.5% (138)

[a]Variables significant at $p < 0.001$ by χ^2.
Number in parenthesis denotes number of patients.

non-Hispanic white groups are listed in Table 7.2. The mean age for Mexican-Americans (72.9) was younger than that for non-Hispanic whites (82.3). The Mexican-Americans were also less likely to have been married and were more likely to have lived alone at the time of admission, as has been reported in previous studies. Mexican-Americans were more likely to be born outside the United States and were less likely to use English as a primary language.

Mexican-Americans also demonstrated a significantly higher degree of mental impairment than non-Hispanic whites (Table 7.3). Total functional status scores indicated that the Mexican-American elderly group was significantly more functionally impaired than their non-Hispanic white counterparts. This was further demonstrated when the total functional status score was divided into categories. Non-Hispanic whites on the average were more mobile and had less trouble transferring, toileting, bathing, and grooming themselves than Mexican-American residents.

Interestingly, the elderly Mexican-American group, when compared to non-Hispanic whites, had significantly higher rates of cerebrovascular accident (stroke) effects at the time of admission (32% vs. 8%, $p < .001$) (Table 7.4). This difference is further magnified when both the primary diagnosis and the additional diagnosis are combined (44.1% vs. 12.0%). Combining diagnoses also revealed higher rates of diabetes mellitus (44.8% vs. 5.6%) and lower rates of hip fractures (4.4% vs. 19.2%) and heart disorders (33.1% vs. 50.7%).

DISCUSSION

The results of this expanded study support the hypothesis that has been suggested by the previously cited investigations: Mexican-American institutional-

TABLE 7.3 Functional and Mental Status Scores on Expanded Mexican-American Study

	Mexican-American	Non-Hispanic White
Mental status:		
Total[a]	8.51 ± 3.1	6.06 ± 1.9
Memory[a]	3.74 ± 0.7	2.80 ± 0.9
Mood[a]	2.80 ± 1.4	1.72 ± 1.0
Consciousness	2.00 ± 1.7	1.84 ± 1.7
Functional status:		
Total[a]	21.4 ± 3.1	15.8 ± 7.1
Mobility[a]	3.57 ± 0.7	2.58 ± 1.2
Eating[a]	3.33 ± 0.9	1.45 ± 1.0
Transfer[a]	3.59 ± 0.7	2.65 ± 1.0
Toilet[a]	3.61 ± 0.6	2.63 ± 0.8
Bath[a]	3.64 ± 0.8	2.68 ± 1.0
Dressing	3.39 ± 0.6	2.98 ± 1.3

[a]variables significant at $p < 0.001$ by χ^2.

ized elderly are more physically and functionally impaired than their non-Hispanic white counterparts. Furthermore, the Mexican-American subgroup has a higher percentage of diabetes mellitus and stroke effects. There may be several reasons for the observation that the elderly Mexican-Americans are entering the extended care facility more impaired.

One possibility may be related to the extensive use of informal support networks, as mentioned previously. This network may be providing, at some level, assistance with activities of daily living, transportation, nutritional support, respite care, social support, and an interface with more formalized support networks. This may allow the impaired Mexican-American elder to reside in the community longer, until higher degrees of impairment are reached. The development of the informal support network may not be a matter of choice. The financial and administrative barriers to nursing home placement may be perceived as insurmountable, and, as such, are not seriously considered by either the Mexican-American elder or the family. Therefore, the informal network may be the only avenue of support perceived to be available and accessible.

Another possibility may be that the elderly Mexican-Americans may be reaching higher levels of disability at younger ages (Crouch, 1972; see also Bastida & Gonzalez and Lacayo in this volume). Therefore, the Mexican-American elder may be physiologically similar, as defined by degree of disability, to the chronologically older non-Hispanic and therefore institutionalized at a younger age (see similar arguments posed by Bastida & Gonzalez in this vol-

TABLE 7.4 Diagnostic Categories in the Expanded Study

	Mexican American	Non-Hispanic White
Major medical diagnosis:		
Cognitive impairment	17.6% (24)	14.2% (20)
Heart disorders[a]	10.3% (14)	31.4% (44)
Stroke effects[a]	31.6% (43)	7.8% (11)
Arthritis[a]	0.7% (1)	15.7% (22)
Cancer	0.7% (1)	4.2% (6)
Hypertension[a]	8.1% (11)	13.5% (19)
Diabetes[a]	25.7% (35)	2.1% (3)
Peripheral vascular disease	2.2% (3)	2.1% (3)
Hip fracture[a]	1.5% (2)	6.4% (9)
Other diagnoses	1.5% (2)	2.1% (3)
Additional diagnosis:		
Cognitive impairment[a]	8.0% (11)	3.5% (5)
Heart disorders	22.8% (31)	19.3% (27)
Stroke effects[a]	12.5% (17)	4.2% (6)
Arthritis[a]	8.0% (11)	16.4% (23)
Cancer[a]	0.7% (1)	5.7% (8)
Hypertension[a]	13.2% (18)	19.2% (27)
Diabetes[a]	19.1% (26)	3.5% (50)
Peripheral vascular disease	6.6% (9)	7.1% (10)
Hip fracture[a]	2.9% (4)	12.8% (18)
Other diagnoses	5.9% (8)	7.8% (11)

[a]Variables significant at $p < 0.001$ by χ^2.
(n) denotes number of patients.

ume). Jackson (1980) has taken the same position regarding the premature aging of black Americans.

The Mexican-American families may also be less able to gather the economic and personal supports necessary to maintain their older members in the home environment. It has also been suggested that although there is an expectation of support on the part of the aged Mexican-American, the willingness to provide this support is not always present within the younger family members (Markides, Martin, & Gomez, 1983). Therefore, the older Mexican-Americans are perhaps being institutionalized more rapidly than their non-Hispanic counterparts, which is reflected in the younger age of the subgroup. If this hypothesis proves to be true, then the combination of the rapidly growing Hispanic elderly population may truly offer a challenge to long-term care service organizations.

The higher rates of diabetes mellitus and stroke effects have also been observed in an ambulatory population (Lopez-Aqueres et al., 1984). The interactions between stroke effects and long-term care placement requires further investigation. The Mexican-American elder may suffer from more severe sequelae due to stroke as a result of co-morbid factors, such as diabetes mellitus. The combination of multiple chronic disease entities and post-stroke functional impairment may overwhelm the informal support system. These factors could result in premature institutionalization for the elderly Mexican-American. In addition, due to the financial constraints, the Mexican-American elder may be less likely to benefit from early and sustained stroke rehabilitation, which could result in greater degrees of permanent functional impairment and greater likelihood of early institutionalization.

The lower rates of hip fracture and heart disease seen in the expanded study have also been observed in ambulatory populations of older Mexican-Americans (Bauer, Diehl, Barton, Brender, & Deyo; Markides & Coreil, 1986). These rates may indicate an ethnic advantage with regard to these diseases or they may suggest that a significant proportion of Mexican-Americans with hip fractures and/or heart disease died prior to admission to the nursing home, resulting in lower rates for these disease entities.

Finally, the study results lend further support to the theory that, although chronologically younger, Hispanics may nonetheless be physically/mentally (in terms of disability) similar to non-Hispanic whites in the institutional setting (Espino et al., 1988).

POLICY AND PLANNING

The long-term care industry has traditionally placed little emphasis on the specific cultural and language needs of the Hispanic elder. Therefore, few programs have been developed to meet the needs of the institutionalized Hispanic elder. Those programs that have been developed have been in the context of the continuum of services offered to noninstitutionalized Hispanics as mentioned above (Cubillos et al., 1988). Institutional caregivers are often monolingual with only limited skills in Spanish. Bilingual employees, though not formally trained, are pressed into serving as translators, which may lead to job conflicts, frustration, and misinterpretation. For example, errors on the English version of Folstein's Mini Mental State Examination may lead the examiner to conclude that the Hispanic elder suffers from dementia, when in reality the elder has failed to understand the questions posed in this standardized mental status examination (Escobar, Bumam, Karno, & Forsthe, 1986). A similar phenomenon may account for the differences in mental status seen in our study group.

Health care practitioners and nursing home administrators must be made aware of the functional needs and medical problems of the aging Hispanic. Caregivers in the extended care facility must be aware of the increased outreach required by this unique ethnic subgroup. Increased attention to initial stroke management and aggressive rehabilitation are crucial.

Efforts must be made to evaluate mental and functional status using appropriate ethnically sensitive instruments. In this regard, translators must be formalized as part of the caregiving team within the extended care facility. They should be trained and required to maintain proficiency in both language and cultural sensitivities of the elderly Hispanic.

Future long-term care policy with regards to the Hispanic aged must focus on increased education regarding the benefits of long-term care, not only for Hispanic aged, but also for their children, who are becoming elders as well. Furthermore, preventive education may also be of benefit, if this population is truly found to be at increased risk for stroke. Materials designed to sensitize all caregivers, both Hispanic and non-Hispanic, to long-term care issues must be disseminated to those persons most likely to come into contact with Hispanic elders. The use of the organized church would be helpful in dissemination of educational materials regarding long-term care options. The mode of education with regard to long-term care must be tailored to the patient's educational level in order to be most effective.

Access to extended care facilities must be made as painless as possible for the older Hispanic population. This includes support for caregivers in accessing resources to facilitate the institutionalization process. Caring community networks providing information on long-term care must take into consideration the needs of the Hispanic groups present in their community.

Additional research must be conducted to determine if a threshold for admission to nursing care facilities can be defined for Hispanics that is different from that for other groups. Exploration of whether health care practices and chronic disease processes such as diabetes mellitus or stroke are significantly different, not only between Hispanics and non-Hispanics in long-term care institutions, but between aged Hispanic subgroups as well, would also be valuable to determine whether elderly Hispanics are, in fact, aging more rapidly than the general population.

Finally, the role of the extended caregiver network in the support of the impaired elderly Hispanic should be defined. Whether or not this network is operational and effective and what supports are needed to maintain and enhance this network are crucial to future long-term care planning for the Hispanic population.

Failure to address the needs of the Hispanic elderly at this time will inevitably result in the need for crisis planning in the not too distant future. It is hoped that through continued dialogue, education, and research, strategies can be developed to help the older Hispanic view their golden years with optimism.

REFERENCES

Bauer, R. L., Diehl, A. K., Barton, S. A., Brender, J., & Deyo, R. A. (1986). Risk of postmenopausal hip fracture in Mexican American women. *American Journal of Public Health, 76,* 1020–1021.

Brens-Jette, C. C., & Remien, R. (1988). Hispanic geriatric residents in a long-term care setting. *Journal of Applied Gerontology, 7*, 350–366.

Crouch, B. (1972). Age and institutional support: Perceptions of older Mexican Americans. *Journal of Gerontology, 27*, 524–529.

Cruz-Lopez, M., & Pearson, R. E. (1985). The support needs and resources of Puerto Rican elderly. *The Gerontologist, 25*, 483–487.

Cubillos, H. L, Prieto, M. M., & Paz, J. J. (1988). Hispanic elderly and long-term care: The communities response. *Pride Institute Journal of Long-Term Home Health Care, 7*, 14–21.

Delgado, M. (1982). Ethnic and cultural variations in the care of the aged, Hispanic elderly and natural support systems: A special focus on Puerto Ricans. *Journal of Geriatric Psychiatry, 15*, 239–251.

Donaldson, E., & Martinez, E. (1981). The Hispanic elderly of East Harlem. *Generations, 5*, 36–41.

Eribes, R. A., & Bradley-Rawls, M. (1978). The underutilization of nursing home facilities by Mexican American elderly in the Southwest. *The Gerontologist, 18*, 363–371.

Escobar, J. I., Bumam, P., Karno, M., & Forsthe, A. (1986). Use of mini mental state examination in a community population of mixed ethnicity. *Journal of Neurological and Mental Disorders, 174*, 602–614.

Espino, D. V., Neufeld, R. R., Mulvihill, M., & Libow, L. S. (1988). Hispanic and non Hispanic elderly on admission to the nursing home: A pilot study. *The Gerontologist, 28*, 821–824.

Espino, D. V., & Burge, S. K. (1989). A comparison of aged Mexican American and non Hispanic white nursing home patients. *Family Medicine, 21*, 191–194.

Fellin, P. A., & Powell, T. J. (1988). Mental health services and older adult minorities: An assessment. *The Gerontologist, 28*, 442–447.

Gallego, D. T. (1988). Religiosity as a coping mechanism among Hispanic elderly. In M. Sotomayor. & H. Curiel, (Eds.), *Hispanic elderly: A cultural signature.* Edinberg, TX: Pan American University Press.

Greene, V. L., & Monahan, D. J. (1984). Comparative utilization of community based long term care services by Hispanic and Anglo elderly in a case management system. *Journal of Gerontology, 39*, 730–735.

Jackson, J. J. (1980). *Minorities and aging.* Belmont, CA: Wadsworth.

Lopez-Aqueres, W., Kemp, B., Plopper, M., Staples, F. R., & Brummel-Smith, K. (1984). Health care needs of the Hispanic elderly. *Journal of the American Geriatrics Society, 32*, 191–198.

Markides, K. S., & Coreil, M. J. (1986). The health of Hispanics in the southwestern United States: An epidemiologic paradox? *Public Health Reports, 101*, 253–266.

Markides, K. S., Martin, H. W., & Gomez, E. (1983). *Older Mexican Americans: A study in an urban barrio.* Monograph of the Center for Mexican American Studies. Austin: University of Texas Press.

Markides, K. S., Boldt, J. S., & Ray, L. A. (1986). Sources of helping and intergenerational solidarity: A three-generation study of Mexican Americans. *Journal of Gerontology, 41*, 506–511.

Mendoza, L. (1981). Los servidores: Caretakers among the Hispanic elderly. *Generations*, 5, 24–25.

Metropolitan Life. (1988). *Hispanic Americans: An emerging group.* Statistical bulletin, 69 (4), 1–6. New York: Author.

Newton, F. C. (1980). Issues in research and service delivery among Mexican American elderly: A concise statement of recommendations. *The Gerontologist*, 20, 208–213.

O'Donnell, R. M. (1989). Functional disability among Puerto Rican elderly. *Journal of Aging and Health*, 1, 244–264.

Sotomayor, M., & Randolph, S. (1988). The health status of the Hispanic elderly. In M. Sotomayor & H. Curiel (Eds.), *Hispanic elderly: A cultural signature.* Edinberg, TX: Pan American University Press.

Torres-Gil, F., & Negm, M. (1980). Policy issues concerning the Hispanic elderly. *Generations*, 5, 2–5.

U. S. Bureau of Census. (1985). *Persons of Spanish origin in the United States.* March, 1982, P-20, No 396. Washington, DC: U. S. Government Printing Office.

Westat Inc. (1989). *A survey of elderly Hispanics: Report for the Commonwealth Fund Commission.* Baltimore, MD: Commonwealth Fund, 1989.

Zambrana, R. E, Merino, R., & Santana S. (1979). Health services and the Puerto Rican elderly. In D. E. Gelfand & A. J. Kutzik (Eds.), *Ethnicity and aging: Theory, research and policy.* New York: Springer Publishing Co.

PART IV

Institutional Care in Ethnic Settings

Nursing home care has been synonymous with long-term care for decades, yet little is known about institutional care and life for ethnic elders. Part IV contains three chapters that present a wide array of issues associated with providing institutional care for ethnic elders, including historical, demographic, epidemiologic, cultural, philosophical, and organizational issues. Additionally, these authors talk about the institutional life of ethnic elders.

In the first chapter in this section, Kaplan and Shore provide a detailed history of Jewish nursing homes in the United States. Included in this chapter is a profile of Jewish homes for the aged, philosophical matters of parent–child relationships, and the relationship between Jewish communities and Jewish homes for the aged. Kaplan and Shore point out that Jewish nursing homes are, like other organizations, affected by different factors: professionals and staff, the residents, and Jewish history and experience. An important point of this chapter is that Jewish nursing homes, like the people they serve, are not homogeneous and continually undergo change.

The second chapter, by Manson, presents an interesting and rare look at institutional care of older American Indians. Manson describes the significant demographic and epidemiologic changes that have shaped and will transform the American Indian population. Next, he provides a detailed account of long-term care for American Indians in institutional settings , the relationship between acute care and chronic or long-term care services and settings, and the types of long-term care services provided by the various facilities. Manson points out that nursing home construction for American Indians is a relatively recent occurrence and describes some of the factors that account for this. On the basis of his review, and throughout the chapter, Manson suggests numerous questions for researchers to consider. It is clear that, despite the detail presented in this chapter, we still know very little about long-term care for older American Indians.

In the final chapter in this section, Kahana and her colleagues look at psychosocial well-being of ethnic elders in two urban nursing homes. Using a sample of Polish Catholic and Eastern European Jewish elderly, along with a comparison group of Western European elders in the same institutions, the authors focused on the impact of living in a culturally congruent versus noncongruent setting. Kahana and her colleagues find support for their hypothesis that residing in a culturally congruent institutional setting is associated with better psychosocial well-being. Several authors in this volume discuss the special features that are or should be included in ethnically sensitive long-term care, especially institutional settings. The chapter by Kahana and her colleagues provides useful evidence of the importance of culturally congruent and ethnically sensitive care.

8

The Jewish Nursing Home: Innovations in Practice and Policy

Jerome Kaplan
Herbert Shore

INTRODUCTION

The democratization process of the North American *social* value system is influenced by the North American *public* value system. This value system is based on an approach by the federal government to equalize groups within the United States. This has led to the tendency to view all old people as homogeneous, thereby doing violence to their culture, heritage, and tradition. Nevertheless, the latter continue to be resilient, with varying degrees of both continuity and change.

The primary intent of this chapter is to examine in detail the long-term care experience of a specific ethnic population with its sizable variation. The Jewish experience with nursing homes in the United States has been selected for a historical, descriptive, and qualitative overview. Also included is a review of recent Jewish, aged, special populations from 1945 to 1990.

This chapter touches upon the overall demographic and socioeconomic profile of the Jewish homes for aged in the United States, numbers served, unique relationships to the Jewish community, role of family to elderly parent, and Jewish Home philanthropy. The interplay of Jewish values regarding the quality of life will also be dealt with as consummate ideals that permeate institutional, community, and family interrelationships. A concluding statement discusses

115

the effect of Jewish Homes on general perceptions about nursing homes, standards, and policy.

TYPES OF ETHNIC HOMES

The origins of the Jewish Homes experience have similarity to other ethnic groups. The sponsors were motivated by religious, national, or other culturally based concerns to provide an environment whereby the aged could share their heritage, celebrate their holidays, worship without fear or ridicule, enjoy their special foods, and feel understood, wanted, protected, and nurtured. Very often they spoke their native language.

The majority of ethnic Homes are under religious auspices, or sometimes even a coalition of religions. Some are under nationality group sponsorship and at times even a coalition of religious and nationality sponsorship. Others serve specific racial groups. Of the more than 4,000 member Homes of the American Association of Homes for Aging, 2,108 are under ethnic or denominational auspices (American Association of Homes for Aging, 1988).

Religious Homes
Homes under religious auspices include, among others, the religious sponsorships of the following: Apostolic, Baptist, Brethren, Catholic, Disciples of Christ, Episcopal, Episcopal/Presbyterian, Evangelical, Jewish, Lutheran, Lutheran Intersynodical, Mennonite, Methodist, Pentecostal, Presbyterian, Reformed, and United Church of Christ. There are others, but this brief listing shows how extensive religious sponsorship is.

National Identity Sponsors
There are homes that have developed under national identity sponsorship. Thus, there are Homes known as the "British American Home," the "Danish Home," the "Deutcher," the "Slovene Home," and the "Welsh Home."

Religious/National Sponsors
At times a combination of religious and national sponsorship evolved. An example is the Czech National Home in Taylor, Texas, which is sponsored by the Czechoslovakian National (Catholic) Church. Or in Cleveland, Ohio, there is the Villa Sancta Anna Home under First Catholic Slovak sponsorship.

Racial Specific Homes
There are some Homes that serve racially specific groups. An example is the Eliza Bryant Center in Cleveland, which serves aged black Americans. Another is the Stephen Smith Home in Philadelphia, which prior to the 1960s had been a facility serving blacks exclusively. It was one of the first to become racially integrated.

Evolvement of Resident Terminology
Nomenclature may be confusing at times. In the United States those aged living in Homes were initially referred to as "wards" or "inmates." As U. S. soci-

ety moved from serving the "indigent" to serving the individual, the person served became known as a resident, client, patient, or guest. The "patient" label is generally associated with hospital care, "client" with social agency, or legal connotations; "guests" with hotel—subsequently "resident" became the description of choice. In housing arrangements, the terms "tenants," "renters" and "residents" have been used, residents generally referring to the fact that the Home or Housing has become the residence of the person living there. Yet the word "resident" is now used for people in nursing homes because of nomenclature in federal law and its regulations.

THE IMMIGRANTS

Though perhaps not thought of in the traditional or strictest sense of ethnicity, many nursing homes have served denominational and national groups, meeting their unique and special needs for religious and cultural preservation and identity (Zeman, 1952).

The founding fathers of our nation and subsequent waves of immigrants, seeking religious freedom and economic opportunity, brought with them systems of law that evolved over centuries and that prescribed local community responsibility for caring for the indigent and the impaired. They also brought with them their native language, customs, traditions, faith, and sense of community. It was a common experience that as immigrants either came voluntarily or were recruited as the necessary labor pools, these newcomers sought their fellow countrymen for emotional, social, and spiritual support. Often because the immigrants could not speak the language, or were in need of temporary shelter and assistance in finding employment, their family and friends lived in close proximity.

In bringing their customs and traditions, immigrants formed societies, associations, and organizations that performed the necessary and special functions to sustain and preserve life and for service to the ill, the aged, the dying, and the dead. If one were to examine the origin of a large number of Homes under Jewish community auspices, similar patterns would emerge (Gold & Kaufman, 1970). As a group of immigrants settled in the area, there were certain religious obligations and moral imperatives that had to be performed. Societies—fraternal membership organizations—were formed to care for the sick and to bury the dead. There were requirements in preparing the body of the deceased, sanctified burial grounds, proper coffins and garments, among other rituals.

Surviving children would have to recite the mourner's prayer. Thus, schools where children could learn prayers needed to be established. The schools were usually affiliated with synagogues. Often the synagogue, which became the center of Jewish life, added a wing where travelers and the homeless could obtain food in keeping with the dietary laws. They would also provide shelter and a hospice for the orphaned and the handicapped (originally thought of as the lame, halt, blind, the elderly, and the dying). The community functions were primarily carried out by the wives of leaders, who created the Ladies Benevolent Aid Societies. In a like fashion there were groups that provided dowries for impoverished young women so they could marry; assured that families had special foods for the Passover Holidays; supported parochial education; and founded Jewish Homes and Hospitals.

The earliest immigrants paralled their American counterparts in life expectancy and longevity. Realistically, old age was an exception rather than the rule, for infectious diseases ravaged populations. Thus, the demographics did not make aging and old age a pressing or critical problem.

Collective Responsibility

These early Jewish immigrants, in addition to their faith and laws, came with the concepts of *Tzedukah* (charity and justice) and *Mitzvah* (good deeds), and a commitment to community obligations. The Jewish immigrants sought the company of their fellow countrymen, who shared their customs, traditions, amd language and who were a source of mutual assistance during the process of acculturation. Throughout their history the Jewish people formed societies, organizations, self-help groups, each of which performed important functions individually and which collectively contributed to the survival of the Jewish people.

THE ORIGIN OF JEWISH HOMES IN THE UNITED STATES

The Jewish immigrants, coming to the United States from Eastern Europe (Bulgaria, Estonia, Hungary, Latvia, Lithuania, Poland, Romania, Russia), most of whom were Orthodox or Traditional, brought with them the model of *Hekdesh* not unlike the poor farm or almshouse. Essentially the communal response was to commingle the lame, halt, blind, orphaned, sick, old, and those affected with mental aberrations, as well as deficiencies. The *Hekdesh*, while it provided care, was a feared fate, the collection pot for the unfortunates, to be avoided at any price, if possible. It met the standard of the times—"good enough" for those who needed a roof over their heads. It provided no amenities, no privacy, and little care. It also was associated with fraternal groups and slowly in some places evolved into campuses that housed orphans and aged, and often also served as lodgings for travelers requiring kosher food, as soup kitchens, and occasionally as a community kosher restaurant (Gold & Shore, 1965).

The Altenheim

Subsequent waves of immigrants, those coming from Germany who were of a more liberal or reform persuasion, brought with them a somewhat different model and experience. Rather than the Hekdesh, they brought the *Altenheim*,

a different concept of respectable retirement in a dignified clublike environment. It was not primarily targeted to serve the impoverished. The Altenheim
rationale was predicated on a philosophy of stern independence. One saved
during one's work life and used these funds to purchase life care in the Home,
rather than being a burden to one's children or family (Gold & Shore, 1965).

Evolvement of the Separate *Hekdesh* and *Altenheim* Movements

These two historical antecedents had their own characteristics (Eastern European, Orthodox *Hekdesh*-like, and German, Reform *Altenheim*-like), and their
separate identities and facilities.

Thus as facilities to serve the Jewish Aged emerged, and were built in the
1880's, in many cities there were two (or more) Homes, an Orthodox and a Reform, and rarely did the twain meet (For an extended example of this occur-
ance, see Folmar in this volume).

The original Traditional Jewish Homes were creatures of the community to
serve the immigrant who might have no family, and usually very few funds.
They were the nameless, faceless "wards" or "inmates" and were to be grateful
for anything provided for them. Individuals entering these Homes turned over
what funds they had for "life care." Their life expectancy was generally in the
60s. The Home provided a room, meals, laundry, and religious services (professional nursing care did not emerge until the late 1940s).

The usual scenario was for a group of highly motivated, caring, and compas-
sionate women who most likely were members of a *Bikur Cholim* (a society to
visit the sick), which recognized the need for a *Mosshav Zekenim*, a home for
the elderly. They raised funds, collected gifts in kind from merchants, and purchased an older residence that served as the first Home. Several older homes in
larger cities have had two or three locations, as they grew and populations
shifted. The earliest Jewish Homes on record are in St. Louis and New York,
dating back to the 1880s. The newest facility under Jewish community auspices
is Heritage Point in Orange County, California, which began operation in
1990.

THE DEMOGRAPHIC CHANGE

The number and percentage of Jewish aged has been in increasing steadily. In
fact, the graying of America is being outstripped by the graying of the Jewish
aged. Between 1970 and 1980, the latter grew 30%. In the mid-1980s people
aged 65 years and over with Jewish identity were estimated to be 15.5% of the
total American Jewish population. This is expected to increase to 17% by the
year 2000 (Schmelz, 1984). The authors suggest that this figure is underesti-

mated. This compares with 11.3% of the total U. S. population and 12.2% of all whites (Rosenwaike, 1986).

As with the general population, the greatest growth is in the oldest of the old years, which is the predominant age for both entrance and residence within a Jewish Home. Chronological aging alone would bear this out, for one-third of the over-65 Jewish population are over 75 years of age and 10% over age 85 (Rosenwaike, 1986).

Prior to the discovery and refinement of the broad spectrum antibiotics, one fourth of the residents living in institutions died every winter, usually from respiratory illness. Pneumonia was known as the "old man's friend" as death relieved the pain, suffering, and loneliness of the elderly. With the virtual elimination of infectious diseases and the surgical and rehabilitative advances as an unanticipated benefit of medical care for the servicemen and women of World War II, care of the aged changed dramatically. And as the number of aged increased, so did community services designed to maintain the elderly in their own homes and in noninstitutional settings.

Further biotechnological advances were coupled with the discovery of psychotropic drugs, which significantly altered the need to hospitalize those suffering from mental illness and impairments. It emptied the state mental hospitals and filled the nursing homes.

Population Blending

While the predominance of the early twentieth century Jewish Homes were traditional (Orthodox services, dietary laws observed, Yiddish spoken), there were a few Jewish Homes where the emphasis was not on Orthodox practices and German was spoken. These Homes were operated separately until the early 1930s. Following the great Depression it became less economically feasible to maintain distinct institutions. As more native born Americans became older, a blending of the population occurred, and Homes began serving the older Jews of an entire city (Buffalo, St. Louis, for example) rather than just the Jews who immigrated from a particular city/entity in Europe (the Bialystoker, or Lemberg, or Sephardic Home) (Gold & Shore, 1965).

Other twentieth-century antecedents of population blending, especially in areas that did not have large Jewish populations, saw regionalization of Homes. Thus, the B'nai B'rith Home in Memphis was developed to serve seven southern states. Variations on regionalization also took root. For example, the Iowa Jewish Senior Life Center in Des Moines serves the state, as does the Milton and Hattie Kurtz Home of Delaware in Wilmington. The Beth Sholom Homes of Central Virginia in Richmond and Eastern Virginia in Virginia Beach serve Virginia, while the three Jewish Homes in Dallas, Houston, and San Antonio serve Texas.

JEWISH ETHICS, THE JEWISH FAMILY, AND JEWISH NURSING HOME RELATIONSHIPS

The Fifth Commandment, "Honor your father and your mother," is an obligation of responsibility to show worthiness toward both parents and parents-in-law. The honoring of parents is a duty. Novick (1990) has pointed out that honor is expressed through services, finances, and respect. Services may mean emotional sport and/or direct care. Finances obviously refers to providing funds to maintain one's life. Respect is intertwined with the Hebrew word *mora*, which means reverence.

Services

In the historical Jewish ethical code, physical presence of parents is implied. On the other hand, this presence does not mean that parents and offspring must live in the same house. Living together is not the usual modern mode. When direct care is needed in one's own home, geographic proximity has its value.

The ethical imperative of directly looking after a parent may be excused in the instance of dementia. Another is when a poor parent–child relationship exists. Whatever the instance, the traditional key has been whether or not the limit of endurance is reached by either the child caretaker or the parent who receives the care.

Finances

The Jewish ethic for financial care of a poor parent by a prosperous child is rooted in the concept of the Hebrew *Tzedakah*. Various interpretations have flowed, to wit: parental right to children's charity takes precedence; charity is limited to one-tenth of the child's assets; and once a child has adequate funds for his/her own sustenance, the poor parents are to receive the rest.

Respect and Reverence

Respect is carried out through reverence of both parents by daughters and sons. It is felt that the giving of a service is to be accompanied by an attitude of respect. All positive effects to sustain a parent's self-worth are the advocated principle.

The Nursing Home

Each of the triad of concepts—services, finances, respect—is intricately intertwined between the aged person in need of nursing home care and the fulfillment of familial/Jewish community responsibility. This interrelationship has created a new element in the evolution of the modern Jewish nursing home.

The Jewish home is now able to provide knowledge and skills on an around-the-clock basis in a manner not ordinarily available within one's own home. Thus, the endurance factor is supplanted and/or supplemented by the care needs factor of the parents. In some instances, it is acknowledged that the limit of endurance by parent or child is a part of a nursing home admission. Because of the aging of the children, this factor is having an impact, even though there has been a growth of formal home support and community-based services.

Biegel and Sherman (1979) have proposed that there be more use of the delivery of services within a neighborhood and the ethnic community. The theory of shared functions (Kaplan, 1983) and research on this topic (Harel, Noelker, & Blake, 1985) show us that the informal support system (primarily family, secondarily friends/neighbors) and the formal support system (agencies, organizations) interface. As more formal supports develop, the potential exists for delays in nursing home admission. Even so, Brody (1981) notes that daughters who provide care also grow older. In addition they enter/remain in the work force in unprecedented numbers. Further, studies of physical health effects, as assessed by self-report, health care utilization, and immune function, suggest increased vulnerability to physical illness among caregivers (Schulz, Visintaner, & Williamson, 1990).

The skills of Jewish nursing home help provide the required services in an atmosphere honed on the respect for the aged parent. Children assist by honoring one's parents through visits, even when a parent is unaware who the visitor is.

In addition to provision of funds by children to help care for an aged parent either directly or as gifts to the Jewish nursing home toward the care of all its residents, the Jewish community does undertake fund raising to assist the elderly Jewish poor who do not have prosperous children, are estranged from their family, or do not have a family.

EVOLUTION: JEWISH HOMES TODAY AND TOMORROW

The Jewish aged range from the old-old, who were early immigrants primarily from Eastern Europe and Germany, to those persons who have arrived in relatively recent migrations from varied countries, to those born in the United States. Thus, wide diversity exists within an ethnic group that is generally perceived by outsiders as homogeneous (Liechtenstein, 1990). Along with this diversification in the aged Jewish population is a wide range of Jewish nursing homes to meet their differing needs. Included in this diversity are a number of Orthodox Jewish nursing homes in different parts of the United States that have sizable Jewish populations.

Among the newer services that have evolved in Jewish Homes are a vast array of community-type services, such as day care for the elderly, counseling and homemaker services, among others. For some Homes, these services have evolved out of family requests for relief from caregiving responsibilities.

Frontiers of Communal Services

For other Homes, newer services have emerged from two sources: the need to serve those on waiting lists and a fulfillment of at least four of the six frontiers of communal services for the Jewish aged identified by Warach (1982). These include: (1) public advocacy on behalf of the aged; (2) renewed needs assessment and new program development; (3) a Jewish community educational program on understanding aging; (4) adequate Jewish community social worker services; (5) development of a comprehensive and coordinated program of diagnosis, case management, home care, and protective services for the chronically disabled, and (6) home care for impaired aged.

In addition to the variables contributing to diversity among aged in Jewish Homes discussed above, is a newer variable—evolving residency composition. There is a trend away from facilities with elderly Jews as their sole residents, as indicated in a study by Friedman (1984) of characteristics of 127 Jewish residential care facilities. An increasing number have pluralistic populations with higher socioeconomic levels and education. He therefore suggests that program offerings should also evolve to meet the changing backgrounds of residents while continuing to maintain Jewish traditions.

Licensed Nursing Home Beds

Nevertheless, there are approximately 28,260 licensed beds in nursing homes under Jewish auspice in the United States, according to the North American Association of Jewish Homes and Housing for the Aging (1988) and it is safe to assume that better than 95% of these are occupied by Jewish residents. Some Homes, built under government programs, such as Hill-Burton Act, have a nonsectarian policy, and some Homes serve the spouse of a Jewish person where there has been an intermarriage. These factors may be the primary reason for this trend stated by Friedman (1984).

With deaths, discharges, and persons on waiting lists who receive services, the number of different individuals served in Jewish Homes in any given year is estimated to approximate 70,000 (Friedman, 1984). These figures are based on Jewish residents of not-for-profit community-sponsored facilities under Jewish auspices only.

In addition there are for-profit, commercial nursing homes that cater to Jewish patients in major metropolitan areas. They usually operate under such names as Star of David or Garden of Eden and are owned and operated to a large extent by caterers, physicians, and rabbis.

Leadership from 1930 to 1990

The Homes for the Aged in the United States has been the primary source of service to the Jewish elderly since the turn of the century. These Homes have established the pattern for future services. The North American Association of Jewish Homes and Housing for the Aged (previously named The National Association of Jewish Homes for Aging) held a significant conference in 1973. At this meeting, alternatives to institutional care were discussed in rational terms. Parallel systems of care were noted. Comprehensive community involvement was stressed. It was noted that service expansion had been taking place for more than 30 years and that the nonprofit Home for the Aged had been in the forefront of the reaching-out services. It was also stated that, as a group, Jewish Homes have given leadership in providing these services and have served as cornerstones in demonstrating the viability of an institution-based approach to many of the popular services of today.

Jewish Homes, for example, have provided the longest continuous U. S. Meals on Wheels service with full, individual diets for an entire community. Another innovation that was Home-based and motivated was that of independent housing, whether through apartments, cottages, or other modes. Major home health aide services were initiated through the auspices of these institutions, as were physical, occupational, and speech therapies to the elderly outpatient. In-house services were also offered, along with the newer added concept of the importance of such therapies for maintenance, and the list could be extended.

These innovations are not altogether new. In 1940, Lewis reported on how a home for aged Hebrews helped find apartment living for those who had lost their money in the Depression and were not able to cope with a "home life." Thus, we have a report of housing alternatives going back to the 1930s. Further description and evaluation of these alternative programs to institutional care during the late '50s through the early '70s can be found in an article by Kaplan (1974) and in an annotated bibliography by Ketcham, Sack, and Shore covering the period from 1940 to 1972 (1974). Shore (1974) also provides us with the basic concept and list of services offered by a Jewish Home that became The Center for Jewish Aged in its community. He further stresses ethical points as he raises questions as to where, when, and how people will receive care based on the availability of the cheapest possible resources, rather than the social, emotional, or ethnic religious preferences of the older person. In other words, at which point does the older person have a right to determine where he wants to live?

How Homes Are Used

An aspect of serving the Jewish aged has been the development of facilities serving "special populations" or those with unique needs. Among these have been the homes and housing for the Jewish Blind, still in existence in New York and Chicago, and the Jewish Blind and Deaf. Modern practices call for the integration of the disabled and handicapped with the general population.

On the other hand, there are a number of facilities built for special groups. Among these are the Self Help Homes for Holocaust survivors and refugees from the Nazi Era to be found in cities like New York and Chicago. Those who fled Germany and who settled in other cities often entered the Home in that city, so as to remain close to family and friends. There are also some facilities for the very religious. An example would be the Home for the Sages of Israel in New York, where the principle activity remains Bible study and the pursuit of learning.

In addition to special populations, Jewish Homes have responded to the recent waves of immigration and have absorbed Cuban, Egyptian, Iranian, South African, and Soviet Jews. Though some of these residents received adequate health and nutritional care during their lifetime, most did not. Thus, in addition to the problems of language and acculturation, these individuals usually require extensive medical, dental, and allied health care. Since many of these individuals were unable to bring their assets with them, they require community support.

Older people use Jewish Homes in several ways. The first is for very short term, holiday, vacation, or respite care. Under these circumstances the older person comes to the Home, while their caretakers (usually children or spouse) go on vacation or are hospitalized. They may use the Home when the older person wants to be in a setting to observe the holidays such as for Passover or the High Holidays (the Hebrew New Year period).

The second is for rehabilitation or short-term convalescence. The older person enters the Home for care and treatment, not usually available in their own homes. This usually follows surgery or may occur for rehabilitation after a hip fracture and repair. It is encouraging to the older persons and their families to know they will "graduate" and return home, and the Home is proud of its alumni.

The third and more usual situation is that of the older person who enters the Home as frail, fragile, vulnerable, and at risk. These individuals remain in the Home until their death. Their average length of stay has been decreasing. They pose the great challenge of meeting their emotional, social, spiritual, and physical needs, as well as their nursing and psychiatric or medical needs.

It has been observed that as entry age has increased, length of stay has decreased and the residents require more extensive care and more high technology intervention. With age and technology increasing, it is likely the Jewish Nursing Home will have to contend with serious ethical issues and will need to carefully examine policies on such issues as living wills, durable powers of attorney for health care, and "do not resuscitate" orders. They will have to become involved with the evolving health ethic of the United States and its impact on Jewish heritage.

The Campus Concept

Jewish Homes in the United States pioneered in the introduction of such services as professional social services (casework, groupwork, activity and recreational therapists), occupational, physical and restorative therapy, psychiatry, sheltered workshops, professional and administration management, and the campus concept.

Jewish Homes, which were established to serve the Jewish older person in need, were also among the first to recognize the importance of environmental designs and special units and/or buildings for dementia patients.

It was logical, then, that following the philosophy of continuity of care many Jewish Homes have developed "campuses." These usually include a nursing care facility, apartments for independent living, housing for low-income elderly (utilizing some government financing such as HUD 202/Sections 8; 231; 236), a senior center, special programs for Alzheimer's patients, nutrition programs, and specialized day care for handicapped elderly. Some Homes offer outpatient, clinic, and assessment services.

The emergence of Jewish-sponsored continuing care retirement communities (CCRC) is a current development. The CCRC model usually includes housing, assurance of health care, and an activity program. These programs may include options of meals, laundry service, light house keeping, transportation, and other services. These may be offered as a package or "unbundled," permitting the consumer to pick and choose the services desired. Other Jewish human service agencies are also multifacility operations but may not necessarily offer all the services on the same campus. They can be found in a number of cities including Boston, Chicago, Detroit, Los Angeles, and San Diego among others.

WHAT DOES THE FUTURE HOLD?

Among the other groups that are present or potential residents are those who may have experimented with psychedelic and hallucinogenic drugs and have mental impairments. A growing number are affected by dementia. AIDS also looms on the horizon. It may be that future residents will include these populations as well as those with lifelong mental impairments and developmentally disabled who are now living into old age.

Many of the Jewish residents of today have more wealth than their children and their grandchildren. On the other hand, there is a sizable pool of needy Jewish aged. Seventy-two percent of all Jewish household heads whose income is $4,000 or less are in the age group of 65 and over and there are 8,000 poor elderly Jews on public assistance in Los Angeles alone (Olitsky, 1986). One of the potential sources of support for care in the future is through the vehicle of long-term care insurance. Some Jewish communities are anticipating these needs and are developing group programs (Boston, Chicago, Louisiana). Thus, another area of continued concern is to serve all members of the community, the economically able, as well as the financially needy.

Since Homes have a limited number of beds, as the number of elderly increases and the Homes have a limited number of beds, Homes will develop case management services with extensive comprehensive outpatient and outreach services. Some models for this are already in place with institutionally based SHMOs (social and health maintenance organizations).

A Suggested Model for the Future

The future suggests a multipronged approach combining medical and social models. One approach is the building service model which includes both the present and potential populations of Jewish Home residents. It would thus also incorporate the growing view that nursing homes may become the chronic disease hospitals of the future while residential facilities (apartments, cottages) may evolve into custodial type care.

The second approach is for the Jewish Home to increase the nonresident services that flow out of the facilities. This model would make available such services as the following: case management, chore service, counseling, congregate meals, daycare (health/social), emergency response service, friendly visiting, health education, homemaker, home health care, hospice, information and referral, Meals on Wheels, mobile health screening, night care, outpatient health clinic, recreation activities, response care, rehabilitation therapies, religious services, senior center, telephone assurance, and transportation with escorts.

Some Homes have done well with this model, but none has all of the above services in place. Heritage Home in Columbus, Ohio, is an exception, with a high number of the elements in this model currently being offered.

CONCLUSION

"Give me your tired, your huddle masses . . ." These words on the base of the Statue of Liberty, written by Emma Lazrus (welcoming millions of immigrants), are the precursors of the Jewish Homes reaching out to tired, huddled, older people. The Jewish heritage of not forsaking the elderly when their strength failed them has led to the establishment of major institutions with innovative programs and services that have set standards and programs for the future.

The responsibility of offspring to their parents, which is expressed in honoring them, supporting them financially when they require it and the children have the means to supply it, and being physically present when such presence is necessary to sustain the emotional health of parents, is a basic tenet of Jewish ethics. When aged parents require a level of care that their children cannot themselves provide, seeking admission to a good long-term care facility may fulfill the imperative of the Fifth Commandment, "Honor your father and your mother" (Novick, 1990:1).

ACKNOWLEDGMENT

The authors acknowledge the assistance of Zev Harel, Ph.D., Professor and Chairman of the Department of Social Work, Cleveland State University for select reference sources.

REFERENCES

American Association of Homes for Aging. (1988). *Directory of Members*. Washington, DC.

Biegel, D. E., & Sherman, W. R. (1979). Neighborhood capacity building and the ethnic aged. In D. Gelfand & A. Kutznick (Eds.), *Ethnicity and aging: theory, research and policy*. New York: Springer Publishing Co.

Brody, E. (1981). Women in the middle and family help to older people. *The Gerontologist, 21*, 471–480.

Friedman, H. H. (1984). Changes in programming for the Jewish aged in residential health care facilities. *Journal of Jewish Communal Service, 60*, 324–330.

Gold, J., & Kaufman, S. (1970). Development of care of elderly: Tracing the history of institutional facilities. *The Gerontologist, 10*, 262–274.

Gold, J., & Shore, H. (1965). The new look in Jewish homes for the aged. *Jewish Digest, 11*, 17–21.

Harel, Z., Noelker, L., & Blake, B. (1985). Planning services for the aged: Theoretical and empirical perspectives. *The Gerontologist, 25*, 644–649.

Kaplan, J. (1974). The institution as the cornerstone for alternatives to institutionalization. *The Gerontologist, 14*, 5.

Kaplan, J. (1983). Planning the future of institutional care: The true costs. *The Gerontologist, 23*, 411–415.

Ketcham, W., Sack, A., & Shore, H. (1974). Annotated bibliography on alternatives to institutional care. *The Gerontologist, 14*, 34–36.

Lewis, E. W. (1940). An apartment project—an experiment in housing for the aged. New York: Paper presented to 13th Annual Conference of the American Association for Social Security.

Liechtenstein, T. (1990). Transmitting and enhancing Jewish knowledge, experience, and unity through professional practice with the aged. *Journal of Jewish Communal Service, 96*, 346–350.

North American Association of Jewish Homes and Housing for the Aging. (1988). *Directory of Jewish Homes and Housing for the Ageing*. Dallas, TX.

Novick, L. J. (1990). Jewish ethics and family responsibility for the elderly. *Journal of Jewish Communal Service, 66*, 387–391.

Olitsky, K. M. (1986). Editorial comment. *The Journal of Aging and Judaism*, *1*, 3-5.

Rosenwaike, I. (1986). The American Jewish elderly in transition. *Journal of Jewish Communal Service*, *62*, 283-291.

Schmelz, U. O. (1984). *Aging of World Jewry*. Jerusalem: The Institute of Contemporary Jewry, Hebrew University.

Schulz, R., Visintaner, P., & Williamson, G. M. (1990). Psychiatric and physical morbidity effects of caregiving. *Journal of Gerontology: Psychological Sciences*, *45*, 181-191.

Shore, H. (1974). What's new about alternatives? *The Gerontologist*, *14*, 6-11.

Warach, B. (1982). Frontiers of service to the aging. *Journal of Jewish Communal Service*, *62*, 299-306

Zeman, F. (1952). *The institutional care of the aged: The scope and function of the modern home for the aged*. Mimeograph. New York: The Home for Aged and Infirm Hebrews.

9

Long-Term Care of Older American Indians: Challenges in the Development of Institutional Services

Spero M. Manson

This chapter considers issues in long-term care specific to older American Indians, with special emphasis on institutionally based service elements. The discussion opens by reviewing the relevant social characteristics of this diverse population. Recent growth trends suggest that a major demographic transition is well underway, with implications for the timing and extent of service needs among an increasing number of older Indians. Attention then shifts to their health status and functional abilities. It is apparent that yet another transition—an epidemiologic one—is in progress, which signals the gradually changing nature of morbidity and mortality in this group of people. Against this important backdrop, the discussion next summarizes the forms of care that have emerged in response to such circumstances. Given the thrust of the present volume, institutional service elements, for example, hospitals, nursing homes, and alternative settings, are highlighted. Finally, this chapter closes with a look at the perceptions that relevant service providers have of older American Indians and long-term care, particularly the institutional aspects. Their views play a large part, formally as well as informally, in the structure and utilization of these services.

DEMOGRAPHIC CHARACTERISTICS

American Indians are undergoing a significant "demographic transition" (U. S. Department of Commerce, Bureau of the Census, 1980, 1984). Overall, the cohort 19 years of age and younger contributes to a broad pyramidal portrait that sharply contrasts with the general population, which is characterized by a significant, steplike decrease in fertility over the last two decades. These quite different trends have important implications for dependency ratios, as discussed below.

Proportionally, the apex of the American Indian population pyramid is much narrower than that of the United States as a whole. Consequently, during the next 15 years, a larger proportion (19.7%) of the U. S. population (versus 13% of the American Indian population) will enter the 65+ age category. However, the best available estimates suggest that, by the end of this century, the number of American Indians 75 years of age and older will at least double. The increased risk for and accompanying expense of treating chronic illness at this age foreshadow a new set of demands on the existing health care systems.

A dependency index or ratio is the proportion of those individuals under 15 years of age plus those over 65 years of age—that is, those theoretically dependent—divided by the total population of individuals 16 to 64 years old—that is, those engaged in wage labor or "productive pursuits." This ratio of dependents to producers or "supporters" is a simple measure of "social burden." Dependency ratios for urban white and urban Indian populations are very similar. In contrast, rural Indian ratios are considerably higher than those of both urban and rural white populations. Indeed, some tribes, such as the Navajo, have dependency ratios in excess of Third World countries like India, Chad, or Brazil (Broudy & May, 1983). High fertility and decreasing mortality—the demographic transition—figure importantly in this trend. It comes as no surprise, then, that rural Indian families experience serious difficulty in supporting their dependent members.

American Indians over the age of 65 live on per capita incomes that are 40 to 59% less than those of whites, regardless of whether they reside in urban or rural environments. Throughout rural America, elderly Indians have 70% or less of the per capita income of their urban counterparts. Nearly one in every two older American Indians (65 years plus), compared to 1 in 5 older whites, exists either at or below the poverty line. This holds true despite essentially no difference in employment between older white and Indian populations. The rural aged, both Indian and white, are more likely to live in a family context (i.e., with close relatives) than their urban counterparts. Similarly, for both populations, the older an individual is, the less likely he/she is to reside with family. It may seem that elderly Indians who live in rural areas have a greater potential for family support than elderly urban Indians. However, this potential is dramatically eroded by their economic impoverishment. Generalizations about "family support" must be seen in this context. Poverty may be one of the major determinants of extended families, by which older Indians live with their children and grandchildren, not only because of cultural norms, but to share and reciprocate scarce, irregular resources.

Advancing age increases the probability that an individual lives alone or in an institutional setting. Roughly one third of the 75+ population, Indian or white, rural or urban, lives alone; however, there are dramatic urban/rural differences in the proportion of 75+ individuals who live in institutional settings. Though older adults (65+) comprise a greater proportion of the rural (5.8%) than urban (4.7%) Indian population, the latter utilize long-term care facilities at twice the rate of the former. This utilization may be an artifact of availability, or that such facilities are more profitable in urban areas. As more rural Indians live to 75 years of age or older, with the decreased ability to live independently, exacerbated by high levels of poverty, many families face unpleasant choices and are unlikely to find the necessary resources.

EPIDEMIOLOGIC TRANSITION

The demographic transition among American Indian populations, that is, a declining but still very high fertility rate coupled with steep decreases in mortality, leads to consideration of an epidemiologic transition. In general, such a model postulates a decline in infectious and parasitic diseases (e.g., the precipitous reductions in infant and maternal mortality documented earlier) with a marked shift toward degenerative and man-made diseases (Manson & Callaway, 1988). Has this shift occurred for the American Indian population (at least for the 28 reservation states covered by IHS statistics)? Certainly there has been a tremendous decline in infectious diseases (Sievers & Fisher, 1981).

Controlling for significantly different population profiles (e.g., a much younger, low-risk Indian population), age-specific mortality rates still indicate a seven-tenths lower ratio for older Indians than non-Indians. If this mortality crossover proves to be accurate, it can have important implications for IHS planning. For example, is this a "cohort effect"? That is, are Indian individuals born around the turn of the century more likely, for whatever reason, to survive in old age whereas individuals born in the 1940s because of introduced factors (e.g., changes in diet and stress) less likely to survive to old age and in effect be more similar to white populations? An incorrect prediction could mean a substantial waste of resources. If it is not a cohort (or cross-section) effect, will American Indians be more likely to survive into their 80s? When other groups, such as whites, enter this age category, they are at greater risk for certain mor-bidities, for example, some forms of organic brain syndrome. Does differential mortality mean that Indians will have higher than expected proportions of or-ganic brain syndrome? Their significantly higher mortality from cirrhosis of the liver, diabetes, motor vehicle accidents, and alcoholism is already well-estab-lished. What will this mean for the demand on social services and health care?

It is important to disentangle possible cohort effects. For example, one study asserts that the Indian population aged 45–64 is at risk in a number of areas in proportions similar to the 65+ Indian population (National Indian Council on Aging, 1981). Given the potential number of individuals about to enter the 65+ age category in the next two decades, are federal and tribal human service systems facing an increasingly larger and higher risk population?

LONG-TERM CARE: INSTITUTIONAL SETTINGS

The Indian Health Service, like public health agencies in the United States generally, is predicated on an acute care model. This model emphasizes the treatment of short-term, nonrecurring diseases typical of children and young adults. As the foregoing discussion of epidemiologic trends among American Indians suggests, the types of illnesses that beset older Indians are different from those experienced by their younger counterparts. Chronic and degenera-tive diseases predominate and are the primary causes of death for the elderly in this special population, as is the case for the majority culture. Moreover, mounting evidence indicates that 71% of all Indian persons over age 60 suffer limitations in their ability to perform activities of daily living due to these con-ditions (National Indian Council on Aging, 1981).

Unfortunately, planning for long-term care and support of older Indians is less often discussed and even more uncoordinated than is true presently for el-derly members of the general population (Manson, 1989a). Indeed, current In-dian Health Service emphasis on youth and family virtually exclude systematic consideration of the health care needs of older American Indians.

Beginning, then, with the most restrictive settings, the acute care general hospital is the cornerstone of primary medical care and rehabilitative services for American Indians. The Indian Health Service, the major provider of these services, presently supports 49 hospitals, most of which are located in Alaska, Arizona, New Mexico, Oklahoma, and South Dakota. These hospitals range in size from 6 to 170 beds, with a total of 2,148 available beds. They offer medical, surgical, obstetric, tuberculosis, and neuropsychiatric care. Under the authority of Public Law 93-638, tribes operate three hospitals. Numerous Indians and Na-tives also receive treatment through contracts with several hundred commun-ity hospitals in areas where the IHS does not maintain its own facilities. During the 1987 fiscal year, IHS hospitals accounted for 2.2 million outpatient visits

(U. S. Department of Health and Human Services, 1988). The leading causes of hospitalization for the same period included injuries and poisonings, digestive system diseases, and respiratory system diseases. Admissions to all hospitals, including those under contract, increased by 115% between 1955 and 1987. Hospital admissions for Indians and Natives 65 years of age and older evidenced the largest percentage increase of any age group during a 10-year period beginning in 1977.

The prominent role of the acute care general hospital in the IHS health program, the increasing prevalence of chronic, degenerative diseases among Indians and Natives, the growing number of older Indians and Natives admitted for hospitalization, and the relative lack of alternative forms of institutional care in Indian communities are an ominous set of conditions that herald a series of critical problems for the system of care.

In spite of the Indian Health Service's reluctance to commit itself, it already may be deeply involved in the provision of long-term care services. IHS hospital staff in several different service areas have indicated that a number of beds, though not formally designated for long-term care patients, in fact are often thought of in these terms. At least two different phenomena are becoming common in regard to the hospitalization of elderly Indians. Physicians describe frequently recurring acute episodes of an underlying chronic disease. Older patients are discharged to home situations that do not have adequate resources to manage their family member's health problems, only to return in a matter of weeks with an exacerbation of a degenerative condition. The same physicians also describe a pattern of repeated short-term hospitalizations that serve an essentially respite function for overburdened families. One health care provider recounted her quandary over whether or not to admit just such a case, lamenting the elimination of "social" admissions.

Has the intersection of these conditions altered thresholds for help-seeking behavior? Has it affected the ways in which Indian and Native people perceive their health problems? IHS physicians acknowledge that the emphasis on urgent and emergent care has begun to reshape the manner and frequency with which Indian people generally, and the elderly in particular, present for service. Specifically, minor problems such as cuts, abrasions, mild burns, digestive upset, and musculoskeletal strains that seldom occasioned much comment are now believed to precipitate frequent clinic or hospital visits. Studies like those conducted by Brody (1985) on lay consultation and referral networks among impaired older adults may shed important light on these dynamics.

Despite the possibility that IHS hospitals may provide some extended care to older Indians suffering from chronic, degenerative disease, inevitably many of them reach a level of functional dependence that requires long-term institutionalization. Unlike the general population, which boasts tens of thousands of nursing homes, skilled and intermediate care facilities are extremely rare in Indian and Native communities. A technical report to the 1981 White House

Conference on Aging indicated that approximately 4,600 older Indians reside in non-Indian nursing homes. For the most part, such facilities are located far from these communities. Their distance and orientation to non-Indian populations present a number of problems for the elderly Indian resident and his/her family. Visiting by friends and family occurs less often as a consequence of difficulties in transportation. Fellow residents and staff typically are non-Indian. The diet and activity patterns of the elderly Indian resident may be quite different from those of their non-Indian counterparts. As a result, most American Indian tribes and Alaska Native regional corporations prefer to construct nursing homes on their own land and to staff the facilities with members of their own groups.

Beginning in 1971 with the first White House Conference on Aging, and in every National Indian Conference on Aging thereafter from 1975 to the present, the topic of nursing homes—the inadequacy of existing facilities and the need for constructing new ones—has occupied a central place in the discussion of elderly Indian needs. These facilities are gradually appearing, albeit slowly, in Indian communities. The first Indian nursing home was constructed in 1969. Six others were erected in the 1970s; two more have been erected in the early 1980s. To date, there are only 10 reservation nursing homes with 435 residents. American Indian and Alaska Native communities are approximately 10 to 15 years behind the general population, which began extensive nursing home construction in the 1960s.

The characteristics of these Indian nursing homes have been summarized previously by Mick (1983). The American Indian Nursing Home in Laveen, Arizona, is the oldest; Morning Star Manor in Ft. Washakie, Wyoming, on the Wind River Reservation, is the newest.

The homes range in size from 20 to 96 beds with a combined patient capacity of 485. The majority of these facilities offer only one level of care, though at least two admit patients with skilled, intermediate, personal, and board and care needs. Occupancy levels are relatively high, with waiting lists at two facilities. The Blackfeet and Curtis homes attribute their lower occupancy rates to active local home health agencies. Seasonal patterns of admission have been noted by a number of the facilities, specifically, higher occupancy rates during winter months. Eighty to 100% of the staff at six of the facilities are Indian. Patient admission criteria vary markedly, from exclusively Indian with tribal reference to unrestricted admissions. The latter occurred in response to initially low occupancy rates. With some exceptions, these 10 nursing homes are located near acute care facilities.

As the different levels of care imply, there is considerable diversity among the 10 facilities in the number and kind of services offered to residents. Most provide occupational, physical, and recreational activity/therapies, though by a wide range of provider types. The ratio of male to female patients in these facilities does not follow patterns for the general population. Females outnumber males by approximately three to one in the non-Indian nursing home population. However, in two Indian facilities, males outnumber females by more than two to one. Two homes report equal proportions, and the remaining three for which there are data indicate that approximately 60% of their residents are female and 40% male. The high prevalence of crippling auto accidents and alcohol-related functional impairment, both of which involve a disproportionate number of males, may account for this discrepancy.

The average age of the institutionalized population in general is 82 years. The lower average ages of residents at 3 of the 10 nursing homes may be due to the same factors that affect the sex ratios. Last, cognitive impairment is the most frequently cited explanation for institutionalization of older adults in the United States. According to the 1977 National Nursing Home Survey, over 56% of all nursing home residents suffer from moderate to severe cognitive impairment (U. S. DHHS, 1977). Yet cognitive impairment is reported to be relatively low among Indian nursing home residents. The three most common diagnoses of the residents in these homes are diabetes mellitus, alcohol abuse, and stroke (Mick, 1983).

The recent advent of nursing home construction in Indian communities reflects a long unmet need. The fiscal incentives that fueled the explosion of nursing home construction in the general population during the 1960s are not present in Indian communities today. However, many tribes are rushing forward with plans for "their own home," which seem to be fueled by a number of factors in addition to need. One of these factors involves the physical presence of the facility and, thus, visibility of effort. Elder care is an emotionally charged issue that speaks to the essence of tribal life and tradition. The nursing home often is portrayed as a tangible expression of community esteem for older members. While true, in some cases it also has become an excuse for disattending to the full spectrum of needs: ". . . but, they have the nursing home." This selective attention is further reinforced by the previously discussed tendency to equate long-term care with institutionalization.

SALIENT RESEARCH QUESTIONS

Given the gradually increasing number of nursing homes appearing in Indian communities, a series of research questions now deserves close scrutiny. Some of these questions concern past speculation as to the reasons for the underutilization of off-reservation, non-Indian nursing homes. Does closer proximity of these facilities to residents' friends and family increase the frequency of visits? Distance and difficulty in securing transportation are offered as the rationale for relatively infrequent visiting by Indian families and friends of residents living in off-reservation, non-Indian nursing homes. Is accessibility the major barrier to regular contact or are there other factors at work, such as guilt about the inability to care for one's older relatives at home, a wish to avoid being confronted with immediate reminders of the inevitable physical consequences of current lifestyles, and beliefs about death and dying that have become associated with nursing homes in many Indian communities? Does the predominance of Indian staff in these facilities result in greater resident satisfaction with the care rendered?

Staff at non-Indian facilities are presumed to be (and, in some instances, indeed have been) culturally insensitive. This insensitivity is cited as one of the major sources of resident and family dissatisfaction with the skilled and intermediate care provided in off-reservation, non-Indian nursing homes. Are the staff in these 10 Indian facilities perceived as more culturally sensitive by residents and families? If so, does this make a difference in overall consumer satisfaction? Are there other factors that affect the perceived quality of care that may be problematic in Indian facilities?

In her survey of eight reservation nursing homes, Mick (1983) reported that administrators described serious problems in hiring and retaining both professional and nonprofessional staff. The former are difficult to attract because of noncompetitive salaries, benefits, and supportive services. Unexcused absenteeism and alcohol-related problems frequently undermine the effectiveness of the latter.

Are the admission and discharge patterns of residents into Indian nursing homes different from the general population? Seasonality appears to play a major role in the occupancy rates of several of the reservation facilities described above. How are services subsequently affected? Skilled and intermediate care facilities are intended to be rehabilitative: Residents are expected to receive services that will enable them to return ultimately to a less restrictive setting. To what extent do Indian nursing homes function in this capacity? Or are they, in the words of a tribal council member, "the last stop"?

What is the decision-making process with respect to the institutional placement of an impaired older Indian family member? The extended nature of Indian families is both a blessing and a burden in this regard. The blessings have been well enumerated; consider some of the burdens. Indian families are presumed to be a reservoir of instrumental and affective support. However, one wonders to what extent size may not be confused with function. There is little doubt that tribal values place great emphasis on familial obligations and responsibilities. Endless examples attest to the selflessness of mothers and siblings in putting the needs of others before their own. Therefore, tremendous pressure is felt by all to retain older relatives in the home at almost any cost. Yet the interminable demands of a frail, impaired older adult strain even this family system.

A study by Manson (1984) revealed that older urban ($n = 76$) and reservation ($n = 155$) Indians perceived physical illness and limitations stemming from related disabilities to be the most difficult type of situation facing them. Moreover, despite the willingness and availability of a large percentage of their social networks to assist them, the study participants indicated that these same individuals lacked the instrumental resources to provide effective assistance. What circumstances, then, lead to the placement of the impaired older Indian family member? In the absence of community-based or in-home supportive services, it often is the case that the middle-aged children assume the responsibility of care in serial fashion, until each has experienced for herself (or much less frequently himself) the burden posed by providing for the elderly person's needs. Systematic studies are needed of this process and of appropriate interventions.

TYPES OF LONG-TERM CARE SERVICES

Two of the 10 reservation nursing homes described above provide board and personal care services. Two others provide only personal care services. No estimates exist of the number of domiciliary facilities that operate in Indian communities apart from nursing homes, though given the general inadequacy of alternatives, there probably are few of them. Congregate housing efforts such as the the Wendell Turkey Shoulderblade Center on the Northern Cheyenne Reservation in Montana appear to be equally rare. Intended for tribal members who are either handicapped or 55 years of age or older, the Center consists of 35 self-contained apartments, two day rooms, a community room, game room, sweat lodge, kitchen, and dining room. Assistance is provided in accomplishing activities of daily living, mental health counseling, religious activities, adult education, congregate meals, and nutritional counseling with special emphasis on diets for residents suffering from heart disease and diabetes.

Special housing for the elderly like retirement villages are becoming more common, but remain the exception in Indian communities. One of the most advanced complexes of this type is maintained by the Confederated Tribes of the Warm Springs Indian Reservation in north central Oregon. It consists of 28 single family housing units designated for tribal members 55 years of age or older. Housing regulations limit the number and age of children and grandchildren permitted to live with the older residents. The housing complex is adjacent to a Senior Center, which provides congregate meals twice weekly and home meals daily if required, two cords of firewood each year, transportation, recreational activities, regular home visits to determine needs and refer as appropriate, in-home services, nutrition education, foot care, and information and referral. This effort is seen as long-term prevention, reducing unnecessary demands on medical and social services, and prolonging independent functioning.

The overarching questions with respect to these types of long-term care services concern the efficacy of their preventive and promotive activities. Do these types of interventions reduce unnecessary demands on medical and social services? To what extent do they decrease functional dependence? prolong relatively independent living? Do they (can they) have positive impact on community views on aging and old age, as the Northern Cheyenne hope?

MYTHS ABOUT LONG-TERM CARE

Like members of the general population, many tribal, Indian Health Service, and Bureau of Indian Affairs personnel subscribe to a series of myths about long-term care (Manson, 1989b). One of the most persistent of these equates long-term care with the nursing home. This perception stems in part from the high visibility and inordinate cost typically associated with institutionalization. However, long-term care comprises much more than just a nursing home. It encompasses all settings—home, community centers, neighborhoods, and churches—in which older people receive supportive care. Another frequent misperception is that long-term care essentially is provided by institutionally based personnel, notably physicians, nurses, and other clinic-oriented health professionals. A third myth about long-term care characterizes it as primarily rehabilitative and protective in nature, probably as a consequence of the related belief that aging is synonymous with illness and dependency. Indeed, long-term care includes these emphases, but it also is intended to prevent avoidable medical and/or social problems, to ensure an optimal degree of independent living, and to promote physical as well as psychological well-being.

A brief survey of 208 IHS providers and allied personnel revealed that their definitions of long-term care almost invariably center around institutionalization: 81% ($n = 84$) of the definitions provided by the respondents named the nursing home as the only ($n = 60$) or primary ($n = 24$) service setting (Manson, 1989b). Those that mentioned a range of possible settings were provided exclusively by community health oriented personnel (e.g., community health nurses, community health representatives, and social workers). Based on their definitions of long-term care, respondents were asked to indicate to what extent they believed that various types of individuals, namely doctors, clinic nurses, community health nurses, and other health care professionals such as community health representatives, social workers, and family are involved in the provision of long-term care. Clearly, institutionally based personnel, for example, physicians and clinic nurses, were seen as having the greatest involvement. The same respondents were asked to rate the extent to which their understanding of long-term care included each of five service objectives (rehabilitation, maintenance, prevention, protection, and prolonged longevity), taken from a definition of long-term care developed by the Division of Long-Term Care, Health Resources Administration, Department of Health and Human Services (DHHS). Rehabilitative and protective services—again, those most often associated with institutional settings—were perceived as central to almost all of their definitions of long-term care.

Another survey of federal, state, and tribal human service professionals ($n = 91$) disclosed similar findings in regard to their general knowledge about the aged and aging processes (Manson & Keane, in preparation). Responding to "The Facts on Aging Quiz" (Palmore, 1988), respondents incorrectly reported that the majority of older adults are not sufficiently healthy to carry out their normal activities (57%), are unable to adapt to change (53%), and are socially isolated (69%). Little wonder that three quarters of the respondents (73%) believed that at least 10% of the aged live in long-stay institutions.

Such attitudes and knowledge affect the planning and delivery of long-term care for elderly Indians. They shape the options that are perceived as available, the priorities that are assigned to them, and subsequent emphases in implementation. Clearly, a number of demographic, epidemiologic, and economic forces are at work that will require the reexamination of these assumptions and rethinking of the appropriate function of institutional resources within a spectrum of care for older American Indians.

IMPLICATIONS

There seems little doubt that, in general, institutional services for older American Indians have suffered from a lack of innovative planning and a historically impoverished system of care. There are bright exceptions, as noted in this paper and elsewhere (Cooley, Ostendorf, & Bickerton, 1979; McCabe, 1987; Mick, 1983). These exceptions, however, share a common context: each is part of a spectrum of long-term care services that promotes the best possible fit between functional abilities and living arrangements. Conversely, mismatches along these lines, dictated in large part by limited choices, may be responsible for frequent disenchantment with institutional care. One of the biggest challenges, then, that face human service planners in Indian communities is the development of more options across this spectrum, not an easy task in light of increasing scarcity of resources.

Another challenge of the planning process is to bridge the policy and philosophical differences that often separate Indian, state, and federal provider agencies. Evidence abounds in regard to the discontinuities in care that arise as a consequence of such differences (U. S. Commission on Civil Rights, 1982; U. S. Senate Special Committee on Aging, 1986). Client eligibility criteria—specifically age, place of residence, tribal membership, blood quantum (percent of Indian blood)—can vary significantly, frustrating even the most skilled case manager's attempt to piece together the necessary elements of care for an older Indian person.

A related problem is access to available services, and not just in the physical sense. A number of recent reports amply document numerous barriers to long-term care, institutional as well as noninstitutional, that are experienced by older Indians. These include but are not limited to lack of information about programs, apprehension in regard to application procedures, transportation, discomfort with telephone contact and/or inability to hear well, and general fear of program staff (Kramer, Polisar, & Hyde, 1990; National Indian Council on Aging, 1982, 1987). Even providers representing severely disabled older Indians acknowledge considerable difficulty obtaining information about available care, despite objective indications of its existence (Valle et al., 1989).

It is also clear that, though the above issues obtain in both urban and rural reservation areas, each of these settings presents different demands and possibilities that affect their relative importance as well as eventual solution (Kramer et al., 1990; Morton & Happersett, 1990). Future efforts at prioritization must begin to take such differences into account, especially in terms of the demographic trends noted earlier.

Finally, a major educational campaign needs to be mounted with respect to current realities of growing old as an American Indian. As previously illustrated, many service providers operate with inaccurate or outdated information about older Indians. Coupled with other stereotypic assumptions, the care they deliver is not likely to be as effective as possible. But this campaign must extend beyond the service system to those whom it serves. Older American Indians and their family members subscribe to their own myths and stereotypes about institutional forms of long-term care. For example, nursing homes are readily acknowledged as necessary for those whose care exceeds the resources and abilities of family, friends, and neighbors (William, 1989). But they also are seen as places to die, where Indian aged wither away from inattention and neglect (Manson & Pambrun, 1979; National Indian Council on Aging, 1980). This need not be the case; many of the promising programs described herein suggest otherwise. The communities of which such programs are a part mirror the same sense of promise and hope.

REFERENCES

Brody, E. (1985). *Mental and physical health practices of older people.* New York: Springer Publishing Co.

Broudy, D., & May, P. A. (1983). Demographic and epidemiologic transition among Navajo Indians. *Social Biology, 30,* 7–19.

Cooley, R. C., Ostendorf, D., & Bickerton, D. (1979). Outreach services for elderly Native Americans. *Social Work, 24,* 151–153.

Kramer, B. J., Polisar, D., & Hyde, J. C. (1990). *Study of urban American Indian aging.* Final report, Grant No. AR0118, Administration on Aging.

Manson, S. M. (1984). *Problematic life situations: Cross-cultural variation in support mobili-*

zation among the elderly. (Grant No. 0090-AR-0037.) Final report submitted to the Administration on Aging.

Manson, S. M. (1989a). Long-term care in American Indian communities: Issues for planning and research. *The Gerontologist, 29,* 38–44.

Manson, S. M. (1989b). Provider assumptions about long-term care in American Indian communities. *The Gerontologist, 29,* 355–358.

Manson, S. M., & Callaway, D. G. (1988). Health and aging among American Indians: Issues and challenges for the biobehavioral sciences. In S. M. Manson & N. G. Dinges (Eds.), *Behavioral health issues among American Indians and Alaska Natives* pp. 160–210. Denver, CO: University of Colorado Health Sciences Center.

Manson, S. M., & Keane, E. M. (in preparation). *Indian health service and tribal service providers' knowledge about aging: Responses to the "Facts on Aging Quiz."*

Manson, S. M., & Pambrun, A. M. (1979). Social and psychological status of American Indian elderly: Past research, current advocacy, and future inquiry. *White Cloud Journal, 1,* 18–25.

McCabe, M. L. (1987). Health care accessibility for the elderly on the Navajo reservation. *Pride Institute Journal, 6,* 22–26.

Mick, C. (1983). *A profile of American Indian nursing homes.* Working paper and reprint series, Long-Term Care Gerontology Center, University of Arizona.

Morton, D. J., & Happersett, C.J. (1990). Health status and lifestyles of Asian and Pacific Islanders and American Indians. *Minority Aging Exchange, 2,* 4–5.

National Indian Council on Aging. (1980). *The first 3 years of a National Indian Task Force operation.* Albuquerque, NM: National Indian Council on Aging.

National Indian Council on Aging. (1981). *American Indian elderly: A national profile.* Albuquerque, NM: National Indian Council on Aging.

National Indian Council on Aging. (1982). *Access: A demonstration project.* Albuquerque, NM: National Indian Council on Aging.

National Indian Council on Aging. (1987). *National housing survey of six Indian tribes.* Albuquerque, NM: National Indian Council on Aging.

Palmore, E. B. (1988). *The Facts on Aging Quiz.* New York: Springer Publishing, Co.

Sievers, M. L., & Fisher, J. (1981). Diseases of North American Indians. In I. Rothschild (Ed.), *Biocultural aspects of disease.* New York: Academic Press.

U. S. Commission on Civil Rights. (1982). *Minority elderly services: New programs, old problems.* Washington, DC: U. S. Government Printing Office.

U. S. Department of Commerce, Bureau of the Census. (1980). *Supplementary report on American Indian areas and Alaska Native villages.* Washington, DC: U. S. Government Printing Office.

U. S. Department of Commerce, Bureau of the Census. (1984). *General social and economic characteristics and general population characteristics.* Washington, DC: U. S. Government Printing Office.

U. S. Department of Health and Human Services, National Center for Health Statistics. (1977). *Characteristics of nursing home residents, health status, and care received.* National Nursing Home Survey. Washington, DC: U. S. Government Printing Office.

U. S. Department of Health and Human Services, Public Health Service, Indian Health

Service. (1988). *Chart series book.* Washington, DC: U. S. Government Printing Office.

U. S. Senate Special Committee on Aging. (1986). *The Older Americans Act and its application to Native Americans.* 99th Congress, 2nd Session, Series #99-2. Washington, DC: U. S. Government Printing Office.

Valle, R., Birba, L., Yelder, J., Sakamoto-Kowalchuk, Y., Forquera, R., Cosgrove, R., & Nelesen, D. (1989). *Linking of ethnic minority elderly with dementia to long term care services.* Report of Contract No. H3-6640.0 to U. S. Congress, Office of Technology Assessment, Biological Applications Branch.

Williams, M. (1989). *Long term care unit survey.* Indian Health Service Leadership Projects. Final report of Grant No. 13.969 submitted by the Aberdeen Area, Indian Health Service, Community Health Service Program and Dakota Plains Geriatric Education Center, University of North Dakota to the Department of Health and Human Services, Bureau of Health Sciences.

10

Adaptation to Institutional Life Among Polish, Jewish, and Western European Elderly

Eva Kahana
Boaz Kahana
Gloria Sterin
Tracy Fedirko
Reva Taylor

This research presents findings of a study focusing on values, lifestyles, adaptation and determinants of morale among two groups of ethnic elders residing in urban nursing homes. The study sample includes Polish Catholic and Eastern European Jewish elders who reside in institutional facilities in the Detroit Metropolitan Area. Comparison data were obtained from Western European residents of the same institutions. Respondents were selected for study based on prior residence in a predominantly Jewish or predominantly Polish ethnic neighborhood.

A major focus of the study is the difference in psychosocial well-being of ethnic elders in culturally congruent versus noncongruent institutional facilities. It is hypothesized that personal characteristics related to ethnicity, such as acculturation, locus of control, and cultural congruence with environment, may predict morale in the face of stresses posed by institutional living.

BACKGROUND AND RATIONALE

As part of the growing recognition of diversity among today's elders, researchers have been increasingly concerned with the influence of ethnic and cultural differences on social life, adaptation, and psychosocial well-being of the elderly in the United States. Social scientists have come to realize that the melting pot of U. S. society has not in fact homogenized elderly of diverse cultural/ethnic origins and that ethnicity continues to serve as a powerful influence shaping lifestyles and defining service needs of older Americans (Abramson, 1980; Bengston, 1979).

It has been well documented that ethnic ties serve as major influences in shaping the social world and social experiences of older adults (Gelfand & Kutzik, 1979; Newman, 1973). Gerontologic research focusing on ethnic elders has generally been concerned with family relations, adaptation to the community (Gelfand, 1982; Gelfand & Barresi, 1987) and more recently with health status and psychosocial well-being of ethnic elders (Markides & Mindel, 1987; McCallum & Shadbolt, 1989).

Ethnicity has been considered by most gerontologic researchers to be a source of multiple jeopardy (Jackson, 1985) placing the ethnic elderly, along with other minorities, in a situation of special vulnerability. Such vulnerability may be associated with their limited personal and social resources, difficulties experienced in seeking and accepting formal assistance, or stigma associated with membership in a cultural or ethnic minority.

A contrary position, supported by data (Kalish, 1986), is that ethnic elders possess special resources in the form of strong personal identities as members of a distinct cultural ethnic group, through strong and enduring family ties, and being embedded in the social fabric of their subculture (Gelfand & Kutzik, 1979; McCallum & Shadbolt, 1989).

An important challenge to our understanding of the well-being of ethnic elders arises as we consider the lifestyles and adaptation of ethnic elders who enter institutional settings. A useful organizing framework for considering unique needs and potential problems of ethnic elders is provided by the conceptual approaches of stress research (Kahana & Kahana, 1984b). This framework suggests that psychosocial well-being of elders is largely determined by life changes or stressful life situations that they confront. Personal resources (such as adaptive skills) and social resources (such as social support) diminish the adverse health and mental health consequences of stressful life situations. Lack of con-

gruence between culturally defined personal needs and environmental characteristics of the institution may be seen as constituting an added source of stress
for the institutionalized aged (Kahana, Kahana, & Riley, 1989).

Institutionalization constitutes a severe stressor to older persons (Lieberman
& Tobin, 1983). Institutionalization poses stress because of loss of previous familiar surroundings, relocation, and demands and restrictions of institutional
living. The impact of such stress is likely to be magnified by diminished personal and social resources of elders who typically require institutional
placements.

There are many reasons that ethnic elderly encounter problems in institutional settings. First, there are strong cultural expectations for family members
to personally care for their elderly members, even the very frail. Thus, the very
fact of institutionalization may be experienced by ethnic elderly as particularly
stressful (Harel, 1986), symbolically reflecting that the norm of mutual obligations has been broken by younger family members.

Ethnic elderly may also be more vulnerable to institutional placement because of the cumulative life crises they have experienced, possibly with adverse
health and mental health outcomes. Immigration, often after experiencing the
trauma of war and/or poverty, along with difficult living conditions in an alien
environment, tends to expose ethnic elderly to more life crises than those encountered by their U. S.-born counterparts (Antonovsky, 1979).

In terms of social resources, ethnic elderly tend to be at a disadvantage. Lack
of language skills or limited educational background render them particularly
vulnerable to stresses of both relocation and institutionalization (Kahana, Kahana, & Kinney, 1990).

Cultural customs and symbols tend to be particularly important to ethnic elderly, so a facility that does not recognize ethnic/cultural customs or display
those symbols would be especially stressful for these elderly. All long-term care
facilities possess at least some features of a "total institution" (Goffman, 1961),
which cut off residents from the outside world. For ethnic elderly placed in a
culturally noncongruent home, such barriers may represent isolation from the
symbolic world that sustains their sense of self.

Gordon (1964) depicts the dominance of Anglo conformity in U. S. society,
which assumes ascendancy of the English language and English-oriented cultural patterns. Countervailing to the above goals of Anglo conformity or assimilation to the melting pot is the ideology of cultural pluralism. This ideology is
welcomed by most ethnics as an opportunity to retain familiar cultural symbols
and a social environment with familiar customs. Placement of nonacculturated
or semi-acculturated ethnic elderly into nursing homes that incorporate familiar cultural and religious symbols may serve ideals of cultural pluralism and reduce stress associated with institutional placement of ethnic elders.

Kalish (1983) has outlined several ways in which ethnicity can affect the individual. These include (1) differential treatment and perception by members of

other groups, (2) differential response by ethnics to members of their own group, (3) differential expectations of self, and (4) direct influences of ethnicity in terms of values and other personal orientations. In the case of institutionalized elderly, staff members who are either mainstream Americans or members of other ethnic groups may have negative attitudes toward ethnic elderly. Thus, Jewish elderly might experience anti-Semitism or Polish elderly might encounter prejudice based on stereotypical views of Polish culture.

Guttmann et al. (1979) indicates that ethnic elderly in institutional settings much prefer staff of similar ethnic background. Ethnic elders often mistrust people whom they perceive as outsiders and prefer institutional placements in facilities sponsored by their own religion or ethnic groups (Fandetti & Gelfand, 1976; Kahana & Kahana, 1984a).

Based on these considerations, the present study sought to explore similarities and differences in characteristics and value orientation of European American elderly living in institutions. In addition, the impact of personal coping resources, and of cultural continuity provided by the institutional setting, were considered as predictors of well-being among ethnic elderly.

The research reported here is part of a larger study of elderly Jews and Poles residing in a large metropolitan area in their respective ethnic neighborhoods. The analyses reported here focus on elderly now living in institutional facilities who had originally resided in these ethnic neighborhoods. Polish and Jewish elderly residents of nursing homes were studied and compared to Western European elderly who had also been previous residents of the ethnic neighborhoods under study.

Polish and Eastern European Jewish Americans are among the most sizable ethnic groups of elders in the United States (Woehrer, 1978). Older members of these groups are predominantly first or second generation U. S. residents. They often reside in ethnic neighborhoods, which reinforce their sense of belonging and ethnic identification. Both of these ethnic groups have been characterized as having strong ethnic identification (Bengtson, 1979). Both groups have also experienced a great deal of stress throughout their life course (Cohler & Lieberman, 1979), which is likely to place these ethnic groups at greater risk of adverse mental health outcomes. There would be special vulnerability among frail and institutionalized elders (Kahana et al., 1990).

It was anticipated, therefore, that Jewish and Polish elderly would have special problems in adapting to the added stress of institutional living. At the same time, we explored value orientations and attitudes about those social institutions that are most likely to sustain identities of these ethnic elders even as they reside in institutional facilities.

For most ethnics the family has served as the all-important unit for identity, loyalties, and social organization (Habenstein & Mindel, 1981). A second central influence in the lives and lifestyles of most Euro-American elders is their religious orientation (Kalish & Creedon, 1986). Particularly relevant to frail and institutionalized elders are distinctive health beliefs and health practices that characterize different ethnic groups (Antonovsky, 1979; Zborowsky, 1952).

Therefore, in considering the three groups of ethnic elders, we explored responses reflecting orientations to family and friends, church and personal health. We were particularly interested in attitudes, beliefs, and orientations that might constitute special coping resources. An added interest in our exploratory study relates to psychological resources that may buffer the adverse effects of institutional living. Studies of European-American elderly have emphasized the importance of self-sufficiency, a concept reflecting internal locus of control (Guttmann, 1986). Yet in our earlier research in institutional settings (Felton & Kahana, 1974), we documented the relationship of external locus of control to psychosocial well-being. In the present study we examine ethnic differences in locus of control beliefs and the relationship of such beliefs to morale among institutionalized ethnic elderly.

SELECTION OF THE SAMPLE

A systematic search was undertaken to find nursing homes housing elderly residents who had previously resided in Hamtramck or Oak Park, Michigan. Hamtramck, an autonomous community surrounded by Detroit, is predominantly of Polish and Ukrainian Catholic ethnic and religious composition. Sections of Hamtramck are now inhabited by older white adults, other areas predominantly by younger blacks, and still others are integrated with blacks and whites of various ages. Oak Park is located in the northwest area of Detroit between two major transportation routes. Most Oak Park residents live in private homes, others reside in senior citizens' housing sites. At the time of this study, about 60% of Oak Park residents were Jewish with a relatively heavy concentration of older adults. Institutions throughout the Detroit Metropolitan Area were included in the study if they reported housing residents over age 65 who had previously lived in Oak Park or Hamtramck. Of 80 potential facilities surveyed, 13 met this criterion. The homes in our sample included nine proprietary facilities, three nonprofit homes, and one public home. They range in size from 20 to 480 residents.

It is noteworthy that the sample of 50 residents from each community represents nearly the total population of institutionalized aged who could be located even with painstaking effort. When compared with the national rates of institutionalization (about 5%), this would indicate that in the studied communities there is a relatively small percentage of aged who utilize institutional services. Only one home was located in either Oak Park or Hamtramck.

All eligible respondents deemed interviewable based on absence of extreme physical and mental infirmity were invited to participate in the study. Lack of command of English did not represent a serious hindrance in interviewing Jewish or Western European residents. Polish-speaking Hamtramck residents were questioned by Polish-speaking interviewers.

CLASSIFICATION OF RESPONDENTS AND ENVIRONMENTS RELEVANT TO ETHNICITY AND CULTURE

Our classification of ethnic groups conforms to Gordon's (1964) definition: a community based on racial, religious, or national background. Respondents were classified as Jewish based on religious affiliation regardless of place of birth. Forty-one Jewish respondents were thus identified, all of Eastern European background. All of the Jewish respondents gave Oak Park, a predominantly Jewish community, as their last address. Polish respondents were identified based on being born in Poland or speaking Polish along with Catholic or Greek Orthodox religious affiliation, and all 33 of these respondents had formerly resided in Hamtramck, a predominantly Polish community.

All remaining respondents were classified as Western European ($N = 28$), based on country of origin and languages spoken. The Western European respondents were a more heterogeneous group and might have previously resided in either Hamtramck or Oak Park; they were either Protestant or Catholic in religious affiliation. A variable denoting acculturation was created by combining place of birth and facility with the English language.

The 103 respondents were residents of 12 different nursing homes. These were classified into 3 groups based on religious/ethnic affiliation versus nonsectarian sponsorship: Jewish, Catholic (Polish), and nonsectarian homes. There were four Catholic homes, three Jewish-sponsored homes, and five nonsectarian homes. In the majority of cases, Jewish respondents were found in Jewish homes, Polish respondents in Catholic homes, and Western Europeans ("Anglos") in nonsectarian homes. Thus, 88% of the sample were residing in what we defined as culturally congruent facilities.

MEASURES

Psychosocial well-being of respondents was measured using the 21-item Lawton Philadelphia Morale Scale (Lawton, 1972). Locus of control was measured using a series of hypothetical problems relevant to life situations of the frail elderly (Felton & Kahana, 1974). Respondents were asked to provide solutions to each of four problem situations: forced relocation, health problems, and self-management. The solutions provided were then scored in terms of "self" or "other" as the locus of control.

The vast majority of Jewish and Western European respondents displayed good command of English as rated by interviewers: 85% of Jewish and 76% of Western European respondents were rated by interviewers as having facility in English. In striking contrast, only 19% of the Polish respondents were so rated.

Polish respondents were significantly less likely to report functional impairment in terms of giving up activities due to health: 53% versus 78% of Western European and 78% of Jewish respondents. This was supported by the observation that more Polish respondents reported spending "no days" being ill than either of the other two groups: 70% versus 50% of Western European and 42% of Jewish respondents. Subjective health rating and interviewers' ratings showed a similar trend.

DEMOGRAPHIC CHARACTERISTICS OF RESPONDENTS

The three groups of ethnic elders are similar in most demographic characteristics. A somewhat greater proportion of Poles are very old (80+), 51% versus 35% of Anglo and 37% Jewish respondents. Marital status was also comparable among groups with few respondents reporting divorce or separation: 2% of Jews, 15% of Poles, and 10% of Anglos. At the time of interview, 15% of respondents were married and just over two-thirds were widowed (69%).

Sixty-two percent are female and 38% are male; 45% had been institutionalized for less than one year, 32% for two or three years, and 23% for four or more years. The Anglo group is somewhat more likely to have been institutionalized for a longer period (four or more years): 36% versus 14% of Jews and 20% of Poles. The groups are comparable on number of living children, indicating that their support networks do not differ. Thirty percent have no children or one child, 30% have two or three, and 41% have more than three children. (Jews are somewhat less likely to have large families, 33% vs. 48% Anglo and 45% Poles.)

SOCIAL SUPPORT AND INTERACTION

Western European respondents were far more likely to report the absence of a confidant than were Jewish or Polish elders: 50% of Western European respondents compared to 33% of Polish and only 18% of Jewish elderly reported having no one close to them. Jewish elderly were the most likely to report being close to their children and grandchildren: 74% versus 42% of Western European and 41% of Polish respondents. On the other hand, Polish elders were more likely to report being close to a nonrelative: 15% versus only 3% of Jewish and no Western Europeans. The Jewish–Polish differences in family cohesiveness may reflect the greater intermarriage rate of children of Poles compared to Jews.

The high frequency of "no confidants" reported, especially by Polish respondents, is likely to reflect difficulty in establishing friendships with persons of different ethnic origins. Thus, although Polish elderly in Catholic nursing homes may have experienced greater congruence in terms of religious and cultural symbols than those in nonsectarian nursing homes, they may have found it difficult to establish friendships with elders who did not share the same ethnic and language backgrounds.

Similar patterns were reported with regard to concrete assistance received (instrumental supports). Forty-four percent of Western European and 48% of Polish respondents received help from no one, compared to only 23% of Jewish respondents, most of whom received assistance from family members (57%). In contrast, 36% of Western Europeans and only 17% of Polish elderly reported receiving aid from relatives. Friends were a very limited source of assistance to any of the elderly interviewed. Polish respondents reported noteworthy assistance from the church (17.2%).

VALUE ORIENTATIONS AND PREFERENCES

A number of questions in our interview focused on understanding the value orientations of institutionalized respondents, their hopes, fears, and personal concerns. In response to open-ended questions about hopes (i.e., what sort of things do you look forward to), the hopes of 26% of Western Europeans centered around health compared to 13% of Jewish and 7% of Polish respondents. These findings may reflect differential value orientations rather than actual health status, as we did not find corresponding differences in self or interviewer ratings of health status among the three ethnic groups. Leisure pursuits were also most salient to Western Europeans: 19% compared with 8% of Jewish and 7% of Polish elders. While the Polish respondents were most likely to center their hopes on leaving the nursing home (38%), this was true of only 13% of Jewish and 4% of Western European respondents. Family-related hopes were somewhat more salient to Jewish elderly (18%) than to either the Polish (14%) or Western European elderly (11%). These differences are consistent with responses indicating the salience of family and interpersonal contact to Jewish respondents. This finding is in contrast to more self-focused concerns on the part of Western Europeans, and an overriding dissatisfaction with life in an institution among the Polish.

Similar value orientation was evident in the personal wishes of respondents from each of the three ethnic groups. Although health-related wishes predominated for all three groups, beyond that, most of the wishes expressed by Poles related to being elsewhere (41% versus 27% of Western European and 17% of Jews). Jewish elders were most likely to express wishes reflecting concern for others: 25% versus 0 for the other two ethnic groups.

In terms of preferred leisure activities, responses were classified as pursuits conducted alone or having an individual focus versus pursuits involving interactions with others. The highly individualistic orientation of Western European elderly was once again demonstrated, with 58% preferring individual pursuits versus 39% of Polish and 33% of Jewish elderly.

When asked how they would spend $500 if such a sum was unexpectedly received, all respondents first responded in terms of meeting personal needs (Western European 48%, Polish 53%, Jewish 37%). Beyond meeting these needs, Jewish respondents and Polish respondents were more inclined to use it to assist others (46% Jewish, 28% Polish, and 17% Western European). These findings are consistent with observations in the literature about the strong emphasis on community-centered values, sometimes even at a detriment to the individual, in Polish and Jewish cultures (Howe, 1976; Kahana & Kahana, 1984a; Lopata, 1981).

QUALITATIVE ANALYSES

Differences among the three ethnic groups came to life as meaningful indicators of adjustment patterns when we consider participants' responses to selected open-ended questions. Among the Polish elderly, a common theme was that of perceived abandonment or even betrayal by children or other family members, which led to institutionalization. For some of these, the trauma of institutional placement was buffered by the attention of a priest or a church member who took a special interest in them. Institutional life was generally portrayed in negative terms, indicating little consolation from adult children, but rather considerable conflict in family relationships. Institutional placement was frequently portrayed as a product of this conflict. Many Polish respondents reminisced about life in "the old country," finding comfort in memories of their youth and well-being in the old, familiar settings. Preoccupied with escape or transfer from the nursing home, few Polish elderly had come to terms with institutional living.

The case of Mrs. P. illustrates the experience and frustration of Polish elderly who are placed in nursing homes that are incongruent with their cultural background.

> Mrs. P. came to the U. S. in 1950 to stay with her daughter. She said "I don't know why my daughter brought me here. I wanted to go to her house. I didn't understand about nursing homes. There is no one here to help (with everyday problems). They all speak English." Mrs. P. does not go to Mass because everything is in English. She cannot talk to her roommate because she is Italian. There is only one other Polish

person in the home. No one on the staff is Polish. Mrs. P. said "they [staff] are all alike—I don't understand any of them," "I cannot talk to anyone," ". . . that's what America did—children don't care for parents. In Poland children respected their parents. In America, when you get sick they throw you out."

A second type of institutionalized Polish elderly was identified among those who had no caring family members.

Mr. M. lost his wife during World War II and never remarried. A niece and nephew, his closest relatives, have apparently swindled him out of his home. Mr. M. commented, "they said on the radio that this is a good place. But I think the care is bad. The people who are served last always get a cold meal. I can't go to anyone to complain. I don't like living with so many sick and senile people who shout and yell and make trouble. It is like a jail here, and I want to be somewhere else. I want to find an older lady who will cook for me. I want my own lady."

Jewish residents tended to retain strong bonds with their children and families even in the nursing home. They were very involved in the lives of their children and grandchildren, even though indicating concern and dissatisfaction about not seeing their children often enough, or about having to live in a nursing home. However, they were less likely than the Polish residents to accuse their children of abandonment, clearly deriving much of their satisfaction and emotional sustenance from their families. The institutional setting appeared to be secondary in their emotional lives.

Typical of Jewish respondents was Mr. J.

Mr. J. entered a Jewish nursing home after suffering a stroke. "My children decided it would be best for me to be here, and what can I say, this is it!" Mr. J.'s three children visit him several times a week. He enjoys sitting on the porch and likes the home. Nonetheless: "A good home-cooked meal is hard to get here—my wife was a great cook." Mr. J. likes the young aides and volunteers, feels the staff is kind and attentive to his needs. His main wish is for his children's good health.

Western European elderly were generally more accepting of institutional placement and institutional life than either Jewish or Polish respondents. They shared a common belief in the desirability of elderly parents and their adult children maintaining independence. Typical of the Anglo's outlook was the desire to not be a burden to the family, coupled with a belief that institutional living is appropriate when a person can no longer live independently.

Mrs. A., a native of Montreal, Canada, related the following:

"The doctors wouldn't allow me to live alone anymore. I fell down the stairs and damaged my right arm and leg, so I can't use them any more. The doctor told me

I had to go into a home, so I said 'okay'. When you have no one to care for you, you do what you are told and make the best of it."

Another respondent of Western European background showed appreciation for living and no bitterness about life in an institution. This attitude was typically found among Western Europeans and Anglos.

Mrs. R. is confined to a wheelchair and her children live far away. Yet she noted "I am living on borrowed time and every day is wonderful."

PSYCHOSOCIAL WELL-BEING AND ITS PREDICTORS IN DIFFERENT ETHNIC GROUPS: QUANTITATIVE ANALYSIS

Overall, mean morale scores do not differ significantly among the three ethnic groups. Nevertheless, there are some consistent differences in the particular morale items endorsed most often by members of each ethnic group. Polish respondents are significantly more likely to endorse items reflecting depression or negative mood tone whereas Jewish respondents are more likely to endorse items denoting worry or anxiety. Comparison of the five factors originally derived by Lawton (1980)—surgency, attitudes toward aging, anxiety, depression, lonely dissatisfaction—confirm these observations.

Significant differences are also observed in locus of control beliefs among the three ethnic groups. Polish elderly indicate greater externality in response to problems salient to institutionalization, that is, relocation and health-related problems. Fully 78% of Polish respondents expressed externality in response to health-relevant problems compared with 36% of Western European and 16% of Jewish respondents ($p < .02$).

The effects on morale of health, ethnicity, culture, locus of control and congruent versus noncongruent environmental settings were examined by means of multiple regression analysis. With morale the dependent variable, the independent variables in the equation are locus of control, congruency, health status, ethnicity, and level of acculturation.

The variable "congruency" was computed from the respondent's ethnicity and the ethnicity of the nursing home. The independent variable "health" was derived from the question "How is your health now"? Ethnicity and culture were computed from combinations of variables that indicated "ethnicity" as described above, and "level of acculturation" was based on facility with the English language.

Previous data on morale of nursing home residents suggest that health has a strong direct effect on morale and that morale of nursing home residents is higher when control is in the hands of someone other than self. In this study, we hypothesize that lower levels of acculturation, health, and congruency will have negative effects on morale of nursing home residents. To examine the individual and joint effects of these variables on morale, a regression analysis was performed. To examine any nonlinear effects of the dummy variables for ethnicity and culture, hierarchical entry of data was performed.

The overall F test is significant ($p < .001$) for the effect of all independent variables, considered together, on morale. Individually, the strongest effect on morale is from health ($p < .00$; beta $= -.47$). The negative relationship indicates (predictably) that poor health decreases morale. Other significant effects on morale were found for "congruency" ($p < .02$); beta $= . - 23$). In addition, there is also a direct effect of acculturation on morale; lower level of acculturation is associated with lower levels of morale ($p < .03$; beta $= -.24$).

DISCUSSION

In considering ethnic and cultural differences in values and responses to institutionalization observed among our respondents, it is important to note that several factors may individually or in combination account for observed differences. Differential rates and patterns of institutionalization may exist between different ethnic groups, introducing a selection factor in institutional placement of respondents from the different ethnic groups. To the extent that children of immigrant parents may have been more geographically or socially mobile, such parents may have been placed in institutions even while being in relatively good physical and mental health. Thus, the relative good health of Polish elderly may be reflecting such a selection factor rather than indicating fewer health problems. The observed combination of relatively good physical health with evident psychological distress about institutionalization suggests that those institutionalized for social reasons feel particularly displaced in a congregate setting.

A second observed ethno-cultural difference appears to reflect differential expectations about institutional life based on differential socialization and value orientation among the ethnic groups (Gelfand, 1986). Accordingly, the observation that Western European elderly are more accepting of institutional life may relate to their endorsement of self-reliance and independence as opposed to the strong value for interdependence in the cultural background of ethnic elderly (Kahana et al., 1990).

A major finding of this research relates to confirmation of our hypotheses about the importance of culturally congruent environmental settings for adaptation of institutionalized ethnic elderly. To the extent that institutionalized and unacculturated ethnic elderly have more limited social resources and coping skills, Lawton's (1980) environmental docility hypothesis leads us to expect that environmental influences would be particularly salient for the well-being of these elders. Our findings also suggest that, at least in institutional settings, ethnic elderly are at a disadvantage. Thus, the double jeopardy interpretation of ethnicity may well fit elderly living in institutional settings.

Most students of ethnicity have come to recognize that multiple and overlapping criteria are needed to establish definitions of ethnic ties (Thernstrom, Orlov, & Handlin, 1980). Hayes, Kalish, and Guttmann (1986) make a compelling case for distinguishing cultural backgrounds of European-American elderly who are traditionally grouped with all other Caucasian elderly in studies of older Americans. The present study took one step in this direction by differentiating European-American elderly of Polish, Western European, and Jewish background. Even as we argue that these more molecular definitions bring us closer to understanding distinctive ethnic cultural influences, we must note that even these narrower units still contain much heterogeneity. The most homogeneous group in our study is the Polish elderly, who share language, national, and religious backgrounds. Jewish elderly share a strong cultural bond based on religion and shared history, but actually were socialized in such differing national contexts as Hungary, Russia, and Poland with concomitant differences in language, food preference, and cultural orientations. Our most heterogeneous group is comprised of the Western European elderly, who differ in religious backgrounds (Catholic or Protestant), language, and national origin.

In our assessment of congruence between institutional settings and resident characteristics, only rough matching of ethnic/cultural background was possible. Thus, we defined Catholic homes as congruent settings for Polish Catholics. This definition is meaningful in terms of the importance of church and religious affiliation, but still leaves areas of incongruence in terms of language and national traditions and often requires that Polish elderly with limited language skills interact with English-speaking staff or residents of different ethnic and language backgrounds.

In evaluating results of our study and results of other research on ethnic elders, we must also remain cognizant of the uncontrolled subgroup and individual differences operating that limit the precision of predictions based on modal differences between ethnic groups (Kalish, 1986).

In the introduction to his book on European American elderly, Guttmann (1986) notes the need for research among ethnic groups on their modes of dealing with stressful life situations. Our findings indicate that while health explains the major variance in the morale of institutionalized ethnic elders, ethnicity-related variables also contribute significantly. Our data confirm the expectation that the sense of belonging to an ethnic group, and its associated way of life, is an important aspect of adaptation, a potentially useful coping resource in moderating the stresses associated with aging and institutionalization.

REFERENCES

Abramson, H. J. (1980). Assimilation and pluralism. In S. T. Thernstrom, A. Orlov, & O. Handlin (Eds.), *Harvard encyclopedia of American ethnic groups.* Cambridge, MA: Belknap Press of Harvard University Press.

Antonovsky, A. (1979). *Health, stress and coping.* San Francisco: Jossey-Bass.

Bengtson, V. L. (1979). Ethnicity and aging: Problems and issues in current social science inquiry. In D. E. Gelfand & A. J. Kutzik (Eds.), *Ethnicity and aging: Theory, research, and policy.* New York: Springer Publishing Co.

Cohler, B., & Leiberman, M. (1979). Personality changes across the second half of life: Findings from a study of Irish, Italian, and Polish American men and women. In D. E. Gelfand & A. J. Kutzik (Eds.), *Ethnicity and aging: Theory, research, and policy.* New York: Springer Publishing Co.

Fandetti, D. & Gelfand, D. E. (1976). Care of the aged: Attitudes of white ethnic families. *The Gerontologist, 16,* 544–549.

Felton, B. & Kahana, E. (1974). Adjustment and situationally bound locus of control among institutionalized aged. *Journal of Gerontology, 29,* 295–301.

Gelfand, D. E. (1982). *Aging: The ethnic factor.* Boston, MA: Little, Brown.

Gelfand, D. E. (1986). Families, assistance and the Euro-American elderly. In C. L. Hayes, R. A. Kalish, & D. Guttmann (Eds.), *European-American elderly.* New York: Springer Publishing Co.

Gelfand, D. E., & Barresi, C. M. (1987). *Ethnic dimensions of aging.* New York: Springer Publishing Co.

Gelfand, D. E., & Kutzik, A. J. (Eds.). (1979). *Ethnicity and aging: Theory, research, and policy.* New York: Springer Publishing Co.

Goffman, E. (1961). *Asylums.* Garden City, NY: Anchor Books.

Gordon, M. (1964). *Assimilation in American life.* New York: Oxford University Press.

Guttmann, D. (1986). A perspective on Euro-American elderly. In C. L. Hayes, R. A. Kalish, & D. Guttmann (Eds.), *European-American elderly.* New York: Springer Publishing Co.

Guttmann, D., Kolm, R., Mostwiu, D., Kestenbaum, S., Harrington, D., Mullaney, J. W., Adams, K., Suziedelis, G., & Varga, L. (1979). *Informal and formal support systems and their effect on the lives of the elderly in selected ethnic groups.* (Final Report, Administration on Aging Grant No. 90-A-1007.) Washington, DC: National Catholic School of Social Service, The Catholic University of America.

Habenstein, R. W., & Mindel, C. H. (1981). The American ethnic family: Protean and adaptive patterns. In C. H. Mindel & R. W. Habenstein (Eds.), *Ethnic families in America: Patterns and variations* (2nd ed.). New York: Elsevier.

Harel, Z. (1986). Ethnicity and aging: Implications for service organizations. In C. H. Hayes, R. A. Kalish, & D. Guttmann (Eds.), *European-American elderly.* New York: Springer Publishing Co.

Hayes, C. L., Kalish, R. A., & Guttmann, D. (Eds.). (1986). *European-American elderly.* New York: Springer Publishing Co.

Howe, I. (1976). *World of our fathers.* New York: Harcourt, Brace, Jovanovich.

Jackson, J. J. (1985). Race, national origin, ethnicity and aging. In R. H. Binstock & E. Shanas (Eds.), *Handbook of aging and the social sciences* (2nd ed.). New York: Van Nostrand Reinhold.

Kahana, E., & Kahana, B. (1984a). Jews. In E. Palmore (Ed.), *Handbook on the aged in the United States*. Westport, CT: Greenwood Press.

Kahana, B., & Kahana, E. (1984b). Stress reactions. In P. Lewinsohn & L. Teri (Eds.), *Clinical geropsychology*. New York: Pergamon Press.

Kahana, E., Kahana, B., & Kinney J. M. (1990). Coping among vulnerable elders. In Z. Harel, P. Ehrlich, & R. Hubbard (Eds.), *Understanding and servicing the vulnerable aged*. New York: Springer Publishing Co.

Kahana, E., Kahana, B., & Riley, K. (1989). Person-environment transactions relevant to control and helplessness in institutional settings. In P. S. Fry (Ed.), *Psychological perspectives of helplessness and control in the elderly*. New York: Elsevier North-Holland.

Kalish, R.A. (1983). *The psychology of human behavior* (5th ed.). Monterey, CA: Brooks/Cole.

Kalish, R. A. (1986). The meanings of ethnicity. In C. L. Hayes, R. A. Kalish, & D. Guttmann (Eds.), *European-American elderly*. New York: Springer Publishing Co.

Kalish, R. A., & Creedon, M. A. (1986). Religion and the church. In C. L. Hayes, R. A. Kalish, & D. Guttmann (Eds.), *European-American elderly*. New York: Springer Publishing Co.

Lawton, M. P. (1972). The dimensions of morale. In D. P. Kent, R. Kastenbaum, & S. Sherwood (Eds.), *Research, planning and action for the elderly*. New York: Behavioral Publications.

Lawton, M. P. (1980). *Environment and aging*. Belmont, CA: Wadsworth.

Lieberman, M. A., & Tobin, S. S. (1983). *The experience of old age: Stress, coping, and survival*. New York: Basic Books.

Lopata, H. Z. (1981). Polish American families. In C. H. Mindel & R. W. Habenstein (Eds.), *Ethnic families in America* (2nd ed.). New York: Elsevier.

Markides, K. S., & Mindel, C. H. (1987). *Aging and ethnicity*. Beverly Hills, CA: Sage.

McCallum, J., & Shadbolt, B. (1989). Ethnicity and stress among older Australians. *Journal of Gerontology, 44*, 589–596.

Newman, W. M. (1973). *American pluralism*. New York: Harper & Row.

Thernstrom, S. T., Orlov, A., & Handlin, O. (Eds.). (1980). *Harvard encyclopedia of American ethnic groups*. Cambridge, MA: Belknap Press of Harvard University Press.

Woehrer, C. (1978). Cultural pluralism in American families: The influence of ethnicity on special aspects of aging. *Family Coordinator, 27*, 329–340.

Zborowski, M. (1952). Cultural components in response to pain. *Journal of Social Issues, 9*, 16–30.

PART V

Models of Ethnically Sensitive Care

This section includes four chapters that discuss successful models of ethnically sensitive long-term care. The first three chapters present features of existing programs, while the last chapter presents a conceptual model of critical features that need to be considered at an organizational and system level. These chapters should be of particular interest to planners and developers of programs and facilities, as well as practitioners who want to emphasize ethnically sensitive care.

In the first chapter, Yeo provides an extensive review of factors associated with lower nursing home admission rates for non-white ethnic elderly. Among the key factors discussed are cost, discrimination, personal choice, and social

159

and cultural differences. Yeo also discusses adjustment of ethnic elders to nurs-ing homes and factors associated with successful adjustment. In the second part of her chapter, Yeo presents components of successful ethnically sensitive nurs-ing home care. She studied several ethnic nursing homes on the West Coast that she identifies as successfully providing care for ethnic elders. Yeo discusses 12 key components to providing ethnically sensitive care.

The second chapter is written by three members of one of the country's most successful ethnically-oriented delivery systems, On Lok. Van Steenberg, An-sak, and Chin-Hansen present detailed information on the philosophy, history, structure, methods of service delivery, and financing of On Lok. On Lok is the prototype for PACE—Program for All-inclusive Care for the Elderly. These au-thors discuss the philosophy behind PACE, the replication of On Lok/PACE, and the special ethnic considerations that must be made. This chapter provides a special opportunity to see many of the core features of an ethnically sensitive long-term care program.

In the third chapter, Folmar presents an interesting case study of two Jewish nursing homes in Cleveland, Ohio. He provides historical background on the cultural and religious underpinnings of each of these nursing homes, overlays structural and organizational issues faced by each nursing home, and addresses the relationship of each nursing home to the other and the larger community. Folmar points out that each nursing home has had to address different religious and organizational philosophies, and basic pressures of competition, coopera-tion, identity, and market share.

The final chapter of this section, by Hernandez-Gallegos, Capitman, and Yee, is different from the other chapters in this section. Instead of presenting in-formation about a specific organization or model, these authors address issues of service use (or underuse) at a system level and in terms of organizational fea-tures more generically. They argue that provider organization features such as personnel practices and service approaches are key issues for understanding un-deruse of services by ethnic elders. This is quite different from the more com-mon approach of focusing on characteristics of the elder. Hernandez-Gallegos, Capitman, and Yee present a conceptual model for understanding the process of service use by ethnic elders and assess its utility by reviewing literature and conducting a survey of providers from various long-term care and support ser-vices agencies. On the basis of their findings they make several recommenda-tions for provider organizations.

11

Ethnicity and Nursing Homes: Factors Affecting Use and Successful Components for Culturally Sensitive Care

Gwen Yeo

The purpose of this chapter is to review the available research literature on the admission and adjustment of ethnic elders to nursing homes (NHs) in the United States and to suggest some of the relevant components that might be examined in providing appropriate NH care for ethnic elders, based on observations and interviews by the author.

This study was partially supported by grants from the Bureau of Health Professionals for Geriatric Education Centers and the Teaching Nursing Home Project from the National Institute of Aging.

BACKGROUND

Ethnic elders in the four non-white categories of Asian/Pacific Islander (P/Asian), black, Hispanic, and native American are significantly underrepresented in nursing home (NH) populations in the United States, according to the available data. In spite of evidence of greater disability among most of these populations, their rates of NH residence are 40% to 80% that of whites (AARP, 1987; Eribes & Bradley-Rawls, 1978; Hing, 1987; Jones-Morrison, 1986; Palmore, 1976; Trevino & Moss, 1984; U. S. Deptartment of Health and Human Services, 1989; Yu, Liu, & Kurzeja, 1985). Although it is not possible to ascertain the trends in NH admission for each ethnic category from the national nursing home surveys of 1973–74, 1977, and 1985 because the same race/ethnic designations were not used for all three surveys, it appears that non-white utilization has been increasing during the past two decades. The rate of NH residents per 1000 population for people 65 and over among "black and other" designations was reported as growing from 21.6 in 1973–74 to 32.6 in 1985. For ages 75 and over, white rates declined during those 12 years, while rates for "black and other" increased from 28.0 to 44.0 for ages 74–84 and 100.5 to 131.9 for those 85 and over (U. S. Department of Health and Human Services, 1989, Table 17).

It seems reasonable to assume that the population of ethnic elders admitted to NHs in the future will continue to increase, given the following projections: (1) the increasing aging of the present ethnic populations; (2) the expanding assimilation of the elders and their families, which would be expected to make NH use more acceptable; (3) growth in their familiarity with service networks; and (4) the potential for a continuing influx of older adults, especially those immigrating from certain Asian countries.

In spite of the fact that cultural issues are frequently recognized as important in the management of chronic illness, even on an outpatient basis (e.g., Clark, 1983; Harwood, 1981; Orque, Bloch, & Monroy, 1983), very little is known about the characteristics of ethnic elders who are admitted to NHs, and almost nothing about the unique issues in their adjustment that might help to give health care providers guidance in their management or care.

Continuity in the lives of elders has been emphasized as a major need to enhance function and quality, with institutional admission representing a major threat to that continuity (Atchley, 1989; Kahana, 1982; Tobin & Lieberman, 1976). Entering the NH environment frequently represents an even more dramatic break in continuity in the lives of ethnic elders than it does for the typical white NH resident. In the NH ethnic elders are generally isolated from their ethnic network and familiar language, values, norms (including diet), and reciprocal role relationships. Fear of this isolation, as well as the lack of cultural models for institutional care of elders, have been suggested as explanations for the lower NH admission among non-white ethnic elders.

Although there are a few examples of ethnically oriented NHs that might reduce the break in cultural continuity faced by elders upon admission, such as those developed for Jewish elders, there are very few designed for non-white ethnic NH residents (Yeo, 1988). (A few exceptions on the West Coast will be discussed below.) Most non-white elders, except those living on Indian reservations or other areas of extremely high ethnic density, then, are typically admitted to NHs in which their group represents a small portion of the resident population and in which the staff have little time, expertise, or resources to meet their needs for cultural continuity.

Present Knowledge

Admission

The increasing underrepresentation of ethnic elders in NHs with age is illustrated in Table 11.1, compiled for the American Association of Retired Persons (AARP, 1987) from the 1980 census.

The differences seem even more significant in view of the fact that lower proportions are married among the four non-white populations 65+ than among whites (AARP, 1987), since being married reduces the risk of nursing home placement (Branch & Jette, 1982; George, 1984; Shapiro & Tate, 1988; Vicente, Wiley, & Carrington, 1979).

In an effort to explore the differential risk of institutionalization by ethnic status, Moss and Halamandaris (1977) summarized the categories of explanation given in Senate hearings on NH care as cost, discrimination, personal choice, social and cultural differences. Based on testimony from health care providers and family members of older minority patients, they concluded that although all four factors may have been operating to some extent among the four ethnic categories, their relative importance in explaining the underrepresentation varied considerably. Among the widely heterogeneous population of P/Asian elders, the most important explanations for not using NH services were language, and social and cultural differences that isolated older P/Asian residents from staff and other residents. Blacks were more likely to identify cost and discrimination practices. American Indians listed social and cultural fac-

TABLE 11.1 Percent of Ethnic Population in Nursing Homes in 1980 by Age

Age	Black	Hispanic	P/Asian	Native Am	White
65+	3	3	2	4*	5
85+	12	10	10	13	23

*Includes all institutions.

tors as most important, with cost and personal choice close behind. Mexican-American elders cited discrimination, cost, and the isolating factors of language and social and cultural differences as barriers.

There is only one available study that attempted to examine these or other factors related to the differential NH representation in a systematic way using an ethnic population. Eribes and Bradley-Rawls (1978) examined the percent of Mexican-American elders in NHs in nine areas in Phoenix to evaluate four possible explanations of lower use. Their data support neither the geographic explanation (i.e., lack of access due to territorial distribution of NHs), nor the economic explanation (there was a negative correlation between NH use and income). Areas with higher than average number of elders living alone also showed a higher proportion in NHs. They concluded that cultural factors explain much of the underrepresentation of Mexican-American elders in NHs.

Espino, Neufeld, Mulvihill, and Libow (1988) report a pilot study of differences among a small sample of Hispanic (primarily Puerto Rican) and non-Hispanic elders on admission to a New York NH. They found the Hispanic sample to be younger, more impaired in mobility and other functions, more likely to be victims of stroke, and more likely to be married (see also Espino in this volume).

American Indian access to NHs is severely limited due to the small number of facilities available on reservations or in Indian communities; only 15 currently exist, requiring that most elders in need of skilled nursing care be placed in NHs in distant communities staffed by non-Indian personnel (Manson, 1989; Rousseau, 1990). As a result, visiting by family and friends was less frequent than in the NHs that have been built on reservations since 1969. An interesting finding on admission patterns in these reservation NHs was its seasonality; occupancy was considerably higher in the winter than in the warmer seasons (Manson, 1989; Manson & Callaway, 1988; see also Manson in this volume).

Cost and Discrimination

Although the relationship of income to NH residence for ethnic elders has not been examined carefully, mixed results have been reported on its effect on the risk of institutionalization in predominantly white samples. Although Palmore (1976) found that elders with higher incomes had higher rates of institutionalization in the Duke longitudinal study, Vicente et al. (1979) found higher rates for poorer elders in a follow-up study of a probability sample of 6,928 adults in Alameda County, California. In the prospective Branch and Jette (1982) study of a statewide probability sample in Massachusetts, Medicaid eligibility was not related to risk either way. In spite of these mixed results, low income is frequently identified as a barrier to appropriate NH care (e.g., Vladek, 1982).

Finding appropriate institutional care when it is needed has been identified as a problem for black elders, which is attributed to cost and discrimination

(Markson, 1979). Based on their analysis of census data, Kart and Beckham (1976) documented a substantial difference in black/white distribution among types of institutions, with blacks predominating in state mental hospitals and whites in nonprofit and proprietary homes for the aged, which they attribute at least partially to discrimination and socioeconomic status (SES). The pattern was found to be especially prevalent in the Southern states and was found to be declining from 1950 to 1970. It should be noted, however, that Wershow (1976) reported a major unexplained inaccuracy with census figures on black residents of NHs in Alabama; in the 1970 data only 36 black NH residents were reported in the entire state, all in public institutions, whereas he documented 197 in one county alone in licensed proprietary NHs.

A study of discrimination in New York City NHs (Friends and Relatives of Institutionalized Aged, Inc., 1984) found that minority aged (black, Hispanic, and "other") occupied 48% of the beds in public facilities. Only 20% of the beds in proprietary facilities and 18% of the beds in facilities owned by nonprofits were occupied by minority elders. These were primarily in those facilities that were predominantly minority. Interviews with discharge planners in New York City hospitals confirmed that they frequently steered older minority patients to the traditional minority facilities in an effort to avoid the process of refusal from private NHs and to move the patients out of the hospital quickly. Efforts of the federal and state governments to enforce the equal access provisions of Title VI of the Civil Rights Act to NH admission were studied by Schafft (1980), who reported very uneven attention to enforcement procedures by state and local officials.

Differential distribution of NH residents to types of NHs by race or ethnicity is not reflected in the latest national data source, the 1985 Nursing Home Survey (U. S. Deptartment of Health and Human Services, 1989). Analysis by this author indicates no difference in the proportion of "white" and "black and other" NH residents in government facilities (8% for both populations) and a very small difference in nonprofit (23% of whites versus 20% of black and other), with the remainder being in proprietary NHs.

Cultural Emphasis on Family Care

In the literature on ethnic aging, little direct attention is given to the reason for underrepresentation of ethnic elders in NHs. When the differential use of NHs is addressed, directly or indirectly, it tends to be attributed to cultural differences in extended family roles and expectations that increase both the acceptability and reality of intergenerational dependence and that reduce the acceptability and need of NH placement for ethnic elders (Carp & Kataoka, 1976; Cheung, Cho, Lum, Tang, & Yau, 1980; Kiefer et al., 1985; Koh & Bell, 1987; Markides & Krause, 1985; Morrison, 1982; Osako, 1979; Sotomayor & Applewhite, 1988; Sotomayor & Randolph, 1988; Taylor, 1988; Wong,

1980). This attribution is referred to as the "cultural aversion hypothesis" by Morrison (1982).

Evidence from a number of observers and various sources suggests, however, that family structure and roles are changing. In many ethnic groups there is a movement toward the patterns of the larger culture. There is less consistent assumption of heavy chronic elder care responsibility by family members and less expectation by elders that they will be completely dependent on family members (Cantor, 1979; Carter, 1988; Cheung et al., 1980; Cuellar, Stanford, & Miller-Soule, 1982; Cuellar & Weeks, 1980; Kiefer et al., 1985; Koh & Bell, 1987; Markides & Krause, 1985; Morrison, 1982; Osako, 1979; Rosenthal, 1986; Sotomayor & Applewhite, 1988; Sotomayor & Randolph, 1988; Taylor, 1988; Wong, 1980). Markides and Krause (1985), in fact, found a positive relationship between depression and association with children among their older Mexican-American sample and concluded that it would be important to incorporate measures of elders' attitude toward dependency along with indicators of the amount of dependency in further research. In Gibson and Jackson's (1987) analysis of responses from a national probability sample of black elders, more than 42% in each of the three older cohorts reported that there were no members of their immediate family within their state; 78% or more, however, said that they received some or a lot of help from church members. Based on her work with black elders, Morrison (1982) warns that the danger of unquestioning acceptance of the "cultural aversion hypothesis" could result in denial of services to minority aged and their families who do not have the capacity to "care for their own" as they would like, and who need NH services.

Two studies of American Indian NHs have concluded that those built on reservations by tribal entities are defined as extensions of family care, demonstrating the continued value and esteem with which elders are treated (Manson, 1989; Shomaker, 1981; see also Manson in this volume). Rather than rejection or disrespect, skilled care in the NH that is not possible in the Navaho hogan is seen as a method of showing greater respect for chronically ill elders (Shomaker, 1981). Some of the methods used in the two Navajo nursing homes owned and operated by the Navaho Health Authority include: being staffed only by Navahos "except for nursing personnel" (Shomaker, 1981, p. 532); both medicine men and Public Health Service physicians visiting the patients; emphasis on Navaho food and traditional activities such as weaving, jewelry and pottery making, and squaw dances; encouragement of families to take elders home over the weekend and during summer; clients being taken to Navaho "sings," fairs, and dances on the reservations; and hogans available at both nursing homes for ceremonials. The facility in Chinle is built in the hexagonal shape of a traditional hogan with windows opening to the vast panorama of the countryside. Shomaker (1981) concludes that caring for elders in the nursing homes is seen as an extension of the family care traditional in the Navaho culture and not abandonment, since families continue to be closely involved with the residents and since care is given by young Navahos who can speak the elders' language.

Other Potential Factors

Some insight on barriers to admission to NHs can be gleaned from the literature on use of other types of long-term care (LTC) services by ethnic elders. To emphasize a few relevant findings, Valle (1989) emphasizes the need for culturally relevant services for the "relatively invisible" population of frail ethnic elders who have higher levels of impairment and who have relied primarily on natural social networks whose members may not be well-informed about available community resources. He suggests: attention to the different levels of assimilation among ethnic elders in the provision of "culturally fair" services in geographic proximity to ethnic neighborhoods, providing outreach, and working with the indigenous community providers. A study of Hispanic and Anglo clients of a case management program in Arizona found the following characteristics among the Hispanic elders: greater impairment levels, somewhat less use of formal services, and strikingly more use of informal services (Greene & Monahan, 1984).

Holmes and colleagues interviewed 205 LTC agencies on possible barriers to service for ethnic elders in 32 counties nationally with heavy density of populations from the four ethnic categories (Holmes, Holmes, Steinbach, Hausner, & Rocheleau, 1979). They found that agencies that serve higher proportions of minority elders value and hire more minority staff, provide specialized training to their staff, have minority representatives on their Board of Directors/Advisory Councils, and are more likely to be located in minority neighborhoods. Torres-Gil and Fielder (1986–87) stress the importance of identification of medical, social, and psychological needs of Hispanic elders in addition to the incorporation of culturally appropriate services in the planning process for adequate long term care services for the Hispanic community.

Adjustment

The literature contains no reports of well-designed research on adjustment of ethnic elders to a NH environment, although case reports of isolation of ethnic elders in a general community NH because of language and cultural differences are not unusual (Brenes Jette & Remien, 1988; Moss & Halamandaris, 1977). In discussing the practice implications of their findings from their classic study on elders' adjustment to institutional living, Tobin and Lieberman (1976) emphasized the need to minimize risk of further deterioration by matching individuals to environments and reducing environmental discontinuity. Dominick and Stotsky (1969) observed NH residents from seven different religious/ethnic backgrounds and concluded that ethnic, cultural and religious ties reduce feelings of isolation, abandonment, and hopelessness.

Chee and Kane (1983) interviewed 11 English-speaking patients and 37 family members in one predominantly Japanese and one predominantly black Los

Angeles NH on their preferences for ethnic factors in the NHs. The six factors reflecting the importance of ethnic food, ethnic programs and activities, ethnic community involvement, and staff and patients from the same ethnic background were all judged very important by the Japanese respondents (4.5 or over on a 5 point scale) but less important by black respondents (2.2 to 3.9 for 5 of the 6 factors). It is notable that the preference for ethnic community involvement was the only factor that averaged 4.0 and over by both black families and patients. Follow-up interviews confirmed the importance to Japanese residents and their families of NH staff's understanding and adapting to the non-Western dietary preferences and value system (such as duty and respect), and their understanding the effect of unique historical experiences (such as internment) of the largely foreign-born Japanese elders.

Morrison (1982) reports a similar study among 181 black, Chinese, and Puerto Rican NH residents in New York City. Using the framework of cultural congruence, Morrison and her colleagues found that: residents from all three ethnic categories agreed that ethnic foods were important; Puerto Ricans were most likely and Chinese least likely to endorse the importance of celebration of cultural holidays, having traditional church services and ethnically oriented music and art, and having staff taught about their culture; Puerto Ricans and Chinese saw having administrators and staff from their background as more important than blacks; and Chinese were least likely to endorse ethnic representation on NH governing boards.

The importance of cultural factors in the adjustment of Hispanic nursing home patients is emphasized by Brenes Jette and Remien (1988), based on their work as clinical psychologists in a 900-bed facility in New York. In addition to the importance of language factors, they recommend recognition of Hispanic elders' religious or fatalistic view of their health and institutionalization, and the importance of the values of *confianza* (trust), *personalismo* (personal relationships), *respeto* (respect owed to elders), *verguenza* and *orgullo* (the sense of shame to be avoided and pride to be upheld), and *obligacion* (duty and responsibility to the family). Negative reactions to poor adjustment to the NH environment include depression among Hispanic elders and withdrawal by family.

Weinstock and Bennett (1969) surveyed residents of a racially mixed NH with racially mixed staff and found that black residents were more likely to communicate their needs to the largely black nursing staff, while the white residents tended to seek out other white staff members. The evaluation of the nursing staff by black residents was also more positive than the evaluation by white residents.

The data from the 1977 NH Survey included staff reports of social contacts and activities. Black and Hispanic residents were reported as less likely to have daily or weekly visitors (48 and 57%, respectively, versus 63% for whites). This becomes significant in light of findings by Greene and Monahan (1982) that frequency of visitation with NH residents was a significant negative predictor of psychosocial impairment, as rated by NH staff.

Questions for Further Research

The literature reviewed above provides few answers to the crucial questions facing planners and long-term care providers who need to prepare for the increasing cultural heterogeneity of current and future elders. In the face of tomorrow's two in every five elders (at least in California) who do not fit the characteristic cultural mold for whom most NHs are designed and administered, the handful of exploratory and preliminary research efforts available to inform us seem almost trivial. No longer is it possible to ignore the increasing rates of admission of ethnic elders to NHs with the casual stereotype that "their families take care of them." We do not know, however, what differentiates those ethnic elders who accept admission to NHs as a consequence of their frailty from those who do not. Do they have less family or other social support? Are they more independent in the style of "Anglo" elders who value autonomy and want "not to be a burden" to their children? The other major set of unanswered questions involves the possible consequences of NH admission for ethnic elders and their families. For example, what happens to family relationships with adult children who may be experiencing high levels of guilt and depression related to the violation of cultural expectations of parent care? How do the elders adapt to the foreign cultural environment of an "Anglo" NH? These and other questions will be important to guide the future research in the field.

COMPONENTS OF ETHNICALLY ORIENTED NURSING HOME CARE

In order to explore the reasons that ethnic elders may choose to be admitted to certain nursing homes, a list of characteristics that might make older adults from ethnic backgrounds feel more comfortable in culturally familiar surroundings was derived from the literature reviewed above. These characteristics were then used in a preliminary set of observation of six institutions identified as successfully providing care for ethnic elders on the West Coast. By identifying the degree to which the institutional settings include the identified components, some light can be shed on the most important features nursing homes could use in providing ethnically sensitive care.

The institutions were chosen because they were among the few who were targeting their services to particular groups of ethnic elders, generally enjoyed good reputations in the communities they served, and could be considered as successful models for providing cultural continuity for elders from their target group in the transition to a NH environment. The settings included NHs targeted to populations described as Asian, Jewish, Russian Orthodox, Japanese, and Chinese, and a residential care facility targeted to Spanish-speaking elders. All are in metropolitan areas of northern California and Washington State. The Jewish and Russian NHs were included because of their excellent record in NH care although their residents are not in the ethnic categories that are the focus of the present paper, nor are they underrepresented in NHs.

With the exception of other Jewish homes and a very small Russian Orthodox facility, these are the only known ethnically oriented NHs in northern California, Oregon, and Washington. The Spanish-speaking facility was chosen in spite of the fact that their facilities are congregate housing and residential care, since no Hispanic NHs could be identified. Interviews were conducted with administrators, other staff, and board members. Findings of this preliminary study are summarized below, by factors that might be found to contribute to an ethnically sensitive model of NH care.

History, Ownership, and Policymaking Authority

In view of the finding by Holmes et al. (1979) that representation of members from target ethnicities was associated with higher utilization in community-based long-term care agencies, this possible relationship was explored among the NHs. All six programs were owned by ethnic non-profit agencies, had boards with target ethnic membership, and were designed to meet needs of ethnic elders. In four cases, the facilities were owned by longstanding ethnic service agencies; in the Russian and Chinese cases, groups were organized for the purpose of developing the NH.

Location

Only one NH (Japanese) is located in a high-density ethnic neighborhood, and two are completely out of a residential area with any ethnic identification. The Russian NH, in fact, is in a suburban area about 20 miles from the San Francisco area where most of the Russian residents lived. Although location has been suggested by many writers to be crucial for utilization, it did not seem to be of major importance in these cases.

Selection and Training of Staff

Administrators, staff, and board members in all the sites expressed strong preferences to have staff from the same ethnic group as the target residents, but because of lack of availability, all found that it was not possible to be that selective in most cases. In the Russian NH, there were Russian speakers on each shift, and that was felt by the administrator to be a success. In the Asian NH, the first administrator who was Asian left at the end of the first year and was replaced by an

Anglo, who has been successful in the role; the other administrators were all of the target ethnicity. The greatest proportion of ethnic staff was found in the Hispanic facility, which had Spanish-speaking staff at all levels of the organization; the next highest proportion was in the very new Chinese NH, which had Chinese staff in most of the supervisory positions and some of the nursing staff.

Training of the staff concerning the special needs of the ethnic elders was reported as important in most of the settings, but there were variations in the formality of the training. The Japanese and Jewish NHs gave special orientation to new staff, while the remainder tended to provide the training in individual feedback or staff development sessions. In the Jewish case, it was especially important to sensitize the staff to the events of the Holocaust and its meaning to survivors. In the Hispanic case, the values of respect, dignity, and patience with the elders was emphasized. In the Russian home, it was especially important that the personal care staff understand the effect of the five major displacements suffered by many of the Russian elders during their lifetimes on the extreme importance of any small material possession they might still retain from their childhood; even just a small piece of paper was a treasure.

Volunteers from the target ethnicities were considered very important in communicating with the residents, especially when staff members were not available, but major differences were found in the number of volunteers participating; in the Asian, Japanese, and Jewish homes there were large numbers.

Admission Policy and Process

The most common policy was to recruit residents in the ethnic community, but not to discriminate among applicants. In the Jewish home all the residents are Jewish, which was the only case where there were no residents outside the target ethnicity. The social worker there reported that they do have occasional non-Jewish applicants, but after the orientation and preadmission visit, none has chosen to be admitted. She attributes this to the realization that some of the Christian events, such as Christmas, will not be observed in that setting.

The Asian NH has a mix of ethnic residents: 60% Japanese, 20% Chinese, and 20% other (Korean, Vietnamese, Cambodian, and Anglo). In both the Russian and Hispanic homes, the majority of their residents are not from their target groups.

Cost

All the NHs interviewed accept MediCal patients but also have residents on private pay status. The Hispanic residential care facility accepts elders on Supplemental Security Income (SSI). They attribute some of their difficulty attracting Hispanic elders to the fact that many who are eligible for SSI are not receiving the benefits, which would help cover the cost of residential care; and many of those who do receive SSI live with their children's families, who rely on the elders' payments to help with household costs, so admission to the residential facility would deprive the families of the elders' income.

The Asian NH raises money in the community with bingo, donations of rooms, and auctions to subsidize the care for low-income elders. Community subsidies are also used in the Japanese and Jewish homes.

Interaction with Family

Interaction with family members was regarded as very important in all of the facilities, but the rates of participation of family members reported varied considerably. In the Russian and Jewish homes, fewer residents had family members close by. In the Asian NH a large number of family members are involved on a regular basis; some visit daily, and there are an estimated six family members present per meal to assist their own and other elders in the dining room.

Language

Even within these ethnically targeted NHs there are still problems with residents speaking different languages, making communication difficult. In the Asian NH at least five language groups are represented; in the Chinese NH residents speak several Chinese languages and dialects. The Jewish home reported that advanced stage dementia patients frequently began speaking in their original language (e.g., Yiddish or German) even if they had not used it recently. Most of the homes did attempt to group residents by language so that they could communicate with each other more easily. The Hispanic home reported special difficulty with monolingual Spanish speakers in dealing with bureaucratic issues, such as regulations.

Food

The importance of ethnic diets was acknowledged by all the respondents, but they also acknowledged the difficulty in meeting all the nutritional requirements and the varied preferences of the residents. In the Jewish NH, all the meals are Kosher, and residents are quick to complain in residents council meetings if they do not like the food. In the Russian home, typically Russian dinners or lunches are served twice a week and on special holidays. In the Asian home there are optional Asian foods available for all meals except breakfast. In the Chinese home, most of the meals are Chinese, and in the Japanese and Hispanic facilities there are ethnic meals several times a week. The Hispanic home staff work with the residents council to develop the menus.

Activity Program

Ethnically oriented activities were provided by all six homes, but the percentage of all activities that had an ethnic flavor differed from one facility to the next. In half the homes, the activity director was Anglo. Volunteers from the ethnic community were very important to provide leadership and assistance for the activities. Traditional holidays frequently provided an opportunity for a special cultural celebration, and also an opportunity to teach residents and staff from other backgrounds some of the history of the group. Traditional crafts, such as Japanese paper folding and making Mexican paper flowers, were featured in their respective sites, as were making symbols to observe religious or ethnic holidays.

In the Asian home the activity calendar was posted in English, Chinese, and Japanese languages, and many of the activities were translated into both Chinese and Japanese when the leader spoke English. Volunteers regularly translated English language papers and read Japanese language papers to the residents. Movies were shown in both Japanese and Chinese. At the time of the interview, the Anglo activity director was beginning a program to let each of the ethnic groups represented among the residents teach each other about the observances of their major holidays.

Religious Observances

In half of the homes, religious observances were a very important part of their programs. In both the Russian and the Jewish settings the religious communities helped to fund and operate the NH, so that their influence would be expected to be important. The Jewish home has a chapel on site that is used for services for both residents and nonresidents. The Russian Orthodox icons and other religious symbols are prominently displayed in some of the activity rooms where services are held. The Japanese home has very strong ties to both the Christian and Buddhist congregations that serve their Japanese residents; both the minister and the priest come weekly to hold services.

Personal and Nursing Care

A strong need for the staff to treat the residents with respect and dignity was emphasized, especially by the Hispanic and Japanese administrators. Importance of understanding residents' culturally related behaviors (e.g., fear among Holocaust survivors) was also expressed.

SUMMARY

Based on the exploration of the application of these 11 components to NH care by facilities already serving ethnic elders, it would seem important that future attempts to reduce barriers to admission and adjustment take into account the identified issues. Those policies that seemed most uniformly endorsed and practiced in the six NHs examined were: a flexible cost policy; recruitment of ethnic staff and volunteers; provision of culturally relevant diet and activities; and training of staff for ethnic-specific values and behaviors. These qualities have all been suggested to some degree by preliminary studies and policy papers and the present study may serve to emphasize their importance for policy planners. However, some of the other suggestions from the literature were not confirmed in the West Coast NHs, such as the importance of geographic placement within an ethnic community, and culturally specific architecture and interior design, although they might be considered self-evident as desirable if the opportunities are available.

There is much we do not know about the factors that affect admission and adjustment of ethnic elders to nursing homes, in order to begin to design nursing homes that contain the fewest possible barriers for ethnic utilization. The findings reviewed in this paper represent a beginning in the attempt to identify the relevant components of a model that could be used by planners, developers, and policymakers to better serve the growing population of ethnic elders.

REFERENCES

AARP Minority Affairs Initiative. (1987). *A portrait of older minorities*. Washington, DC: American Association of Retired Persons.

Atchley, R. C. (1989). A continuity theory of normal aging. *Gerontologist, 29*, 183–190.

Branch, L. G., & Jette, A. M. (1982). A prospective study of long-term care institutionalization among the aged. *American Journal of Public Health, 72*, 1373–1379.

Brenes Jette, C. C., & Remien, R. (1988). Hispanic geriatric residents in a long-term care setting. *Journal of Applied Gerontology, 7*, 350–365.

Cantor, M. J. (1979). The informal support system of New York's inner city elderly: Is ethnicity a factor? In D. E. Gelfand & A. J. Kutzick (Eds.), *Ethnicity and aging: Theory, research, and policy*. New York: Springer Publishing Co.

Carp, F. M., & Kataoka, E. (1976). Health care problems of the elderly of San Francisco's Chinatown. *Gerontologist, 16*, 30–38.

Carter, J. H. (1988). Health attitudes/promotions/preventions: The black elderly. In J. S. Jackson, P. Newton, A. Ostfield, D. Savage, & E. L. Schneider (Eds.), *The black American elderly: Research on physical and psychosocial health*. New York: Springer Publishing Co.

Chee, P., & Kane, R. (1983). Cultural factors affecting nursing home care for minorities: A study of black American and Japanese-American groups. *Journal of the American Geriatrics Society, 31*, 109–111.

Cheung, L. Y., Cho, E. R., Lum, D., Tang, T., & Yau, H. B. (1980). The Chinese elderly and family structure: Implications for health care. *Public Health Reports, 95*, 491–495.

Clark, M. (Ed.) (1983). Cross-cultural medicine. *Western Journal of Medicine, 139*.

Cuellar, J. B., Stanford, E. P., & Miller-Soule, D. I. (1982). *Understanding minority aging: Perspectives and sources.* San Diego: San Diego State University Center on Aging.

Cuellar, J. B., & Weeks, J. R. (1980). *Minority elderly Americans: The assessment of needs and equitable receipt of public benefits as a prototype for area agencies on aging: Final Report.* San Diego: Allied Home Health Agency.

Dominick, J. R., & Stotsky, B. A. (1969). Mental patients in nursing homes: Ethnic influences. *Journal of the American Geriatrics Society, 17,* 63–85.

Eribes, R. A., & Bradley-Rawls, M. (1978). The underutilization of nursing home facilities by Mexican-American elderly in the Southwest. *Gerontologist, 18,* 363–371.

Espino, D. V., Neufeld, R. R., Mulvihill, M., & Libow, L. S. (1988). Hispanic and non-Hispanic elderly on admission to the nursing home. *Gerontologist, 28,* 821–824.

Friends and Relatives of the Institutionalized Aged, Inc. (FRIA) (1984). *Racial discrimination in New York City's residential health care facilities.* New York: Friends and Relatives of the Institutionalized Aged, Inc.

George, L. (1984). The institutionalized. In E. Palmore (Ed.), *Handbook on the aged in the United States.* Westport, CT: Greenwood Press.

Gibson, R. C., & Jackson, J. C. (1987). The health, physical functioning, and informal supports of the black elderly. *Milbank Quarterly, 65,* 421–454.

Greene, V. L., & Monahan, D. J. (1984). Comparative utilization of community based long term care services by Hispanic and Anglo elderly in a case management system. *Journal of Gerontology, 39,* 730–735.

Greene, V. L., & Monahan, D. J. (1982). The impact of visitation on patient well-being in nursing homes. *Gerontologist, 22,* 419–422.

Harwood, A. (Ed.). (1981). *Ethnicity and medical care.* Cambridge, MA: Harvard University Press.

Hing, E. (1987). Use of nursing homes by the elderly: Preliminary data from the 1985 national nursing home survey. *NCHS Advance data from vital health statistics 135,* Washington, DC: U. S. Dept. of Health and Human Services.

Holmes, D., Holmes, M., Steinbach, L, Hausner, T., & Rocheleau, B. (1979). The use of community-based services in long-term care by older minority persons. *Gerontologist, 19,* 389–397.

Jones-Morrison, B. (1986). *The risk and access of black elderly to institutional and non-institutional continuing care services.* Paper presented at the annual meeting of the Gerontological Society of America, Chicago.

Kahana, E. (1982). A congruence model of person-environment interaction. In M. P. Lawton, P. G. Windley, & T. O. Byerts (Eds.), *Aging and the environment: Directions and perspectives.* New York: Springer Publishing Co.

Kart, C. S., & Beckham, B. L. (1976). Black-white differentials in the institutionalization of the elderly: A temporal analysis. *Social Forces, 54,* 901–910.

Kiefer, C. W., Kim, S., Choi, K., Kim, L., Kim, B., Shon, S., Kim, T. (1985). Adjustment problems of Korean American elderly. *Gerontologist, 25,* 477–482.

Koh, J. Y., & Bell, W. G. (1987). Korean elders in the United States. *Gerontologist, 27,* 66–71.

Manson, S. M. (1989) Long-term care in American Indian communities: Issues for planning and research. *Gerontologist, 29,* 38–44.

Manson, S. M., & Callaway, D. G. (1988). Health and aging among American Indians:

Issues and challenges for the biobehavioral sciences. *Behavioral Health Issues Among American Indians and Alaska Natives*. American Indian and Alaska Native Mental Health Research, Monograph No.1, 159–209

Markides, K. S., & Krause, N. (1985). Intergenerational solidarity and psychological well-being among older Mexican-Americans: A three-generation study. *Journal of Gerontology, 40*, 390–392.

Markson, E. W. (1979). Ethnicity as a factor in the institutionalization of the ethnic elderly. In D. E. Gelfand & A. J. Kutzick (Eds.), *Ethnicity and aging: Theory, research, and policy*. New York: Springer Publishing Co.

Morrison, B. J. (1982). Sociocultural dimensions: Nursing homes and the minority aged. *Journal of Gerontological Social Work, 5*, 127–145.

Moss, F. E., & Halamandaris, V. J. (1977). *Too old, too sick, too bad*. Germantown, MD: Aspen Systems.

Orque, M. S., Bloch, B., & Monroy, L. S. A. (Eds.). (1983). *Ethnic nursing care: A multicultural approach*. St.Louis: Mosby.

Osako, M. (1979). Aging and family among Japanese Americans: The role of ethnic tradition in the adjustment to old age. *Gerontologist, 19*, 448–452.

Palmore, E. (1976). Total chance of institutionalization among the aged. *Gerontologist, 16*, 504–507.

Rosenthal, C. J. (1986). Family supports in later life: Does ethnicity make a difference? *Gerontologist, 26*, 19–24.

Rousseau, P. (1990). Task force on minority health issues: American Indians and Alaskan Natives. Paper presented at meeting of the American Geriatrics Society in Atlanta.

Schafft, G. (1980). Nursing home care and the minority elderly. *Journal of Long Term Care Administration, 8*, 1–31.

Shapiro, E., & Tate, R. (1988). Who is really at risk of institutionalization? *Gerontologist, 28*, 237–245.

Shomaker, D. M. (1981). Navajo nursing homes: conflicts of philosophies. *Journal of Gerontological Nursing, 7*, 531–536.

Sotomayor, M., & Applewhite, S. R. (1988). The Hispanic elderly and the extended multigenerational family. In S. R. Applewhite (Ed.), *Hispanic elderly in transition*. New York: Greenwood Press.

Sotomayor, M., & Randolph, S. (1988). A preliminary review of caregiving issues and the Hispanic family. In M. Sotomayor & H. Curiel (Eds.), *Hispanic elderly: A cultural signature*. Edinburg: Pan American University Press.

Taylor, R. J. (1988). Aging and supportive relationships among black Americans. In J. S. Jackson, P. Newton, A. Ostfield, D. Savage, & E. L. Schneider (Eds.), *The black American elderly: Research on physical and psychosocial health*. New York: Springer Publishing Co.

Tobin, S. S., & Lieberman, M. A. (1976). *Last home for the aged: Critical implications of institutionalization*. San Francisco: Jossey-Bass.

Torres-Gil, F., & Fielder, E. (1986–87). Long-term care policy and the Hispanic population. *Journal of Hispanic Policy, 2*, 49–65.

Trevino, F. M., & Moss, A. J. (1984). *Health indicators for Hispanic, black, and white*

Americans. DHHS Publication No. (PHS) 84-1576 Hyattsville, MD: National Center for Health Statistics.

U. S. Department of Health and Human Services. (1989). *The national nursing home survey: 1985 summary for the United States.* Data from the National Health Survey Series 13, No. 97. DHHS Publication No. (PHS) 89-1758. Hyattsville, MD: National Center for Health Statistics.

Valle, R. (1989). U. S. ethnic minority group access to long-term care. In T. Schwab (Ed.), *Caring for an aging world: Inter-national models for long-term care, financing, and delivery.* New York: McGraw-Hill.

Vladek, B. (1982). Sounding boards: Nursing home care in the United States. *New England Journal of Medicine, 307,* 883–889.

Vicente, L., Wiley, J. A., & Carrington, R. A. (1979). The risk of institutionalization before death. *Gerontologist, 19,* 361–367.

Weinstock, C. & Bennett, R. (1969). Problems in communication to nurses among residents of a racially heterogeneous nursing home. *The Gerontologist, 8,* 72–75.

Wershow, H. J. (1976). Notes and comment: Inadequate census data on black nursing home patients. *Gerontologist, 16,* 86–87.

Wong, E. F. (1980). Learned helplessness: The need for self-determination among the Chinese American elderly. *Journal of Ethnic Studies, 8,* 45–52.

Yeo, G. (1988). *Responding to the cultural and ethnic needs of elders requiring institutionalization.* Paper presented at the annual Gerontological Society of America meeting, San Francisco.

Yu, E. S. H., Liu, W. T., & Kurzeja, P. K. (1985). Physical and mental health status indicators for Asian-American communities. In *Report of the Secretary's Task Force on Black and Minority Health,* (vol. II). Rockville, MD; U. S. Dept. of Health and Human Services.

12

On Lok's Model: Managed Long-Term Care

Carol Van Steenberg
Marie-Louise Ansak
Jennie Chin-Hansen

On Lok Senior Health Services emerged as a community solution for a serious problem in a culturally diverse, urban neighborhood. On Lok's service area holds within it Nob Hill, Fisherman's Wharf, North Beach, Chinatown, and San Francisco's Financial District. In the midst of such picturesque San Francisco landmarks live more than 18,000 older adults. Many have very limited incomes, speak little or no English, and have serious chronic illnesses. Often they reside in small, rundown hotel rooms tucked above and behind the district's stores and offices. Despite the need, few long-term care resources were available in the community to these elderly before On Lok was created in 1971.

Over the years, On Lok has adapted its program to the changing needs and ethnic mix of its area. In the process, On Lok has become increasingly sophisticated about the delivery of long-term care and about health care financing. Today On Lok's program services 325 nursing-home-certified elderly in San Francisco. The ethnic mix is 87% Asian or Pacific Islander (mainly Chinese-Americans), 9% Anglo (mainly Italian Americans), 1% Hispanic, 1% American Indian or Alaskan Native, and 2% Other. There are more than twice as many women (71%) as men (29%) among the program's enrollees. In short,

On Lok's participant group mirrors the ethnic composition of the older, Medicaid-eligible population of its area.

On Lok also is the prototype for PACE—Program of All-inclusive Care for the Elderly—the national Medicare and Medicaid demonstration examining whether On Lok's model can be replicated in other communities. With On Lok's close guidance, each PACE site applies the managed care techniques developed in San Francisco, receives all-inclusive capitation payments from Medicare and Medicaid, and looks forward to permanence at the end of a three-year demonstration period. Together these PACE sites are testing the On Lok model in a wide range of ethnic communities.

PHILOSOPHY AND HISTORY

On Lok's goal from the beginning has been to provide a humane, cost-effective alternative for the frail elderly living within the Chinatown, North Beach, and Polk Gulch areas of San Francisco. The underlying philosophy is:

- To provide care that meets the needs of and is satisfying to older persons and that costs no more than that provided in the "traditional" system.
- To enable maximum self-help by the older person, work with family and friends to meet additional needs, and then provide services for otherwise unmet needs.
- To help the older person remain out of institutions as long as it is socially, medically and economically feasible.

On Lok opened one of the first adult day health centers in the country in 1973. Major events in the development of On Lok's comprehensive system include:

- 1971: Initial study to determine community need for long-term care and to develop a long-range plan for comprehensive, community-based care encompassing prevention, rehabilitation, and housing.
- 1973: Opening of On Lok's first day health center, modeled on England's day hospital approach, with funding from the Administration on Aging as a research and demonstration project.
- 1974: Medicaid pilot program to test adult day health care as a long-term care alternative; passage of California legislation based on On Lok's success to make adult day health a permanent statewide MediCal benefit in California.
- 1975: Addition of second center, in-home care, home-delivered meals, and housing assistance.
- 1978: Expansion of the model to include complete medical care and social support for nursing-home-eligible elderly, with funding from the Office of

Human Development Services and the Health Care Financing Administration (Medicare reimbursement for service demonstration, under Section 222 waivers).

- 1980: Opening of On Lok House, providing 54 units of HUD Section 202–subsidized housing for frail elderly persons and On Lok's third day health center.
- 1983: Change of the service program's financing system for cost-based reimbursement to capitation payments (fixed monthly per person premiums) from Medicare, Medicaid, and the individual (with assumption by On Lok of full financial risk), under a three-year Medicare and Medicaid demonstration (Section 222 and Section 1115 waivers).
- 1985: Congressional authorization granting On Lok "permanent waivers" of Medicare and Medicaid regulations, allowing it to continue indefinitely.
- 1986: Feasibility study for the national effort to replicate the On Lok model, the Program of All-inclusive Care for the Elderly, or PACE, with funding from the Robert Wood Johnson Foundation, and federal legislation enabling up to 10 other sites to receive waivers like On Lok's to operate the model.
- 1990: Opening of 1000 Montgomery, providing 36 market-rate, single-room-occupancy residences for the frail elderly, child care facilities, and a fourth day health center; beginning of waiver demonstration programs by first four PACE sites (in Portland, Oregon; Boston, Massachusetts; Columbia, South Carolina; and Milwaukee, Wisconsin).

STRUCTURE AND IMPLEMENTATION

As noted in the historical overview, On Lok has had waivers since 1983 allowing prospective monthly payments from Medicare, Medicaid, and/or the individual (based on the individual's entitlement). With these funds, On Lok meets all the health and health-related needs of its 325 very frail, elderly participants.

Eligibility for On Lok's program is limited to persons who are:

- Over the age of 55.
- Certified by the State of California as eligible for nursing home care.
- Residents of San Francisco's Chinatown, North Beach or Polk Gulch neighborhoods (a three-square mile area).

Persons who enroll in the On Lok program are called "participants," rather than clients or patients, in keeping with the program's philosophy of maximizing independence and self-care. Before joining On Lok, a prospective participant receives an assessment by several members of On Lok's multidisciplinary team. This assessment takes place in the person's home and during two or three trial visits to one of the day health centers. The team's initial assessment results in a treatment plan recommended to the prospective participant and the family. If this plan is acceptable, formal enrollment in the program occurs as soon as a representative from California's Department of Health Services confirms the applicant's acuity level (i.e., need for intermediate or skilled nursing facility care).

An individual who enrolls in the On Lok comprehensive program is "locked in" for Medicare and Medicaid purposes. That is, the individual agrees to receive all health care services solely from On Lok's providers, and Medicare and Medicaid benefits in the fee-for-service system are suspended. These benefits can be reinstated if the person chooses to disenroll, but the vast majority of participants (90%) remains enrolled in the program for life. Just 2% disenroll due to dissatisfaction with the program.

In contrast to a traditional system of case management, On Lok consolidates, rather than brokers, service delivery (Zawadski & Eng, 1988). In a brokerage system, a professional team assesses a participant's needs, develops a treatment plan, and then, directly or through a separate case manager, arranges for yet other providers to deliver services. All these functions are consolidated in On Lok's extensive multidisciplinary team. Together On Lok's physician or nurse practitioner, nurse, occupational and physical therapists, dietician, day health center supervisor, recreation therapist, social worker, health worker and driver assess participant needs, formulate care plans, directly deliver most services (including primary care), manage the care given by contracted providers, monitor treatment results continuously, and adjust the care plan as needed. Figure 12.1 illustrates the range of services managed by the team.

Operationally, how does this work? And what difference does it make to the frail older person and the family? Consider two real case histories. The first one, "Mrs. C.," involves an older person identified and followed as a part of a comparison study to evaluate On Lok's Medicare and Medicaid demonstration (1983–1987); the person featured in the second, "Mrs. W.," is an On Lok participant (Shen, Takeda, Kasch, & Van Steenberg, 1989).

Mrs. C. lived outside On Lok's catchment area and therefore was not eligible to join the program. Several years before the comparison study, she had suffered a stroke, which totally paralyzed her left side. After a period of rehabilitation, she could walk very slowly, using a cane and a leg brace. In October 1984, when first interviewed by the research team, she was living alone in her own apartment with a home health aide assisting her four days a week, three hours each day. During the summer of 1984 she had begun to fall occasionally, particularly at night when she needed to make a trip to the bathroom. Each fall resulted in her admission to a skilled nursing home facility. Each time she had been able to return home—until October 1985. Then her physician determined that because she had fallen four times in five months, she was no longer safe at home alone. Since she could not afford 24-hour attendant care, she remained

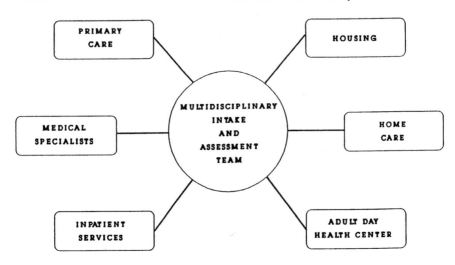

FIGURE 12.1 On Lok service components.

in the nursing home. Mrs. C. was greatly grieved by giving up her apartment and selling her personal belongings. Alert and oriented, she found being with so many sick and confused people very difficult. She became withdrawn and depressed, continuing to mourn her loss of independence.

In contrast, Mrs. W. joined the On Lok program in 1980, nine months after her stroke. At that time she was confined to a wheelchair and needed assistance with all home chores as well as with all activities of daily living except eating. Mrs. W.'s daughter, with whom she was living, was providing her care as well as rearing three small children. Mrs. W. found it difficult to communicate because of her stroke and her behavior problems caused her family considerable stress at home. After she began attending On Lok's day health center five days a week, her functional status improved. Five years later, in 1985, Mrs. W. fell and fractured her shoulder. In the hospital awaiting surgery, she suffered another stroke. Since surgery then was too dangerous, she was transferred from the hospital to a skilled nursing home facility under contract with On Lok. Her On Lok physician and other members of the team saw her several times a week at the nursing home and within two months her condition had stabilized enough that she could be discharged. Still, she required more care than her daughter could give her at home. The team decided that she could manage in communal housing if she attended the day health center seven days a week and had an attendant available to check on her during the evenings. Each day, at the center, her therapies and medical follow-up were provided. Despite two subsequent stays—for a fracture to her right arm and the removal of her gall bladder—she continued to live in communal housing and came to the center daily. She was able to walk with assistance using a cane and a short leg brace. Her behavior problems were resolved, and she became content with her present situation. Her relationship improved with her daughter, who no longer felt burdened by her mother's care, and she enjoyed her grandchildren.

Although Mrs. C. and Mrs. W. had similar conditions and dependency needs, On Lok's array of services and constant monitoring allowed different outcomes and levels of satisfaction. In contrast to Mrs. C., who was confined to a nursing home for most of the three-year study period, Mrs. W. spent only two months in a nursing home. Of the two, Mrs. W. had more serious medical problems, yet she was able to continue living in the community. She could not return to her daughter's home, but she could regain a positive relationship with her daughter and her grandchildren. She continued to enjoy the company of other seniors both in her communal housing and in the day health center. As a result of her continued residence in a home environment and her involvement with others, Mrs. W. did not suffer the isolation and emotional stress imposed by Mrs. C.'s lengthy confinement in the nursing home.

PRINCIPLES OF THE ON LOK/PACE MODEL

As illustrated by Mrs. C.'s situation, six principles underlie the On Lok/PACE model. The first is a focus on the very impaired and frail elderly who require ongoing care for the rest of their lives. In other words, On Lok has intentionally chosen not to serve all the elderly in its geographic area but to concentrate on a specific high-cost long-term care population, namely, those with few alternatives to permanent nursing home placement. The average age of those enrolled in On Lok's comprehensive PACE system is 82, and they have an average of more than seven medical diagnoses each. Among the most common diagnoses are dementia (44%), hypertension (54%), cerebral vascular disease, including stroke (40%) and coronary heart disease (37%), and arthritis (42%). These medical conditions result in major impairments in the participants' activities of daily living: 84% in bathing, 67% in walking, 66% in transferring (e.g., from bed or a chair), 62% in dressing, 58% in toileting, and 23% in eating.

Community residence is a second key element. The clients' continued residence in the community and the community's ongoing participation in the program are emphasized. Maintaining the participant's lifestyle and respecting cultural preferences are of high priority. For example, participants may choose between Chinese and Western-style meals at the centers and for home-delivered meals. On Lok staff assist participants in continuing favorite pastimes. With the help of staff, for example, several participants are the guests from time to time of a neighborhood Italian restaurant. Community groups come into the centers to offer entertainment and educational programs.

Third, comprehensive medical, restorative, social, and supportive services are included. All acute and long-term care options are available on a 24-hour basis to respond properly to this population's multiple, interrelated problems. On Lok's service range is much broader than traditional Medicare and Medicaid benefits. Nursing, physical and occupational therapies, meals, nutrition counseling, social work, recreational therapy, and personal care are all provided in the day health centers, which are open seven days a week. In-home care includes personal as well as skilled care. Physicians, who are On Lok employees, provide primary medical care to all participants. In cooperation with other members of the team, the physicians serve as gatekeepers to the use of medical specialists and inpatient care.

Service integration through consolidation and team control is the fourth principle. On Lok's multidisciplinary team determines service need and mobilizes any service required since fee-for-service restrictions do not apply. No limits are imposed a priori for any service. Team members deliver the majority of outpatient service themselves and oversee all contract services, including medical specialty services, inpatient care in hospitals and nursing homes, medical specialists, and laboratory, x-ray, and pharmacy services. The program's own staff delivers day-to-day services because direct delivery enhances the team's ability to assure continuity and quality of care. On Lok's contracts with medical specialists, local hospitals, and nursing homes all specify that contractors must work closely with program staff. For example, On Lok's home health nurse visits participants in the nursing home on a weekly basis to monitor their care.

The fifth principle is integrated funding. Resources from Medicare, Medicaid and the private individual are pooled to provide services. Use of these funds is not subject to any usual payment restrictions. For example, preventative care, usually not allowable under Medicare, is regularly provided at On Lok and physical therapy can continue as long as the team believes it helps the participant, whether in maintaining or regaining abilities.

Finally, the On Lok/PACE model requires provider assumption of financial risk. The provider organization must be able to manage risk, that is, to monitor clients, services, and costs and readily adapt to change. The assumption of financial risk provides a powerful incentive to increase the service system's efficiency and effectiveness.

SERVICE DELIVERY

On Lok's team has the mandate of keeping quality of care high while controlling program costs. On Lok's program meets all external licensing and quality assurance standards, including periodic audits from various agencies involved. Currently, On Lok has ten different licenses: four for its adult day health centers, four community clinic licenses, a home health agency license, and a health maintenance organization license. In addition, On Lok has a Medical Advisory Committee and an Ethics Committee, each of which includes community representatives.

By preserving or enhancing participants' health and independence, the team minimizes the use of hospital and nursing home care. They reduce acute episodes by intensively monitoring participants' medical and social conditions (e.g., blood pressure, nutritional intake, and medication compliance) and anticipating risks like falls, skin breakdown, and psychosocial problems. Education and retraining in mobility and activities of daily living strengthen participants' functional capacities, build independence, and thus reduce the need for supervision and assistive support. Providing low-cost services in the least restrictive setting (day health center or participant home) maximizes participant quality of life while decreasing the use of high-cost services. Although On Lok participants are frail, have been certified for nursing home care, and often have significant disabilities, their hospital use is remarkably low. Between 1987 and 1989, the average hospital days per 1,000 per year for On Lok participants was 2,534 (Kunz, Shen, & Ansak, 1990). For comparison, the usage rate in 1987 for all persons over the age of 65 (most of whom were healthy) was 3,030 per 1,000 per year (GHAA, 1989).

FINANCING

On Lok currently is the only provider to assume full financial risk, under capitation financing, for an exclusively nursing home certifiable population. In On Lok's financing model, Medicare, Medicaid, and private individuals make capitation payments based on their cost responsibility in the fee-for-service system, with a built-in savings. For this sum, On Lok is responsible for providing all the services needed by the program's participants, no matter how high their service utilization may be. If it costs more to care for a participant than is provided by the capitation payment, On Lok must absorb the losses. On the other hand, On Lok can retain any savings that are realized.

The Medicare capitation payment is a variant of the Adjusted Average Per Capita Cost (AAPCC) methodology developed for the 1982 Tax Equity and Fiscal Responsibility Act (TEFRA) to reimburse risk-based HMOs. Whereas TEFRA HMOs have standardized per capita rates of payment that are adjusted by four demographic cost factors (age, sex, welfare status, and institutional status), the On Lok program uses a single, higher Medicare cost adjuster, which more accurately reflects its population's frailty and utilization experience. For calendar year 1991, Medicare paid On Lok $914.49 per participant each month.

On Lok negotiates its Medicaid rate annually with the State of California's

Department of Health Services (DHS). As do all other California prepaid health plans, On Lok submits to DHS a rate proposal that incorporates its service utilization patterns and costs per unit of service. The State evaluates On Lok's proposal in light of California's costs for a nursing home population. For FY '90–'91, DHS paid $1,800 each month for participants eligible for full Medicaid coverage.

Participants not eligible for Medicare or Medicaid pay one or both portions of On Lok's capitation rate privately, but less than one percent of enrollees is completely private-pay. Not surprisingly, individuals who enter the program as private pay often quickly spend down their assets and become Medicaid-eligible.

On Lok assumed full financial risk in 1983 not because it wanted to but because it *had* to in order to continue operating. While Medicare was interested in a shared risk arrangement with Medicaid and On Lok, California's DHS (the Medicaid agency) was not. Without California's participation, Medicare refused to share risk with On Lok. On Lok could not secure private reinsurance because the insurance industry did not have adequate actuarial data on long-term care. Consequently, On Lok had to self-insure. By setting aside 5% of revenues each month, On Lok's Board of Directors established a risk reserve fund to cover catastrophic costs and a transition period should On Lok have to return to fee for services. By 1991, the risk-reserve fund exceeded two-month's operating costs.

REPLICATION

Congress (P.L. 99-272) made On Lok's financing and service demonstration a permanent program in 1985, allowing its waivers to remain in effect so long as the program operates successfully. In 1986 On Lok received a grant from the Robert Wood Johnson Foundation to explore replication of the model.

Later that year Congress passed legislation that enabled limited replication of the On Lok model through Medicare and Medicaid capitation financing. This law (P.L. 99-509) provided that "the Secretary of Health and Human Services shall grant waivers . . . to not more than 10 public or nonprofit private community-based organizations to . . . provide comprehensive health care services on a capitated basis to frail elderly patients at risk of institutionalization . . . . Any waiver granted . . . shall be for an initial period of 3 years. The Secretary may extend such waiver beyond such initial period for so long as the Secretary finds that the organization complies with the terms and conditions." In 1990, Congress extended the number of replication demonstration programs for which waivers would be available to 15.

Today, with the assistance from John A. Hartford and other private foundations, as well as the Robert Wood Johnson Foundation, On Lok is implementing PACE (Program of All-inclusive Care for the Elderly), the replication project. On Lok is working with organizations in California, Colorado, Hawaii, Illinois, Massachusetts, New York, Oregon, South Carolina, Texas, Washington, and Wisconsin to help them implement the PACE model.

Unlike On Lok, these organizations can share risk with Medicare and Medicaid during their first three years of operation under the demonstration waivers. As provided by P.L. 100-203, Section 4118, the replication sites are to assume more of the risk each year of the demonstration period such that, at the end of the three years, they will be at full financial risk, like On Lok.

As of October 1990, four sites had begun demonstrating the comprehensive acute and long-term care program, with capitation financing. These new PACE demonstrations are Elder Service Plan, in Boston, Massachusetts; Palmetto Seniorcare, in Columbia, South Carolina; Providence Elderplace, in Portland, Oregon; and Community Care for the Elderly in Milwaukee, Wisconsin. Another four are expected to begin operations under waivers by the end of 1991. Whereas On Lok's participant population and workforce have been predominantly Chinese-American, none of the first eight PACE sites serves a mainly Asian community or has an Asian staff.

ETHNIC AND OTHER SPECIAL CONSIDERATIONS

The On Lok model was developed for and has been geared to the poor elderly who live in the inner city. As is now being documented in the PACE replication, the On Lok model is not ethnic-specific. One site is even testing whether the model transcends economic lines, that is whether PACE appeals as well to middle-income elderly suburban residents. The first eight PACE sites' primary ethnic groups vary from African-American, to Hispanic, to White Anglo Saxon Protestant.

Although the model is not ethnic specific, the PACE staff must be sensitive to ethnic issues if they are to operate the program successfully. Because care is managed very intensively, excellent communication with participants and their families is a must. The team's understanding of cultural nuances is critical in establishing a treatment plan acceptable to participants and with which they will comply. Financially, community support is essential for On Lok and for the other nonprofit organizations that operate on the PACE model.

On Lok began without a fixed model, and throughout its 20 years of existence has developed its programs as community needs have been detected. In the PACE replication, service program parameters and financing methods have been established, of necessity. At the same time, a great deal of flexibility is possible and each site is encouraged to use this flexibility to adapt the program to local circumstances.

In working with the sites, On Lok staff draw upon their experience in adapting the program to participants' cultural values. They ask questions about the participants' value systems and help PACE site staff sort through the implications of these values for day health center attendance, family involvement, counseling, outreach and marketing, hospital and nursing home care, and other treatment planning issues.

Each PACE site incorporates specific ethnically oriented methods into the program planning and caregiving process. For example, On Lok's team must be familiar with the cultural beliefs of the Chinese related to medicine, illness, death, and dying and with their family structure to work effectively with the participants.

To further illustrate, many Chinese believe in herbology. Making teas and soups made with various herbal concoctions is a traditional health practice. The team does not discourage participants in using herbs (in part because experience shows such advice is ignored); instead, the team encourages participants to tell them what herbs are being used. Such information is vital since many of the herbs contain derivatives similar to compounds found in Western medicines. Armed with this knowledge, the team can watch for side effects, the physicians prescriptions can be made so as to minimize the possibility of overdosage, and drug interactions can be considered.

The role of food in the treatment of illness is another important consideration at On Lok. Many participants believe illness reflects disharmony in "yin" and "yang" within the body. Chinese traditional beliefs hold that yin and yang may be brought back into balance through the ingestion of various foods, with specific foods recommended for particular symptoms. What difference does this make to the team? As with herbs, it is important for the team to know what the participant is consuming. In some cases, the team will need to address the matter with the participant. For example, salty foods are often used to counter the symptom of dizziness. In a participant with hypertension, this practice may have serious consequences! Under such circumstances, the team would talk with the participant, and perhaps the family, about the situation and would monitor any changes in the participant's condition closely.

Traditional Chinese do not separate mind and body as is the case in Western culture. Mental health problems are not acknowledged unless they are severe; then shame and fear figure largely. Thus, when a participant who ascribes to traditional Chinese values is depressed, he or she talks about physical pain. The approach at On Lok is to treat the symptoms identified by the participant and while doing so try to uncover any recent events that may have triggered an emotional reaction. Has something happened recently within the participant's family? Has a close friend died? Is the participant about to be evicted? In other works, rather than discussing the participant's feelings directly, as might be appropriate with more Americanized participants, a "back-door" strategy is used to help the participant resolve the disturbance.

The team works closely with the participants' families in the caregiving process. Typically the structure of Chinese immigrant families is different from that of American families. A daughter-in-law married to a younger son may be the primary "hands on" caregiver, for example, yet have no authority to make decisions about the participant's situation. Those decisions may well belong to the eldest son, who never takes a role—or shows interest-in day-to-day care. Each family is different. In order to work effectively on the participant's behalf, the team must discuss these roles and relationships with the family to determine who is responsible for what.

During Chinese New Year's (a two-week period), a death is perceived as bringing bad luck for the family for the year. Participants would rather not even talk about poor health during this time and are likely to refuse treatment. Consequently, if a participant of Chinese descent becomes very ill and needs to be hospitalized during New Year observance, staff must be prepared to offer additional support and counseling to the participant and the family.

Cultural factors are also important in On Lok's housing. Because of the Chinese belief in spirits, Taoist monks were once brought into On Lok House to cleanse the residential facility of spirits. Most of On Lok's participants are immigrants who have not been accustomed to living in very much space. Generally, they have few belongings and little, if any, furniture. Consequently, when 1000 Montgomery was refurbished in the late 1980s, it was designed as a single-room occupancy "hotel," with community space on each floor, rather than as a series of one-bedroom apartments with kitchens. Storage space was built into each room, and each room was furnished with a bed since residents were not likely to have a suitable bed or a chest of drawers to move into their accommodations.

Approximately half of On Lok's participants are monolingual in Chinese, while others are more comfortable speaking Italian or Tagalog, than English. To ensure appropriate communication, On Lok's staff is multilingual; among the languages spoken are several dialects of Chinese in addition to Mandarin, Italian, Tagalog and Spanish. Most, but not all, staff also are fluent in English. Assignments of staff and participants to On Lok's four day health centers are made with these linguistic considerations in mind. Marketing and educational materials for participants and their families are produced in Chinese as well as English. Staff training is provided in Chinese as well as English.

To facilitate community support at On Lok, its board composition reflects the major ethnic groups in the community and the participant population, and On Lok's volunteer force is multi-ethnic. Board members and volunteers act as liaisons to the community and as interpreters of/advocates for the community's needs.

Establishing positive relationships with local physicians is a special consideration in operating this model. Because all program enrollees must receive primary care from the program's staff physicians, community physicians may perceive the program as a threat to their private practices. Their resistance usually subsides once they understand the program and realize that it serves only the very frailest of the elderly, namely the patients who cause physicians the greatest headaches and for whom they can do the least without the help of others. However, the delicacy of this educational task should not be underestimated. At On Lok, this is a continual process. Having chosen for its Medical Director a physician in private practice in the community who is highly regarded helps a great deal! In addition, On Lok includes many of the community's physicians on its panel of contract medical specialists. Others serve on On Lok's Medical Advisory Committee, the Ethics Committee, and the Board of Directors.

Finally, it needs to be recognized that not all of the community's frail elderly—regardless of their ethnic background—are interested in enrolling in a total system such as PACE, which requires giving up one's own personal physician. The financial considerations for middle-income persons not eligible for Medicaid are significant, as well. Although the private-pay out-of-pocket cost of participating in PACE is lower than the cost of nursing home care, it can be as high as $1,800 per month. Many middle-income individuals would rather take their chances in the fee-for-service system until admission into a nursing home can no longer be avoided.

REFERENCES

Ansak, M. (1990). The On Lok model: Consolidating care and financing. *Generations,* *14,* 73-74.

GHAA News. (1989). *Managed HealthCare.* November 6, 25.

Kunz, E. M., Shen, J., & Ansak, M. (1991). Managed Care for the Frail Elderly through PACE. *Group Health Institute Proceedings.*

Shen, J., Takeda, S., Kasch, K., & Van Steenberg, C. (1989) *On Lok's Risk-Based CCODA: An Experiment in Long-Term Care Capitation, Final Report, 1983-1986.* San Francisco, CA: On Lok Senior Health Services.

Zawadski, R. T., & Eng, C. (1988). Case Management in Capitated Long-Term Care. *Health Care Financing Administration Review: Annual Supplement, 9,* 75-81.

13

A Higher Purpose: Jewish Tradition and Model Long-Term Care in Cleveland
Steve Folmar*

INTRODUCTION

Jewish nursing homes in America rank well above average in the provision of high-quality care. This care is typically set in relatively modern facilities that are often regarded as the standard of excellence. It should not be surprising then that Jews use nursing homes more than other groups generally do.[1] The elevated rate of nursing home residency also reflects a cultural preference for nursing home care over other forms of care for the elderly, provided that it is in a "Jewish" environment.

The hallmark of Jewish long-term care services is not simply that they have model services but that they offer them on a continuing basis. Just as the high quality or innovative services of one institution stand as examples for other

*Funding for the research and writing of this chapter was generously provided by The Cleveland Foundation (#83-571-31R), The Jewish Community Federation of Cleveland, and The National Institute on Aging (National Research Service Award 5 T32 AG00155-02). I am grateful to the Western Reserve Historical Society for access to archives and to many people affiliated with Menorah Park Center for the Aging and the Montefiore Home who shared their insights with me. A number of colleagues read earlier drafts of this chapter and made valuable comments: Don Stull, Chuck Barresi, Eliza Pavalko, Mike Foster, Phyllis D'Agostino, and Glen Elder. Finally, I thank Phyllis Taubman for transcribing interviews.

nursing homes, the structural features and processes behind Jewish long-term care also exemplify qualities meriting emulation. Thus, while the major thrust of this book is to examine specific services, programs, or funding mechanisms, the purpose of this chapter is to illustrate how one ethnic group's community-level organization enables the continuous delivery of a high-quality package of services.

This otherwise overlooked dimension of "model services" is relevant to other ethnic groups in its illustration of a method to provide not one particular service at one point in time, but high quality services in general, over an expanse of time, that keep pace with the changing needs of the elderly. By placing a high priority on serving the elderly and mobilizing the necessary resources, the Jewish community of Cleveland, Ohio, achieves and maintains a remarkably high level of technical quality in its services. Certainly, this is not the only available model, but is the one agreed upon by the Jewish community through the processes of examination, debate, and consensus building.

These processes have evolved within the changing historical, cultural, and socioeconomic context of the Cleveland area. An understanding of this ethnic group's unique ability to repeatedly update its services must be informed by the history of its two nursing homes, Menorah Park Center for the Aging and the Montefiore Home.[2] Key elements in that history are the cultural dimensions that support institutional care of the elderly as well as the structural and organizational features of the nursing homes and the local and national Jewish communities that support them.

This chapter is divided into four sections. The first briefly describes the two nursing homes. The other three are laid out in historical sequence, beginning with a brief historical portrait of the early years of long-term care in the Jewish community of Cleveland. Against this demographic, social, and cultural backdrop, we consider the ideological differences that gave rise to the social ranking (see Hatch, 1989) of the Reform and Orthodox branches of Judaism.

Originating from different parts of Europe and rooting themselves in America during distinct periods of migration, the Reform and Orthodox communities found themselves vying for status in a two-tiered system of social stratification symbolized by their ability to care for the elderly. As a defining symbol of social honor in both communities, the provision of care to the elderly became the focal point of competition that arose between the two nursing homes. The Reform community's social, cultural, and economic advantage over the Orthodox was reflected in the higher status enjoyed by the Reform home for the aged for nearly half a century.

But this competition is only a part of the story. As time progressed, the cultural distinctions between the two communities have blurred and the status of the nursing homes derived more from other factors than from their identification with Reform or Orthodox Judaism. Nonetheless, the hierarchical nature of the relationship between the two nursing homes persisted. By the time their relative positions eventually reversed after the Second World War, factors internal to the organizations of the nursing homes, not the external relationships between their supportive communities, determined the character of the homes and ultimately their relative prestige. It is here, in the organization of their nursing homes and in the Jewish community itself, that a model for excellence is most clearly manifested. When our attention turns to the years following World War II, organizational features of the Jewish community and of the nursing homes emerge as the driving force behind their attempts to address the challenges of the day.

Arguably the long-term care industry is just entering a new era, faced with a new set of challenges. No less is the Jewish community grappling with problems that demand new solutions. In conclusion, the focus of this chapter turns to some of the imminent challenges facing the Jewish long-term care effort. Bold predictions about the future of Jewish long-term care are left to others; instead, I will outline the process by which the Jewish community is evaluating the need for services and how it will likely respond to that need.

The original materials for this chapter are derived from three sources: observations during my four years as the Director of Research at one of the two Jewish Federation–supported nursing homes of Cleveland; formal, semistructured interviews with lay and professional leaders of the Jewish long-term care effort in Cleveland; and the archives of the two nursing homes.

MONTEFIORE AND MENORAH PARK

The Montefiore Home is currently located in one of the older, eastern suburbs of Cleveland; Menorah Park Center for the Aging is about six miles farther east, in a newer suburb. Together they serve about 500, or 56% of the 900 institutionalized, elderly Jews from the Cleveland area (Jewish Community Federation of Cleveland, 1986). Many of the 400 residents of other nursing homes are there temporarily as they await admission to Montefiore or Menorah Park. Both nursing homes are strictly sectarian, are based on social models of care, have equal access admissions policies with reference to income, offer skilled and intermediate nursing care, accept Medicaid and Medicare financing, receive substantial subvention from the Jewish Community Federation of Cleveland, and serve the geographical area of greater Cleveland.[3] Their services include a wide array of social activities, for example special events, workshops, and arts and crafts. Well-staffed, professional social service departments attend to the social well-being of the residents. Comprehensive health care services are provided by highly professional nursing departments and full-fledged departments of medicine. There are important differences between the two homes, however.

The major distinction in service delivery is in their community outreach programs. Menorah Park reaches out to the community with respite and day-care programs and operates a congregate housing facility whose tenants may use Menorah Park's extended post-hospital stay facility. Montefiore's extended care is used by the general community. Put together, the services of these two nursing homes represent a nearly complete package of high-quality, professional health and social services for the elderly Jew.

THE EARLY YEARS

Origins

The Montefiore Home, the older and smaller of the two, has already celebrated its centennial. Among the first homes for the aged in Cleveland, Montefiore was established in 1882 as a refuge for healthy but indigent elderly Jews and served a population from the Appalachian Mountains to the Mississippi River (Montefiore Home, 1883).

The Montefiore Home was established by Cleveland's earliest Jewish immigrants. This contingent, with whom Montefiore continues to identify, came from Western Europe and was active in founding the Reform Movement (Gartner, 1978). It was culturally distinct from the later Orthodox immigrants of Eastern Europe. Not only were the two groups separated by differences in degree of religious observance, national origin, and the timing of their arrival to America, but also by their degree of assimilation to American culture and their economic status. The ideological separation of the Reform and Orthodox communities came to symbolize all of these differences. Importantly, these differences added up to a clear two-strata social hierarchy, with the Reform Jews enjoying the superior social position.

This social distinction influenced the services provided for the elderly. One informant for this study recalls how Menorah Park came into being in 1906:

> The Orthodox community sought to have Cleveland people of all branches cared for with some recognition of their religious needs . . . Considering the fact that there was an inadequate number of beds available for the growing population of elderly, they set out to raise funds to supply that need. When they had raised approximately $5000 . . . they approached Montefiore and . . . [requested that Montefiore] . . . enlarge their bed capacity . . . and the only requirement . . . was to supply additional observant beds. Since Montefiore turned down the acceptance of the fund . . . the [Orthodox] community set out to establish a second nursing home which would fill their needs as to capacity, as to observance. This brought into being the Jewish Orthodox Home for the Aged . . . which later became . . . Menorah Park.

Cultural Foundations

Despite their differences, both wings of the Jewish community defined the place of elderly people in Jewish society similarly. Derived from values and practices that became distinctive features of Jewish settlements in Western Europe and the shtetls of Eastern Europe (see Zborowski & Herzog, 1952), the social status of the elderly was (and is) embodied in the dual principles of *mitzva* and *tsdokeh*.

The *mitzva*, or commandment, to "Honor thy Father and thy Mother," which is common to Christianity, is highly developed in Jewish culture. In the words of Zborowski and Herzog (1952, p. 199):

> The deference and respect rendered to the old by the young is part of the emphasis on being adult. Life is viewed as a constantly expanding area of gratification. It is a constantly expanding area of responsibility too, but the shouldering and discharge of responsibility is in itself a gratification. As one grows more and more adult—that is, older and older—he is able to do more and more, and to command more and more respect.

Moreover, informants for this study confirm that this *mitzva* pertains to all people older than oneself. One of the most meaningful ways to demonstrate deference to elders is to provide for them when they are in need. Since the meaning of parental deference is extended to include all the elderly, the provision of welfare to them necessarily falls on the shoulders of the community and is therefore organized as a formal institution.

Translated variously as "social justice," "righteousness," or "charity," *tsdokeh* is the second principle that applies to the social status of the elderly. It simply describes the Jew's duty to provide for the needy through deeds and contributions. *Tsdokeh*, ideally, should be performed for the intrinsic value of giving, but in practice is also associated with accruing religious merit and by extension, social status. A person gains status relative to others both by assuming the role of giver and by giving generously.

Tsdokeh is considered integral to a person's "Jewishness." The wealthy accrue social status in large measure because wealth enables them to be charitable. The more generous they are, the better. As described by one informant, "One should give until it hurts." It is expected that a person should give (tithe) at least 10% of his or her income to charity, and as much as 20%, 30%, or even more for the affluent and wealthy.

Charitable giving takes on a number of forms, ranked according to whether the gift encourages self-reliance and preserves dignity. To help a person to help himself (such as offering him a job) is the highest form of giving. Outright public donations that obligate the receiver are the lowest form. If a person of higher social status, such as an elderly person, receives charity from a younger person, discretion is the rule (Zborowski & Herzog, 1952). This moral creed guided the development of homes for the aged in the Jewish communities of Europe; "the dignity of age can better endure the impersonal than personal benefaction" (Zborowski & Herzog, 1952, p. 203).

The high standard of care characteristic of Jewish nursing homes is made possible not only because they are well financed, but because, according to informants, the aim is to provide care that would meet the needs of the affluent even though the client may be poor. This is contrasted with other (non-Jewish) nursing homes' attempts to provide care that meets the material needs of the poor. Why set one's sights so high? Beyond the social and religious obligation to honor the elderly through *tsdokeh*, Jewish nursing homes structure a personal connection between client and provider. Care providers act on the possibility that they may become the custodian of one of their own—a parent, an aunt, a friend. This possibility is more than theoretical as administrators, staff, and board members of both nursing homes have had close friends and relatives live out their days in one of the two facilities.

Social Ranking

The cultural edict "to give charitably" was set in a competitive social environment in Cleveland. Since the system of social honor regarding the elderly was common to both communities, the rules of that system could be used to differentiate the two homes. In effect, a uniform interpretation of *mitzva* and *tsdokeh* set the ground rules for ranking the two communities, since common criteria were lacking in other institutions.

Moral or social superiority could not be claimed on purely religious grounds, since each faction rejected the other's religious interpretations. But primacy in the social order could be claimed by the one that reflected the higher level of charity, which was visible in the quality of the surroundings and the care offered the residents. One informant put it this way:

> Going back . . . to 1920 thereabouts, you had a high standard home for the aged in Montefiore Home and not a very high standard Orthodox Old Home [Menorah Park's predecessor]. That affected the social position of people who supported those two institutions.

Up to the end of World War II, this rivalry continued, with Montefiore recognized as the more prestigious of the two, backed by the more enlightened, influential, and affluent of the two communities. Like homes for the aged across the nation, both continued to provide custodial care for the socially marginal but basically healthy elderly with limited professional health, medical, and social services.

THE RECENT PAST

The Changing Composition of the Elderly Population

Several historical events after World War II radically altered the profile of the Jewish elderly and consequently the types of services they needed. Well known to gerontologists are the health and demographic dynamics of burgeoning numbers of sick and disabled elderly. Nursing homes began to replace homes for the aged. In the Montefiore Home (1883; Western Reserve Historical Society, 1946) the population increased from 19 to 108, but the percentage of "well-aged" residents fell from 89% to 8%. This demographic shift had a direct bearing on social networks of people needing institutional care, since the needs of even the more affluent chronically ill could not be met at home. For the first time, large numbers of elderly with sound social networks and economic resources sought institutional care.

Less well known was how the War, with its devastating effects on Jews, affected the organization of Jewish communities in the United States. Several informants discussed how, after World War II, Jewish communities organized much more effectively, determined never to endure persecution again. While many Jewish community services had been brought under the umbrella of Jewish community federations earlier in the century (Gartner, 1978), the scope of federations broadened and their power consolidated (Polivy, 1986).

The Rise of the Jewish Community Federation

Significant functions of the Jewish Community Federation of Cleveland, like other federations, are the organization of general fund raising and the distribution of funds to Jewish welfare and service institutions. Another major function, at least of the Cleveland Federation, is to provide research that estimates the degree of need for current and future services. That the consolidation of federation influence coincided with the expansion of the sick and disabled population was fortuitous, for the Cleveland Federation has played a primary role in advancing the effort to provide the best services possible to elderly Jews.

Professionalism and Reorganization

It was also shortly after the Second World War that Cleveland's Jewish nursing homes began a 40-year history of offering not only excellent care, but model programming. While it enjoyed a reputation as a well-managed organization up to the 1940s, new administrative leadership in the 1950s led Montefiore toward becoming a noted innovator. Two major shifts were particularly influential. One was a shift toward greater professionalism, in particular among the social services. Professional social workers were hired to manage cases, beginning with the admissions process, and social work students began doing their field placements there. The "social" model of care extended to new services, such as day care for disabled adults and innovative work programs and living arrangements.

The other shift was organizational. Previously, the Board of Trustees of the Montefiore Home controlled the bulk of the power to make decisions, ranging from individual admissions to major programmatic thrusts. As the needs of the elderly had become more complex, the expertise to meet these needs moved beyond the grasp of Board members, whose professional interests were not in the field of aging. But the new administrator, with his formal training, considerable vision, and forceful personality, had the necessary expertise and established the director of the home as the major decision maker.

He did, however, maintain a strong relationship with the Board. This organizational combination, which is key to the promotion of first-rate services, allowed the home to more effectively explore new directions in social and health services for the elderly.

The balance between a strong administrator and a powerful, active lay community is the model for organizational leadership in the Cleveland Jewish community. The success of the organization depends largely on this relationship. Ideally, administrators are chosen for their commitment to long-term care and to the Jewish community as well as for their leadership qualities, vision, and managerial skills. As the professional leader of the facility, the executive officer is expected to set the standards and goals the organization will attempt to achieve. It is he or she who must cultivate the Board's commitment to the program, but maintain control over the overall direction.

Commitment of the Board

The commitment of the Board members is what propels the institution forward. Their involvement is ultimately necessary for the financial backing for new initiatives. Cultivating the Board's involvement takes considerable skill on the part of the executive director. The Jewish model is set apart from other long-term care facilities in that a skillful administrator has a major say in who is elected to the Board. This has obvious advantages for establishing a productive relationship.

One key to fostering dedication among Board members is to tie the Board and the nursing home into its Jewish self-identification. The process of identifying the nursing home, and particularly the Board of Trustees, with Jewishness reached its fullest expression in recent years at Menorah Park. All Board meetings, for example, are imbued with an aura of religiosity. One of the first items on each agenda is a *D'var Torah*, a reading of religious text accompanied by some analysis of the text. Often the interpretation of the text is related directly to the care of the elderly. It is in these readings that the Board ties the everyday operational aspects and programmatic planning of the institution to religious principles. As one staff member summed up in her *D'var Torah*, the Board and staff need constantly to be reminded of the "higher purpose" of their pursuits. By calling on a higher principle, they enhance their feelings of self-worth and cement the commitment of Board and staff to needs that transcend material wants (see Hatch, 1989).

The balance between Board and executive officer must be delicately maintained. An executive officer who wrests too much control from the Board risks alienating them and their financial support. Likewise, too much power concentrated in one or a few Board members can be dangerous. An informant explicitly links the decline of the Montefiore Board (years ago) to the "autocratic" control exercised by one its own members during the same period the administrations of the two homes changed hands, leaving Menorah Park with the stronger, more visionary leader. This informant held the view that this was the reason that many talented and resourceful lay people signed onto the Menorah Park Board, making it the stronger and socially preferred of the two.

While it previously enjoyed a national reputation for excellence, Montefiore Home came to be viewed as "second fiddle" to Menorah Park. Not accidentally, its decline in reputation coincided with a decrease in prestige associated with being on its Board. This perception is symbolically embodied in the aging building itself, now over 50 years old.

As described above, Menorah Park was originally established as the Jewish Orthodox Home for the Aged just after the turn of the 20th century, when recently immigrated Eastern European Jews could not persuade the Montefiore Home to increase its capacity or to adhere to kosher dietary rules. The reputation of Menorah Park as "the Cadillac" facility in the Cleveland area, which was founded on a particularly strong administrative/trustee relationship, crystallized when it moved to its current facility in 1968. In what was considered a state-of-the-art building, Menorah Park installed a comprehensive set of on-site health and social services (described above), intended to minimize dislocation stress to the residents. Later Menorah Park introduced outreach long-term care services such as respite care and day care for the memory impaired that were pioneering efforts in the Cleveland area.

Newness: A Core Symbol

An important symbolic aspect of Menorah Park's new building was the newness itself. Integral to the definition of "the better" of the two nursing homes is its physical presentation. Sources affiliated with Montefiore Home are quick to point out that their building is old and therefore "depressing." Contrasted to that is the "nice atmosphere" at Menorah Park, which depends mainly on its newer construction and design. Not coincidentally, Menorah Park's reputation as the better facility was confirmed when it opened its building in 1968.

How important to the reputation of a nursing home is form versus substance? One professional staff member summed the answer to this question in two statements. First, he pointed out that, "people will give money for buildings more so than for programs," then elaborated with an illustration of how newness speaks directly to public perception:

> You can't judge the actual nursing care. You can judge whether there's an odor or not or how the building looks, but you can't judge whether a nurse is good or not

on a cursory view. Part of . . . what people do . . . with the newness is that they equate newness of facilities with "high-tech." And if you're "high-tech," then you're skilled in terms of staff. If you have a nice, modern facility, then your staff's going to be up-to-date.

The importance of "newness" and receiving the best care available is, of course, balanced with other considerations, for example, urgency. The desire for high-quality care has led to a long waiting list for admission to Menorah Park. Approximately 90 to 100 people are on the waiting list at any one time and some wait as long as a year or more for admission to Menorah Park. Montefiore has a much smaller waiting list, about 10. The advantage to the community is that clients can gain quicker entry there in emergencies.

Competition and Cooperation

The size of their waiting lists is indicative of the relationship between the two nursing homes. Originally, the distinct religious and cultural traditions that gave rise to Montefiore and Menorah Park and the heated rivalry between them reflected passionate differences surrounding issues of observance, assimilation, social status, and cultural differences between the two communities. For many years Menorah Park played "second fiddle" to Montefiore. The force of this largely social distinction compelled Menorah Park's board and staff not to be outdone by the Reform community. The influential, creative, and resourceful Orthodox community responded to their lower social position by fashioning a home of their own in Menorah Park that would come to enjoy a national reputation for excellence in long-term care. Of course, one could only expect Montefiore eventually to respond, in kind. It has. It is erecting a new facility, where it will offer services new to the Jewish community such as hospice care. It would not be risky to predict that the social order of the two homes will soon be reversed once again.

The historical competition between the two homes and their supporters is widely recognized to have been active in the past, but is not as pronounced today. The sharp lines that separated the Orthodox from the Reform community in the early part of this century have become blurred as the Orthodox community has assimilated, intermarriage between the communities has increased (as has interfaith marriage), children of Reform parents have embraced Orthodoxy, and so on. Opinions vary widely on how competitive an atmosphere remains between the two nursing homes. Some argue that they are highly competitive, others say that they are extremely cooperative. Certainly, they are both. One source captured this dual aspect of their relationship in the metaphor "sibling rivalry."

The primary example of interagency cooperation occurred when the Montefiore Home purchased for its future building a parcel of Menorah Park's property. The purchase was made possible when Board Members of Menorah Park took an active role in negotiating the transfer of the land and in raising the capital necessary to build the new Montefiore.

A lasting meeting of minds, however, was not achieved. Philosophical differences between the two Homes have become symbolized by contrasting perceptions about the grounds they occupy. Some supporters and staff of Menorah Park construe the situation as Montefiore residing on Menorah's campus. The opposing viewpoint held by Montefiore lay and professional leaders is that there are separate but adjacent campuses. The view that they share the same campus is seldom expressed.

Negative aspects of a continued competition are the obstacles posed to establishing joint programming that could save money, maximizing the talents of existing personnel, and so on. But there is a positive, adaptive side to this competition as well. The very fact that two nursing homes exist presumes that they will be compared. The facility finding itself judged inferior will strive to improve, even to surpass the other in the quality of its services. Fortuitously, the opportunity to shift positions, and to renew the service delivery package, presents itself periodically when one building becomes outdated and the decision is made to put up a new facility.

THE FUTURE

Projections

The need for long-term care services in the Jewish community will continue to grow. The Jewish community is older than the general population of Cleveland. Already its population over age 65 is about 19%, while the elderly population of America will not achieve that proportion for another decade (Jewish Community Federation of Cleveland, 1988). The rate of institutionalization of Jewish persons aged 65 and older in Cleveland approaches 7.5% (Jewish Community Federation of Cleveland, 1986), 50% greater than the rate of institutionalization among the general public (5%), reflecting a propensity in this population to use formalized long-term care services. The need for high-quality services in the face of these facts is exacerbated by significant out-migration of young Jews. The Jewish population of Cleveland fell from 70,000 in 1980 to 65,000 in 1987, leaving many older people with some or all of their grown children living out of the area (Jewish Community Federation of Cleveland, 1988).

Meeting the Challenge

The commitment to deal with the increasing and changing needs of the elderly is aggressively pursued by the Jewish Community Federation, the primary agency responsible for organizing the collection, receipt, and redistribution of charity. In its fund raising campaigns, the Federation can expect to top $25 million annually, despite the limited target population of under 65,000. Indeed, not only did the 1989 campaign exceed that figure, but another $11 million was committed to building Montefiore's new facility!

Two major items help to define the long-term care agenda of the Jewish community of Cleveland for the near future. The first addresses the means by which a shrinking general population can serve growing numbers of the elderly. The range of options being weighed is framed both by considerations of promoting living-at-home programs for the elderly and by careful study of the continuum-of-care model. These options are under deliberation, following a well-established pattern in the Cleveland Jewish Community. The ultimate outcome will depend, as it has in the past, on how key individuals manipulate the organizational structures of the nursing homes and the Jewish community. The abilities of leaders to visualize and promote various alternatives will influence the community to respond in various ways depending on how well they feel the program will serve the community need.

The second major item on the agenda is one of identification. Emerging from the decision to relocate Montefiore to the campus currently occupied by Menorah Park, this issue potentially has fundamental and lasting ramifications for the quality of long-term care in the Jewish community. The problem of identification takes at least two forms. One prominent opinion holds that relocation would create a ghetto of sick, elderly Jews. Such a dark forecast is widely discounted by active participants in Montefiore's relocation, but only time will tell if having 500+ nursing home beds in a neighborhood highly concentrated with Jewish elderly will create a public image problem.

More critical is the problem of maintaining separate identities for the two nursing homes. Already an active but informal debate about whether or not the two nursing homes will eventually merge has arisen. For every person that believes that the two nursing homes will never merge, another predicts that merger will happen within a decade.

If this debate becomes formalized, its resolution will have profound implications for the Jewish long-term care effort in Cleveland. The fact of having two separate organizations deliver that care has been one of the main reasons that Jewish long-term care in Cleveland has been at the cutting edge of service delivery on an ongoing basis. The healthy "sibling rivalry" between Menorah Park and Montefiore coupled with the staggered timing of their establishment and construction histories has fostered an environment in which nursing home care could undergo more or less continuous renewal. Assuming that a merger did occur, no less momentous would be the implications for the organizational structure of the one nursing home. To be sure, the talent pool available for Board leadership would all be available to the one organization, but the talent might also go to other Boards if there is not room for them all to realize their potential in one organization. Direct implications for the care of the elderly would also be of concern. A number of lay and professional leaders believe that the 335 beds at Menorah Park is about the maximum that one organization can handle without becoming too institutional. All involved want to be careful not to make a decision that will negatively affect their "higher purpose," the pursuit of excellent care for their elderly.

ENDNOTES

1. For example, 7.4 of every 100 Cleveland area Jews aged 65 years or more reside in nursing homes, compared to 5 in 100 among the remainder of the commuinity (Jewish Community Federation of Cleveland, 1986).
2. Steinitz (1986) offers a broad overview of the development of Jewish American service to the elderly.
3. Menorah Park also has an agreement with the Jewish Community Federation of Akron, Ohio to provide a small number of beds for residents of Akron.

REFERENCES

Gartner, L. P. (1978). *History of the Jews of Cleveland*. Cleveland: Western Reserve Historical Society.

Hatch, E. (1989). Theories of social honor. *American Anthropologist, 91*, 341–353.

Jewish Community Federation of Cleveland. (1986). *Report of the nursing home beds study committee commission on services to older persons*. Unpublished report.

Jewish Community Federation of Cleveland. (1988). *Survey of Cleveland's Jewish population, 1987*. Report 7 of the Population Research Committee. Cleveland: Jewish Community Federation of Cleveland.

Montefiore Home for the Aged. (1883). *First annual report of the Board of Trustees and Directors of the Aged and Infirm. Israelites Home, District No. 4, O. K. S. B., Located at Cleveland, Ohio; Also a Concise History of the Organization of the Home from February 16th, 1880 to July 1st, 1883*. Cleveland: Mount and Co., Printers.

Polivy, D. K. (1986). The Jewish Federation movement. In M. N. Dobkowski (Ed.), *Jewish American voluntary organizations*. New York: Greenwood Press.

Steinitz, L. Y. (1986). Jewish communal response to older people's needs. In M. N. Dobkowski (Ed.), *Jewish American voluntary organizations* . New York: Greenwood Press.

Western Reserve Historical Society. (1946). MSS 3835, The Montefiore Home; Records 1882–1972. Container 1, folder 3, *The Montefiore Home in 1948*.

Zborowski, M. & Herzog, E. (1952). *Life is with people: The Jewish little-town of Eastern Europe*. New York: International Universities Press, Inc.

14

Conceptual Understanding of Long-Term Service Use by Elders of Color

Winnie Hernandez-Gallegos
John Capitman
Donna Yee

This chapter explores how provider organization features, such as personnel practices and service approaches, play an important role in explaining underutilization of the aging network by elders of color. First, a model is presented for understanding the dynamic processes that affect service use by elders of color. The model looks at the roles of provider organizations in mediating service use by elders of color and the reciprocal influence of individual characteristics on provider organizations. This chapter also looks at how service orientation and cultural awareness affect service use by elders of color.

This project was supported, in part, by award number 90AT0388 from the Administration on Aging, Department of Health and Human Services, Washington, D.C. 20201. Grantees undertaking projects under government sponsorship are encouraged to express freely their findings and conclusions. Points of view or opinions do not, therefore, necessarily represent official Administration on Aging policy.

The literature suggests that relatively little is known about how the aging network is accommodating cultural diversity through personnel practices and service approaches. In an attempt to fill these gaps, this chapter also reports on a project funded by the Administration on Aging. Aging network agencies and service providers in five areas were invited to focus group meetings to discuss challenges and opportunities to address issues in provision of services to elders of color. This chapter briefly describes the methodology for data gathering and discusses the outcomes of the participant survey. Finally, conclusions and recommendations are presented.

A CONCEPTUAL MODEL FOR UNDERSTANDING SERVICE USE

Given the context of the aged population's increasing diversity, the projected demands, and the need to improve the efficiency and effectiveness of the delivery of long-term care services at the federal, state, and local level, it is evident that service use and the factors associated with use need to be better understood. For each of the racial/ethnic groups considered, there is accumulating evidence for higher rates of poverty, chronic illness, and disability in everyday activities. While it appears that elders of color use more acute care services and fewer long-term care services than do white elders, there are very few comparative multivariate studies that examine the relative contributions of health status, availability of informal care, and economic and cultural factors to these apparent differences in utilization. There were no studies identified in this literature review that fully describe the help seeking and responses to care offerings by elders of color. It is unclear whether elders of color underutilize the aging network because they don't seek care or as a result of interactions with agencies once they do seek care. It thus appears that current models for explaining service use need to be reexamined.

Several models have emerged to explain medical service use by elders. Two models that have received the most attention are the behavioral model of health care utilization proposed by Andersen and Newman (1973) and the medical care process framework developed by Donabedian (1973). Briefly, the Andersen and Newman framework views service utilization as dependent primarily on individual determinants, although some of these predictors reflect broader socioeconomic factors. The model clusters individual determinants in several categories: (1) enabling factors such as income, insurance coverage, and regular source of care; (2) predisposing factors such as age, gender, living arrangements; and (3) need factors such as health status, functional limitations, cognitive functioning.

The Andersen and Newman model does not place sufficient attention on the national and state policies that determine service availability and accessibility or the features of local communities. Perhaps the central problem in using this model in explaining service use by persons of color, however, is the failure to consider the behavior of provider organizations as gatekeepers and caregivers in creating openings or barriers to access through their approaches to service delivery. Donabedian's (1973) model builds on the Andersen framework by including service providers as important factors influencing service use. Donabedian posits that health care utilization is the result of a process in which users and providers respond to a need and in concert create a service use incident. While Donabedian's approach to explain service is more inclusive by adding the behavior of organizations as a factor influencing service use, it nonetheless fails to recognize the provider's behavior within the broader system features. Additionally, the framework leaves unaddressed the influence of organizational factors on service use, such as staffing mix and provider orientation to diversity. It seems appropriate to offer a modified model for understanding the use of aging network services by elders of color and elders from other underserved ethnic/cultural sub-groups.

The proposed model in Figure 14.1 indicates that *Service System Features* and *Community Features* are major factors in how *Provider Organizations*, are defined and how they operate. Service use by individual elders is in turn determined by how *Provider Organizations* both reach out and respond to the predisposing, enabling, and need features of individual elders. Our discussion will focus on two components: *Provider Organizations* and *Individual Determinants*. Almost no attention is devoted to two other factors noted in the model, *Service System Features* and *Community Features*, although they may play crucial roles in determining lower participation rates by elders of color.

These issues have been addressed in greater detail by others in the field (Binstock Grigsby, & Leavitt, 1983; Crown, 1984; Cutler, 1989; GAO, 1990). What follows is a brief description of each of the components as proposed in this framework. The direction of the arrows in Figure 14.1 indicates the relationship and interaction that takes place in the process of service delivery and utilization. An explanation of these relationships is presented in the discussion of each of the components.

Service System Features

This component of the model refers to aspects of the larger national or state system in which services and funding mechanisms are defined and service availability at the community level is determined. Service delivery is directly affected by federal, state, and local public policy. The reauthorization of the Older Americans Act, for example, is approved by Congress, including the level of funding and the types of services to be provided through the aging network. The influence of this component on service providers is direct and, by our estimation, not a reciprocal one. The political process is open to revision of

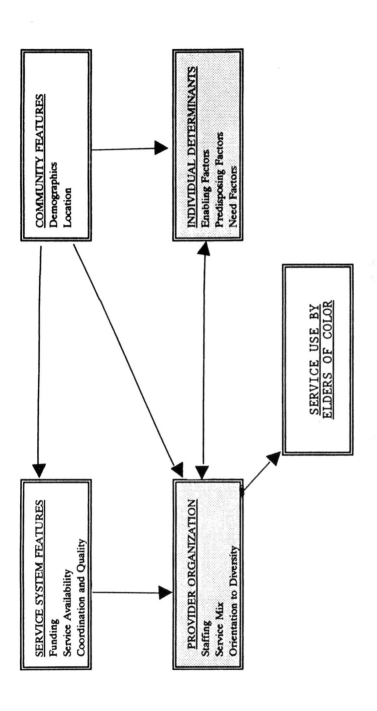

FIGURE 14.1 A model for understanding service use by elders of color.

public policies: the repeal of the Medicare Catastrophic Amendment in 1989 is the most dramatic recent example. Nonetheless, the majority of constraints and opportunities faced by providers in the delivery of care are generated by federal, state, and local policies.

Community Features

The model highlights the influence of community factors on the other three components of the model. Identifying factors such as the representation and dispersion of ethnic/racial subpopulations are critical to this framework. For example, the debate over the 1980 U. S. census focused on the accuracy of census representation of communities. Funds for many social and health services are allocated based on the economic status, racial composition, and age distribution of each community. Another feature referenced in this component of the model is the location (region, urban/rural) of elders. Additionally, local political or other circumstances, such as levels of unemployment or general economic conditions, also affect service providers.

Individual Characteristics

As indicated above, the factors in this component of the model include enabling (income, health insurance coverage, etc.), predisposing (age, gender, race, cultural/ethnic norms, values), and need (functional impairment, health status, etc.) factors as proposed in the behavioral model of Andersen and Newman (1973). The relationship as depicted by the direction of the arrows in Figure 14.1 is reciprocal. Underscored is the interplay of individual characteristics (e.g., language skills and level of acculturation as in the case of foreign-born elders, or a personal history of having been exposed to discrimination and racism) and how provider staff responds to these individual characteristics. Provider staff orientation to diversity (e.g., sensitivity to cultural differences, recognition of cultural values and norms in preferences) and the influence these factors contribute are also highlighted. The literature suggests that elders of color consider, in decisions to use services, issues such as cultural insensitivity of providers, failure of programs to satisfy cultural preferences, lack of sensitivity to the feelings of elders, and lack of bilingual/bicultural staff to facilitate communications (Gallagher, 1988; Kapke, 1988; Kramer, Polisar, & Hyde, 1990; National Indian Council on Aging, 1982). This suggests that at the very core of the relationship between elders of color and provider organizations are two main issues that may ultimately frame decisions to provide services and to use services: perceptions and attitudes. That is, provider responses to individual characteristics and responses by elders of color take place in the context of interpersonal exchanges, of communication, actions, and reactions.

Provider Organization

This element of the model stresses the influence provider organizations have in mediating service use. Provider organizations, through policies for assessing and addressing individual characteristics, such as eligibility determination, need assessment, or ongoing monitoring and reassessment, act as gatekeepers to the delivery system. Outreach efforts, local coordination of services with other provider agencies, and attention to the quality of care being provided are features that enhance access to services. In addition, organizational orientation toward diversity in personnel and clinical practices are critical to the client/provider relationship.

The direction of the arrows in Figure 14.1 indicates a reciprocal relationship between the elder and the provider organization. For example, an assessment process will determine whether income, health, cognitive, or functional deficits exist. A decision is made by the provider to respond or not respond to the assessed needs soon after the assessment. The result of the assessment may be a care plan with authorization for type and scope of services, or the placement of the individual on a waiting list. The reasons for wait listing a potential client may include a shortage of staff or unavailability of bilingual staff person to provide services. In any case, the organizational response determines who gets served and who does not.

Service Use by Elders of Color

The last element of this model, as suggested in Figure 14.1, marks a distinct departure from contemporary explanations of service use. While the elder consumer of services may make the ultimate decision to participate in a given program, it is suggested that service use is the *outcome* of dynamic interactions among all four components. Service use does not result from an automatic, mechanistic relationship between the elder of color and the provider organization; rather, service use results from a mediated relationship. Not only are system features at play, but in addition community and provider organizational features exert influence on service use by elders of color. For example, the availability, location, scope, and mix of services is frequently predetermined prior to service use.If a service is not available, service use cannot occur or other less appropriate service may be substituted. Additionally, other provider features such as outreach activities, availability of bicultural or bilingual staff, and provider orientation to diversity determine how providers influence service use. The model posits that the final outcome, measured as service use by elders of color, results from a dynamic process between communities, provider staff, and the older consumer herself.

UNDERSTANDING PROVIDER STRATEGIES TO DIVERSITY

The *National Aging Resource Center: Long-Term Care at Brandeis University*, coordinated a project in October 1989 with the *National Resource Center on Minority Populations* at San Diego State University. The purpose of the study was to explore how the aging network is adapting to the increased diversity among the aged, in terms of both staffing and service components. The study combined two approaches. The first approach was to conduct focus group meetings in five sites as a means of identifying the issues associated with staffing and service delivery to elders of color. In order to more systematically begin to understand the level of diversity in staffing in the aging network and the issues of providing culturally inclusive services, a survey of focus group participants was conducted. Both activities informed the development of the typology presented in this section. Because of space limitations, only the results of the survey are discussed in this chapter (for additional information of the results of the focus group meetings see Capitman, Hernandez, & Yee, 1990).

Selecting Communities

In order to collect information from a wide cross section of the aging network, the following criteria were developed for selecting the communities for this project: racial/ethnic mix of aged population in the area; geographic spread of areas being served; urban/rural mix of the areas served; and development of the aging network (spectrum and availability of services). State Unit on Aging and Area Agency on Aging cosponsorship was coordinated at each of the five sites that agreed to participate: Dade County in Florida, Santa Clara and San Mateo Counties in California, the State of Nevada, Selma and surrounding rural communities in Alabama, and Chicago and Cook County, Illinois. Each of the sites had distinguishing characteristics. Of all sites, Chicago was the largest city. The Selma AAA covered a ten-county, primarily rural area. Both Dade County and San Mateo/Santa Clara Counties had a mixture of urban and suburban areas.

Selecting Participants

A planning committee, comprised of local aging network representatives and locally convened by the SUA/AAA, generated the names of service provider organizations who would be invited to participate in the survey and focus group meetings. Invited were SUA/AAA staffs; the range of Title III–funded service providers; other state, county, and city organizations including mental health providers, housing and other social service programs, such as information and referral services; nursing home and home health care providers including both proprietary and nonprofit facilities at all service levels; and skilled home care providers such as Visiting Nurses Association; and other nonprofit community service providers, such as free-standing community-based organizations or geriatric health programs. In all, over 120 persons, representing 95 organizations, attended the focus groups.

Survey of Focus Group Participants

Service delivery organizations invited to the focus group were mailed a survey prior to the meeting to be held in their region. The survey included questions in the following five areas: (1) general description of agency and services provided; (2) racial breakdown of the agency's work force; (3) demographic description on populations served; (4) issues in the recruitment, retention, training, managing, and promoting staff of color; and (5) issues in coordinating and providing services in a multicultural community. The overall response rate of 91% was achieved through personal telephone calls offering assistance or clarifications to participants. The respondents included providers from senior centers, support services, nutrition programs, health clinics, case management and information referral agencies, nursing homes and other supportive housing, paraprofessional home care, and home health fields. There were some differences across sites in the distribution of respondents by type of agency (population focus, size, nonprofit vs. proprietary) and mix of service. It is not clear the extent to which the respondents are representative of the aging network at each of the sites. Therefore, survey respondents do not constitute a "statistically representative sample" but a convenience sample. Nonetheless, all respondents were engaged in the provision of services either to the general aged population or to elders of specific racial/ethnic groups. At the same time, there were notable variations in the detail of response across agencies and communities. Survey respondents did not consistently provide sufficient detail on the racial and ethnic breakdowns of the staffs within each job title. Because of these factors, a qualitative approach was taken in the analysis.

PROVIDER STRATEGIES: A TYPOLOGY

The qualitative analysis of the surveys occurred in several steps. Responses on agency services and populations served were used to group participating agencies into:

- Providers focused on serving the general aged population. Respondents in this group were social service and long-term care providers that did not include a focus on a specific ethnic or racial group as part of their mission.

• Providers focused on serving elders from specific racial or ethnic populations. These agencies were described as having been founded to meet the
social, health, or economic needs of a particular ethnic/racial group.

Within each of these two broader groups, attention was then turned to overall analysis of service population and staff demographic distributions, definition of issues associated with recruitment, retention, training, promoting, and
managing staff of color, and how cultural diversity was being considered in service approaches and care coordination. The goal was to identify broad group-
ings of agencies with regard to the orientations to multiculturalism. We did not
seek to assess the adequacy or appropriateness of these approaches in terms of
service use, program costs, or other features analyzed. Notable variation existed
among the first broad category, providers that focused on serving the general
aged population. These providers varied in the degree to which elders of color
were being served, persons of color occupied staff roles at every level of the organization, and personnel practices and service approaches reflected an appreciation of differences. This variation appeared unrelated to the age, size, service
offerings, or sponsorship of these provider organizations. Within the second
broad category, those providers focused on serving specific ethnic/racial groups,
there was also significant variation across the five sites of the study. These respondents were identified in three communities. Respondents with a focus on a
specific racial/ethnic group were not found in Selma and in Las Vegas. It is unknown the degree to which this reflects the funding policies within each state,
or whether in fact, these agencies exist and did not participate in this project.

The survey responses suggested that within diverse communities aging network providers had come to adopt differing orientations to diversity reminis-
cent of varying approaches to work force diversity noted among businesses.
Building on a framework developed by Foster, Jackson, Cross, Jackson, and
Hardiman (1988), aging providers could be said to have adopted differing strategies to accommodating diversity in the aging population and in the employment markets. Five primary strategies were identified. The following discussion
provides a description of these strategies.

Monocultural Aging Service Providers

These were found across the five areas. One characteristic common to these
agencies was the reported opinion that cultural diversity was not an issue requiring special attention within the organization at this time. None of these
agencies noted service to culturally diverse communities as part of their mission. These agencies did not expand on how and why diversity is considered in
managing a work force. These respondents were the least likely to provide complete demographic data on their staffs. When provided, the available information suggested little or no diversity in staffing, with persons of color exclusively

at the paraprofessional direct service level. No agencies in this group reported persons of color in any key or policymaking positions, such as directors, assistant directors, supervisors, or case managers. The majority of responses regarding promotion and management of persons from diverse backgrounds cited that these had not arisen as issues for the organization. Where respondents did elaborate, these answers tended to focus on employee characteristics such as lack of skills necessary for promotions and inability to write the language. General agency characteristics were sometimes cited as barriers to promotion: restricted upward mobility due to size of the agency; and restricted to lateral mobility because of staffing patterns.

This group did not comment about care coordination or service issues related to specific ethnic or racial groups. Elders of color were generally referred to as "minority" elders while at the same time responding that statistics on the populations served were not kept on an ongoing basis, or could not readily be disentangled from the "non-white" categories. Regarding anticipated changes in demographics and how these affect future services patterns, the majority responded with descriptions on the rapid growths in the "old-old" age group of elders, the increasing frailty of elders served and the increased demand resulting from increases in the population. The majority anticipated that future demands may result in a need for additional staff or additional building space to house staff. A portion did not anticipate having to make any changes. Several respondents seemed to address possible reasons for underservice of elders of color in the context of issues in care coordination. Overall, the responses did not include reference to any agency programs or materials developed to reach elders of color, such as special outreach efforts, or coordination with other providers for interagency referrals.

Nondiscriminatory Aging Service Providers

These providers recognized cultural diversity explicitly through mission statements and other policies. Respondents identified issues regarding affirmative action and made references to cultural differences. These providers appeared to have a culturally diverse work force, although most of that diversity occurred at the direct service level (both professional and paraprofessional staff members). Respondents in this group favored developing strategies for addressing cultural diversity within the community and the work force, however, they did not describe actual programs, services, or policies implemented to address these issues in their agency or community.

The special approaches or unique experiences in recruitment from diverse populations cited did not focus attention on qualifications of the applicant pool in general but reflected thoughtful consideration to alternative approaches such as: appealing to other minority professionals in the community and to faculty at state universities; contacting vocational schools and community colleges regarding work–study programs and requesting graduate lists; and soliciting referrals from current staff. Some referenced the agency's reputation for providing good benefits, salary, and supervision to be factors that promote recruitment. Language barriers were discussed by some respondents, although they expressed the view that this barrier arose primarily in recruiting for paraprofessional roles only. Some responses reflected unsuccessful attempts to recruit staff who were also bilingual and/or bicultural.

Respondents described a number of factors that they believe need to be considered in attempting to retain a culturally diverse staff: fair salaries and benefits; administrative support for increasing staff educational levels; good communications among staff and administrators; sufficient bilingual staff so that fair work loads can be ensured and such staff persons are not overextended; scheduling that can accommodate culture-specific holidays and other events requiring time off; and participatory management and team building.

Many respondents focused on how individual attitudes and interpersonal relations need attention in retention of a diverse staff: helping staff overcome racial/ethnic prejudices; helping sensitize and educate staff to individual differences due to ethnic, religious, and cultural backgrounds. Respondents in this group often noted that there had been training efforts concentrated on cultural diversity and care for the aged. Some respondents believed that it was difficult for their agency to sustain a real focus on these issues. One respondent noted that "The system pays lip service, sponsors a training program, then leaves it alone or up to the individual's initiative and follow-up."

Management and promotion issues focused on agency features such as: good communications; sensitivity to interpersonal conflicts that may stem from differences; and examining reasons for turnover. Others cited internal policies for promotions that posed barriers and mentioned ways to address these, such as encouraging staff to go for training or more education.

Respondents in this group made reference to the increasing diversity in populations served. Some respondents articulated service problems faced by elders in specific racial/ethnic group, such as: high proportion on Latino elders without any insurance coverage; acculturation difficulties by recent immigrants in particular; differential incidence of depression among ethnic groups. Generally, the comments reflected knowledge of cultural values to be considered in serving a multicultural community and sensitivity and awareness of some of the difficulties elders experience in seeking help. Other respondents pointed to the need to develop specific programs and goals, however, they seemed unsure about how to implement these ideas. Responses by this group on most items reflected that diversity was an explicit topic discussed in their organizations. The responses generally contained an analysis of how these issues could be addressed; however, no specific strategies were offered.

Multicultural Aging Service Providers

Few agencies were grouped in this category, although such agencies were found in each of the five sites. This group of respondents is characterized by active commitment and explicit priority for addressing cultural diversity in personnel and service approaches. These aging providers noted specific policies, programs, and materials designed to meet diversity goals. Most of these respondents provided data on the racial breakdown of staff and elders served. These respondents had extensive representation by persons of color at all levels of their work force.

Respondents described clear efforts to diversify the work force as evidenced by detailed and comprehensive strategies and policies such as: special recruitment efforts including coordination with minority networks and organizations, recruitment in local communities, schools and shopping centers, and cultural events; utilizing minority recruiters, as well as using internships and on-the-job training; publicizing needs in targeted newspapers, on radio and television stations, and in ethnic-specific community groups; and offering stipends to second-year graduate minority/bilingual students who serve two years with the agency.

Most respondents cited specific policies or comprehensive plans to encourage retention, such as: educational opportunities and tuition refund programs; development of career ladders and opportunities for promotion; social activities that support both intragroup and intergroup experiences; evaluating needs of each racial/ethnic group represented in the staff; recognizing contributions and special skills; and creating opportunities for staff of color to serve as trainers. These respondents can be characterized as having thought through how management practices and decisions affect retention of persons of color.

Respondents in this group focused on the importance of involving staff actively in designing training materials and selecting topics and approaches to ongoing staff development. Many believed that specific training on multiculturalism was needed and had developed programs that incorporated culture/ethnicity issues as components of training requirements for staff at all levels. Some of the topics mentioned in discussions of multiculturalism training included: dispelling myths about different cultural groups; exploring personal attitudes and behaviors with people of different races and backgrounds; examining racial/ethnic group differences in feelings about aging, illness, social support, service delivery, and death; and normative behaviors and values of other cultures.

This group of respondents, while having a majority of white clients, were able to respond with statistics on persons of color served. Most respondents described their care coordination and service approach as addressing diversity through a work force responsive to the needs of multicultural elders. Almost all the responses included reference to the need for bilingual or bicultural staffing and inclusion of persons from diverse backgrounds in all service roles to ensure continued attention to these issues.

These aging service providers mentioned specific programs and/or materials developed to increase participation by elders of color and their families. These programs included: specific outreach to communities of color through development of close links to media, churches, and racial/ethnic group–focused service providers; materials including brochures, advertisements, admissions forms, and program guidelines translated into different languages; materials focused on special concerns or issues for specific racial/ethnic groups; expanded services and/or opening satellite offices in multicultural communities; inclusion of community leaders in care planning or information/referral networks; sponsorship of special events, community training programs, or educational forums located in diverse communities or focused on issues of particular concern to specific groups; and flexible hours to accommodate community needs.

Sustaining Focus Aging Providers

Respondents representing providers placed in this group described an ongoing struggle to meet the needs of their unique community: these providers were committed to alleviating the distress in their target population. Overall, this group of respondents shared some of the same issues as those reported by agencies serving the general population, such as: having a small pool of professionals from which to recruit; competition among other culturally focused agencies for trained staff while operating within limited budgets; and having to deal with applicants who have limited fluency in English. This group of respondents was characterized as having less diversity in their work force. Also, clients served by this group of respondents were primarily from the same racial/ethnic background as the staff.

Strategies for recruitment seemed more focused on continued enhancement of their traditional applicant pool: agency-sponsored social events; networking with community leaders; inviting the press to agency functions to give more exposure to ethnic agency needs and services; use of ethnic communities' newspapers; and formal arrangements with nearby universities and colleges to provide field placements for both undergraduate and graduate students. Overall, strategies seemed also to stress relationships with other agencies and other communities.

These respondents tended to cite general features of their work setting as the primary barriers to retention. Examples included lower salaries, poor benefits, and competition with other agencies. This group of respondents mentioned frequently the importance of working relationships and good communication as factors that helped retention. A few responded that staff retention is not a problem when there is open communication and training is provided to staff at all levels. Comments about training reflected that this was an important priority to the respondents. Training approaches included: having bilingual staff train in English and the other languages spoken by other staff of color; and using major training events in the area, such as the American Society on Aging's summer series training program, other gerontology conferences, and workshops sponsored by the aging network.

Several respondents answered that the small size of their agency limited promotional opportunities. All of these respondents served one major group of elders, including: Pacific Asian, African-American, Native American, Jewish, and Latino elders. Some agencies had even more narrowly defined target groups: Japanese-American, Pacific/Asian refugees, or Greek-American elders. Most of the care coordination and service approach issues identified by these respondents centered around language. Others cited the complexity of the network and the difficulty this poses for coordinating care. To address this complexity some providers, as did ethnic providers in Chicago, formed a coalition as a means for addressing these issues and as a mechanism for articulating needs to the State Unit on Aging and the Area Agency on Aging.

Expanding Focus Aging Service Providers

Only a few respondents described their agencies in ways that suggested this category. All of these were relatively longstanding providers to a specific racial/ethnic group in their respective communities. Over time these agencies had come to recognize that their unique approaches to service could benefit a broader community. Their orientation to diversity included developing staffing models that reflected a similar range of racial/ethnic groups as their populations, while sustaining a primary focus in a community. These respondents identified some of the same issues as the groups described above, but they also made specific references to activities and programs that reached out to the general population.

Most of these respondents shared specific approaches for recruitment such as: advertising in ethnic newspapers and mainstream newspapers as well as in professional journals; networking with ethnic and white professionals; and encouraging minority staff referrals. These agencies, in general, shared an explicit goal to actively recruit staff that is sensitive to monolingual elders. At the same time, these providers also reached beyond their ethnic community to recruit white and other staff.

These respondents often referenced inclusive management practices such as: explicit expectations articulated regarding mutual respect among staff; written communications to staff in English and in native language; flexible working schedules to accommodate cultural holidays; encouragement of staff to share knowledge and skills; special training for white staff to sensitize them to working with elders of color; and encouragement of management to understand the different cultures, customs, and folklore that are associated with having a diverse work force. While they noted many of the same strategies identified by the Sustaining Focus agencies, these respondents identified some additional challenges of managing a culturally diverse work force, such as sustaining employee motivation given fiscal constraints.

Each of the respondents in this group served elders from other ethnic/racial communities and articulated specific goals for delivery of services to these other communities. These respondents were explicit about the issues of acculturation among the elders of color. For example, one respondent in Santa Clara/San Mateo described the special needs of Isseis, or first-generation Japanese elders, as differing from those of Niseis, who are second-generation Japanese-American elders. Overall, these agencies made reference to the increasing diversity in the populations they served and made reference to the implications these changes will have on their current staffing patterns.

DISCUSSION

The survey results provided some preliminary qualitative data on the differing ways that organizations have found for responding to cultural diversity among the aged. Quantitative data for testing the links between personnel policies, service approaches, and agency use by racially or culturally isolated subpopulations were not collected, however, these findings suggested the kinds of hypotheses that need to be considered in a more focused approach. While this study is preliminary and further research needs to be conducted, several aspects of the service-delivery process come into clearer focus.

One of the major findings underscores the crucial role that attitudinal factors play on service use by elders of color. The first major result was the extent to which provider responses appeared to fit into distinct categories along the dimension of orientation to cultural diversity. Provider features were measurably different from one group to the next, suggesting that provider orientation has concrete consequences on how proactively and creatively cultural diversity issues in staffing and service approaches are addressed. There was a high correlation between personnel practices, such as recruitment and staff retention efforts, to the explicit designation of diversity as a priority for the organization—the higher and more clearly stated the priority, the greater the work force diversity. Similarly, the extent to which diversity was defined as an important dimension to consider in the planning and implementation of services was highly correlated with how providers assessed and developed strategies to increase service use by elders of color, such as outreach efforts or contact with local community leaders.

RECOMMENDATIONS

Many of the agencies participating in this project have long been providing services in multicultural communities, and their approaches to the challenges posed by diversity can serve as excellent practice models. Results from both the survey and focus group meetings highlight SUA and AAA initiatives already underway to address work force diversity and enhance services to elders of color. The findings also underscore areas on which continued attention is needed such as the dearth of information of the long-term care work force and the populations served by the aging network. It is recommended that aging network systematically collect data on:

- (1) Service needs by elders of color; (2) the network's labor force characteristics; and (3) aging network providers with a focus on areas served, elders targeted, and types of service available.

To strengthen ongoing initiatives and to support those implemented by other service providers in the community, aging service providers are encouraged to:

- Incorporate methods for ongoing or periodic self-review on the progress of these activities; and
- Develop specific goals that support ongoing review of existing interagency relationships; and review referral patterns, including reasons for rejection or pending status.

In the context of interagency relationships, it is recommended that the aging network focus particular attention to providers dedicated to serving primarily elders of color and:

- Examine methods for long-term care vendor selection;
- Provide technical assistance to these organizations; and
- Continue examination of service mix, service availability, and gaps that not being addressed.

The findings also point to the difficulties inherent in the process of recognizing, articulating, and incorporating diversity in personnel and clinical practices. Recognition of this difficulty requires that the aging network develop and implement approaches that promote opportunities for participation by persons of color so that the process of addressing diversity issues incorporates their perspective. The network should continue to:

- Promote activities that focus on the link between personal beliefs and the design and delivery of care; and
- Strengthen and broaden the scope and roles of agency boards and other governing bodies, and diversify board membership to include persons of color who are community leaders as well as elder consumers of services.

It was clear from the survey results that the process of evaluating how care is being delivered to elders of color in turn also takes into account how services are delivered to other older consumers, how care coordination with other community agencies is accomplished, the scope of services offered, and geographic areas served. Likewise, examination of work force diversity at management and service levels leads to a review of recruitment policies, retention efforts, promotion practices, and the identification of personnel practices that need revision. All of these issues come into greater focus when concerns related to cultural diversity are addressed.

REFERENCES

Andersen, R., & Newman, J. F. (1973). Societal and individual determinants of medical care utilization in the United States. *Milbank Memorial Fund Quarterly/Health and Society, 51*, 95–121.

Binstock, R. H., Grigsby, J., & Leavitt, T. D. (1983). An analysis of "targeting" policy options under Title III of the Older Americans Act. National Aging Policy Center on Income Maintenance, Brandeis University.

Capitman, J. A., Hernandez, W. M., & Yee, D. L. (1990). Cultural diversity and the aging network: An exploratory survey. National Long-Term Care Resource Center, Florence Heller Graduate School, Brandeis University.

Crown, W. (1984). Targeting Title III of the Older Americans Act: An analysis of the existing and alternative interstate allocation formulas. National Aging Policy Center on Income Maintenance, Brandeis University.

Cutler, N. E. (1989). Minority targeting in the Older Americans Act, 1978–1988: From the "greatest economic need to Meek *v.* Martinez." National Resource Center on Minority Aging Populations, Center on Aging, San Diego State University, College of Health and Human Services.

Donabedian, A. (1973). *Aspects of medical administration: Specifying requirememts for health care.* Cambridge, MA: Harvard University Press.

Foster B. H., Jackson, G., Cross, W. E., Jackson, B., & Hardiman, R. (1988). Workforce diversity and business. *Training and Development Journal,* April, 38–42.

Gallagher, K. (1988). Methods to increase the participation of minority elderly in programs funded under the Older Americans Act: Final report for the Gerontological Society of America. Denver, CO.

General Accounting Office. (1990). *Older Americans Act: Administration on Aging does not approve interstate funding formulas.* HRD-90-85.

Kapke, K. A. (1988). *The health status and health service needs of the elders of the Oneida Indian Tribe.* Milwakee, WI: Final Report of the 1987 Postdoctoral Fellowship Project in Applied Gerontology. University of Wisconsin–Milwaukee.

Kramer, J. B., Polisar, D., & Hyde, J. C. (1990). *Study of urban American Indians.* Los Angeles: Final Report from research grant #ARO118. The Public Health Foundation of Los Angeles County.

The National Indian Council on Aging, Inc. (1982). ACCESS—A Demonstration Project, Entitlement Programs for Indian Elders, Final Report.

PART VI

Planning, Policy, and Practice

This final section includes four chapters that raise issues and suggest planning, policy, and practice agendas with regard to ethnicity and long-term care. These chapters provide background and illustrations of important issues that will benefit planners, policymakers, and practitioners. The information and recommendations in these chapters should aid in the development of ethnically sensitive programs and financing. Moreover, these chapters suggest important directions for professionals to focus their efforts.

The first chapter, by Lacayo, points out that our general conception of "elderly" must be revised downward for older Hispanics. Older Hispanics seem to see themselves as old prior to age 65. Moreover, she points out that there is a general lack of data on the health of older Hispanics. This lack of data, she argues, hampers efforts to design or reform health programs for today's and tomorrow's older Hispanics. Lacayo suggests points of intervention and presents policy issues that planners, policymakers, and practitioners need to be sensitive to. Among these issues are problems of access to health and long-term care, a lack of understanding of rights to health and long-term care, and training of professionals to understand the needs and special circumstances of ethnic seniors.

In the second chapter in this section, Kart points out the tremendous diversity that exists among the older black population. Using national data from the 1984 Supplement on Aging of the National Health Interview Surveys, he demonstrates the great variation in functional ability and the degree to which need for help is met by informal and formal sources. Kart shows that one of the more popular behavioral models used to understand service use is not very powerful. In much previous research, health has been used as a measure of need for services. As with other research Kart finds that this measure is the strongest predictor of service use by older blacks. Kart suggests that the lack of utility of this model is due primarily to the failure to consider several barriers to service use that ethnic elders experience. He stresses that researchers, policymakers, and practitioners must consider these barriers and the diversity within the black elderly population when studying older blacks and in the development of long-term care programs. Further, he cautions us on the use of the current limited behavioral models in assessing equity in access to health and long-term care.

Wright and Mindel contend that there are three major issue areas at the root of discussions on the direction of long-term care policies: economic, health, and service use. They discuss these issues for ethnic elderly in general and, where appropriate, point out differences between ethnic groups. These authors discuss long-term care policy development and show that these policies are generally not sensitive to the special circumstances of ethnic elderly. Finally, they make several recommendations that will create ethnically sensitive government policies and programs.

In the final chapter, Stull presents findings from a study of ethnic elders' preferences for long-term care services and financing. He points out that white, black, and Hispanic elderly in his sample often have very different patterns of service use, anticipated service use, and preferences for features of delivery systems. Moreover, a substantial number of ethnic elders are willing and able to purchase some form of insurance that covers long-term care over and above that paid for by Medicare. Stull suggests that public–private partnerships in long-term care financing, including expansion of Medicare and private long-term care insurance, may be viable directions for financing long-term care for ethnic elders. Educating ethnic elders on Medicare and medigap coverage and informing the insurance industry and policymakers of ethnic elders' preferences and financial ability are important considerations for future long-term care financing.

15

Hispanic Elderly: Policy Issues in Long-Term Care

Carmela G. Lacayo

INTRODUCTION

Hispanic elderly are one of the fastest-growing but most underserved segments of our population. The Hispanic elderly are among those most in need of adequate long-term care, both formal (government-assisted) and informal (provided by family, friends, or other caregivers). Despite their urgent need for long-term care, older Hispanics in this country underuse health and other social services. Limited familiarity with the social service system, limited ability to speak English, the scarcity of culturally sensitive, bilingual/bicultural services and service providers as well as discrimination have been traditional, formidable barriers to aged Hispanics' service use. These barriers are still prevalent. This chapter will try to explain why this is so and what can be done about it.

DEMOGRAPHICS

At the outset it is important to define "Hispanic elderly." Most government offices define old age as 65 years or for some purposes 60 years and over. Approximately one million Hispanics over 65 lived in the United States in 1988. It is estimated that this group will grow by 217% between 1987 and 2015, to a total of over three million people, compared to a 50% increase among all U. S. elderly (U.S Department of Commerce, 1988). U. S. Hispanics age faster than older Anglos. Nearly two-thirds of sampled older Mexican-Americans saw themselves as old beginning at or below 60 years of age (Lacayo, 1982; see also Bastida & Gonzalez; Espino in this volume). Earlier functional aging can be attributed to harder working conditions, poorer nutrition, including prenatal nutrition, and poorer health care (Dowd & Bengtson, 1978; Kurtz, 1970). Hence, a more practical definition for old age in Hispanics is 55 years and over. Using this definition means official statistics on older Hispanics underestimate the true size and needs of this group. Given the limitations on available data for the age group 55 and older, the ensuing discussions will be limited primarily to the age group 65 and older.

Ethnographics

The Hispanic population is diverse, consisting of native born, legal, and undocumented immigrants, with varying lengths of residency in the United States. Hispanics are a heterogeneous group that varies regionally and culturally. Mexican Americans make up 53% of the total U. S. Hispanic population over 65; Cuban-Americans 14.5%; Puerto Ricans, 10.8%; Central and South Americans, 5.6%; and those of "Other Hispanic Origins," 15.8% (U. S. Department of Commerce, 1988). Geographical concentrations exist, such as Mexican-Americans being dominant in the Southwest; Cubans, in the Southeast; and Puerto Ricans, in the Northeast. The large influx of South and Central American refugees in the 1980s, an increase of 67% between 1982 and 1988 (U. S. Department of Commerce, 1988), has brought large numbers of older Salvadorans, Guatemalans, and Nicaraguans to areas not thought of as traditional Hispanic population centers, like Illinois, Michigan, and Louisiana.

Poverty

In 1988 aged Hispanics were more than twice as likely to be poor as older Anglos: 22.4% versus 10.0% (U. S. Department of Commerce, 1988). Older Hispanics had a reported unemployment rate in 1987 of 5.2%, more than double that of the Anglo population (2.4%). These figures do not include individuals considered "drop-outs" or "discouraged workers" (those who have abandoned hope of securing or stopped looking for a job) (U. S. Department of Labor, 1989). Employment rates are also much lower for the Hispanic elderly (12%) than for all elderly (17%) (Commonwealth Fund Commission, 1989). Older Hispanics reported that median earnings from employment were only 75% of that of the comparable Anglo population. These discrepancies are partly due to educational disadvantage, as 31% of all Hispanic men 65 years or older and 31.5% of older Hispanic women were functionally illiterate, with less than a fourth grade education, in 1987 (U. S. Department of Commerce, 1988). They are also due in part to types of employment compared to other elderly, Hispanics participate more in the unskilled, service, and farm areas of employment than in the skilled and managerial fields.

Health Insurance

Many Hispanic elderly have not worked in jobs where Social Security credits were earned; others lack information regarding their eligibility (Andersen, Lewis, Giachello, Aday, & Chiu, 1981). Social Security and Supplemental Security Income represent almost three out of every five dollars (57.3% of total support) income for Hispanic elderly compared to two out of every five dollars (40.1%) for aged Anglos. Only 19% of aged Hispanics are covered by a private pension, compared to 45% of the total older U. S. population. Approximately 19% of all Hispanic elderly receive neither Social Security nor pension income (Commonwealth, 1989; Lacayo, 1980).

Hispanics historically have been part of the working poor who receive no health benefits from employers. No public or private medical insurance is reported by 8% of Hispanic elderly compared with one percent of all elderly (Commonwealth, 1989). Medicare is the type of health coverage most often reported by all Hispanic elderly subgroups (49%) except Puerto Ricans (38%). Puerto Rican elderly rely more heavily on Medicaid (46%). Overall, Medicaid is the second largest source of health coverage reported (33%), followed by private health insurance (21%) (Commonwealth, 1989; Lacayo, 1980). Even though Medicare is the major mode of access to health care for the Hispanic elderly, less than half of the older Hispanic population has Medicare. For them, increases in Medicare supplemental insurance are formidable due to their overwhelming poverty. The threat of a costly long-term illness is all too real for Hispanic elderly and their families. The fact that Medicare does not cover long-term care services or preventive services such as eyeglasses, hearing aids, and physical checkups presents a major barrier to receipt of these services.

Older Hispanics are also in poorer health than their Anglo counterparts. One measure of this is the number of "disability days" they experience. In 1986, 31.5% of older Hispanics reported being bedridden for 1 to 30 days, compared to 21.9% of elderly Anglos. Moreover, Hispanic elderly also reported averaging 37.0 restricted activity days due to poor health, six more days than aged Anglos. Yet the average number of doctor visits for aged Hispanics (8.0) in that year was less than that for older whites (9.1) (U. S. Department of Health and Human Services, 1986). This last point demonstrates a persistent characteristic of older Hispanics: their underuse of available services.

Language

The survival of Spanish as the language of choice among older Hispanics may be a primary factor in older Hispanics' underutilization of services. Three important reasons Spanish remains the language of choice are: the recent arrival of many of the Hispanics to the United States; living in communities within the United States that are relatively self-sufficient, with Spanish the principal language (a case in point is the proliferation of Spanish mass media); and the proximity of the United States to Mexico. New arrivals and frequent contacts with individuals from Mexico help the Spanish language to maintain itself in the United States. Forty percent of elderly Hispanics speak only Spanish (Commonwealth, 1989; Lacayo, 1980), with a larger percentage reporting difficulties understanding forms written in English. A common belief of U. S. residents, that all immigrants should learn English, ignores the fact that learning a new language may be extremely difficult for an elderly person (Trilla, 1982). This belief can also facilitate discrimination, as individuals may feel that it is unnecessary, expensive, and/or wrong to provide bilingual and bicultural services to those in need.

HEALTH RESEARCH ON OLDER HISPANICS

The lack of quantitative analysis of these issues obstructs the development of an adequate data base that can be used to plan and direct health care programs essential to the older Hispanic (Lopez-Aqueres, Kemp, Staples, & Brummel-Smith, 1984). Few nationwide samplings of older Hispanics, or Hispanics in general, have been done. Many studies have not even considered Hispanics as a separate ethnic group, Hispanics being included in both white and black ethnic categories (Espino, Neufeld, Mulvihill, & Libow, 1988). Studies including a Hispanic ethnic classification often fail to differentiate between the different Hispanic subgroups. This results in an incomplete and often imprecise picture of "Hispanic" needs (Aday, Chiu, & Andersen, 1980; Newton, 1980; Schur, Bernstein, & Berk, 1987). In addition, minority aging research has focused little attention on the issues of multiple causation and intercorrelatedness of variables, including the separate effects due to race or minority-group status from those due to class (poverty).

A fundamental obstacle is the lack of data available from government sources such as the U. S. Census (Eribes & Bradley-Rawls, 1978). Only since 1988 has the U. S. Census Bureau integrated "Spanish origin" into its race categories of "white/black/other." Annual Census reports on Spanish origin population data began only in 1985; however, many of the Census Bureau's reports still do not separate data by Spanish origin.

Empirical data on the health and disease profiles of older Hispanics nationwide is also lacking. The Hispanic Health and Nutrition Examination Survey ("Hispanic HANES") conducted by the Department of Health and Human Services in 1982–1984 yielded one of the first national profiles on Hispanic health. The *Report of the Secretary's Task Force on Black and Minority Health* (U.

S. Department of Health and Human Services, 1985) gave no data specifically related to Hispanic elderly; information reported on disease prevalence and death rates by disease were based on the total Hispanic population, with no age designations.

Formal and Informal Care

Another area of missing data is the extent to which the needs of older Hispanics are being met by current long-term care programs and available public services, including the role the Hispanic's extended family and informal support system plays in furnishing long-term care services. Ethnographic literature has long supported the view that the Hispanic family takes care of its elders. However, more recent findings have presented opposing views of the dynamics and structure of the Mexican-American family. The onslaught of urbanization and industrialization has caused an erosion of what would be considered the "traditional Hispanic family." Lacayo (1980, 1982) found that only 11% of Hispanic elderly lived in extended families situations. This is far below the estimated 50% living in extended family settings in Los Angeles prior to 1950.

Lacayo (1980) found that fewer than 6% of Hispanic families provided financial support to their elder family members. The exorbitant cost of most long-term care is prohibitive for the vast majority of aged Hispanics and their equally poor families. The family can no longer provide the level of services and resources to its elderly members that it once did. Even when such resources are available, the Hispanic elderly may be particularly reluctant to ask for support to avoid burdening their own often impoverished families (Greene & Monahan, 1984).

Greene and Monahan (1984) documented the differences between Tucson Mexican-Americans' use of formal and informal care compared to an Anglo control group. The Mexican-American group showed lower use of formal care (1.81 services vs. 2.72 for the Anglo group) and higher use of informal support (6.14 services versus 3.52). This persisted even though the Hispanic elderly showed more functional impairment, both physically and mentally, at younger ages than their non-Hispanic counterparts (Greene & Monahan, 1984; Lacayo, 1982; Espino et al., 1988). This agrees with the statistical representation of Hispanic typically seen in long-term care. They are the ones who are the most impaired, and who have either overwhelmed their informal supports or have no informal support system (Espino & Burge, 1989).

Additional health research on the Hispanic elderly is crucial. Key areas for study include the demographics of disease among this group; primary types of disabilities; mental health; the economics of illness; and reasons for the reported low use of health services. Comprehensive data are essential for designing or reforming adequate programs to alleviate older Hispanics' income and health difficulties, and for designing health promotion programs to prevent fu-

ture generations of Hispanic elderly from facing the same serious difficulties today's elders suffer.

POLICY ISSUES

Access

Now that we have summarized the barriers (poverty, lack of health insurance,
language, scarce bilingual/bicultural services, fear of deportation, lack of effective outreach, and discrimination) that continue to hamper Hispanic elders' securing long-term care, we will discuss policy issues and program needs that
could help ameliorate this situation.

Changes in the U. S. work force will also greatly affect the availability and
quality of long-term care available to older Hispanics and other elderly Americans in the 1990s and beyond. The number of Hispanic women in the labor
force will grow by 69% (to 2 ½ million) between 1988 and the year 2000, more
than four times the increase in the total working population (U. S. Department
of Labor, 1989). This means fewer family caregivers will be available to provide
long-term care services to Hispanic elderly at home. It is incongruous for our
society to ask the Hispanic family to do what the rest of society does not and
cannot do; that is, to stay home to care for an older family member needing
long-term care. This is an especially unreasonable demand to make of a poor
population, all of whose able members must work to survive. Despite common
misconceptions, the Hispanic elderly do not generally substitute less costly traditional health care, such as use of folk healers (*curanderos*), drinking of herbal
teas, and the like for more costly conventional health care (Andersen et al.,
1981; Greene & Monahan, 1984).

Civil Rights

The middle-class orientation of health care systems, in general, is perceived by
many minority groups to be discriminatory in itself and, hence, contributes
heavily to the alienation felt by the Hispanic patient (Donabedian, 1972;
Strauss, 1969). The perception of discriminatory behaviors may be real or imag-
inary, but this is irrelevant to the issue. It is not the authenticity but the nature
of the perception that ultimately determines service use. The result of this perception? Older Hispanics forgo needed health care.

Stronger civil rights enforcement is required to eradicate the discrimination
against older Hispanics and other elderly minorities on the part of long-term
care facilities. Vigorous civil rights enforcement should be carried into the
nursing home arena, as well as in employment of long-term care workers. This
is one of the key first steps that can be taken to meet the minority elderly's

long-term care needs. Hispanic elderly and other minority elderly will continue to be inequitably served if the doors to congregate care institutions are closed to them.

The continued increase in undocumented immigrants requiring health care who face probable language and money barriers, plus the uncertainty of eligibility and deportation if their status is discovered create additional difficulties in service delivery. Even legal immigrants and native-born residents often have difficulty obtaining services because they don't know about them (Lacayo, 1980). There is evidence to suggest that even with outreach, the "neediest of the needy" are not getting information or services.

Outreach

Speaking little or no English is a primary factor in older Hispanics' lack of knowledge about long-term care options. Lack of Spanish-speaking staff, interpreters, materials, and outreach in Spanish limit the knowledge of, access to, and use of currently available services. Illiteracy (both in Spanish and English) and poverty compound the knowledge problem (Greene & Monahan, 1984). And the conclusion that must be reached is that in order to provide the services needed by older Hispanics, services and outreach must be available in Spanish. Redesigning outreach programs to be culturally sensitive and available in Spanish is imperative. Information and better outreach in Spanish on Social Security benefits, Medicaid, and Medicare, including their eligibility requirements, should help increase the number of Hispanic recipients in the future. Further, information on available community services, such as respite care, nutrition programs, senior centers, and so on needs to be made available in Spanish. Innovative outreach techniques like bilingual radio and television announcements should be utilized. These techniques are especially effective with older Hispanics, for whom radio and TV are the communications media of choice (Lacayo, 1980).

Communication between providers and clients is certainly a precondition to the satisfactory outcome of social services. The language barrier between Spanish-speaking Hispanics and English-speaking health care providers presents an obvious impediment to quality health care services (Greene & Monahan, 1984; Lacayo, 1980; Quesada, 1976). The only future remedy to this problem is to increase the pool of bilingual and bicultural providers (Trilla, 1982; see also the chapters by Hernandez, Capitman, & Yee; and Espino in this volume for additional information on these issues).

Geriatric Education

In California, the state with the largest Hispanic population, only 1.7% of physicians were Hispanic in 1980; the number nationally was around 2.3% (Muñ-

230 Planning, Policy, and Practice

oz, 1988; Root, 1987). These numbers are far below the Hispanic representation in the United States (8.1%) and Californian (23.4%) populations. This trend has not changed appreciably in the last ten years, and is not expected to change much in the 1990s. Although bilingual individuals are available in many health care settings, they are typically relegated to lower status, lower paid jobs, such as nursing aides or orderlies. Insufficient educational programs and lack of adequate professional role models to aid Hispanic students, especially in urban educational systems hamper improvements and increases in Hispanic representation in the health care professions in the near future (Muñoz, 1988). Efforts must be made at all levels of education to assure that Hispanics and other minorities have an equal opportunity to the educational system. Greater attention to promoting geriatric training for Hispanic nurses, physicians, dentist, pharmacists, social workers, dieticians, and other health care service providers is needed. They can add another positive dimension to long-term care, by being more knowledgeable and sympathetic to the bicultural needs of older Hispanics who require long-term care services.

Administrators and planners in particular must be included in this instruction because, as has been indicated in the literature (Santos, 1987), the health care profession is no longer dominated by doctors and other providers but by corporate management-oriented professionals. Part of the current awareness and concern for minority geriatric training stems from the recognition on the part of management and fiscal planners of the link between successful patient rapport and cost effectiveness. With the growth of the Hispanic population in particular, awareness of the Hispanic elderly's needs becomes fiscally imperative, as well as socially justifiable.

Geriatric educators should continue outreach efforts to the Hispanic community. Additionally, transition programs like the Summer Health Careers Programs should be supported for minority students who enter health professions schools and need assistance to improve study habits and science skills. Other suggestions by Hispanic educators include: (1) increased economic aid availability for economically disadvantaged students entering the often expensive health-related educational programs; (2) collaborations among public schools, minority communities, and the medical profession to ensure better academic preparation and a strong interest in the health professions; and (3) continuing education opportunities for minority health professionals to upgrade professional abilities (Acosta, 1987).

Retraining midlife and older workers in health care professions is also crucial to solving the long-term care dilemma. Since 1979 the number of young U. S. workers has been declining. But job participation among people aged 55 or over will rise at a faster rate in the 1990s than that of the overall pool of workers. Between 1988 and 2000 more than two million persons aged 55+ will join the work force (U. S. Department of Labor, 1989). Their experience, stable work histories, high motivation to work, and desire for flexible working hours make them an ideal group for retraining as in-home health aides and for other health occupations. Peer counseling and other kinds of support services by the Hispanic elderly for their peers have proved effective. Peer assistance must play an increasing role in long-term care, because of the aging of the work force in the coming decades.

SUMMARY

Since it is unlikely that the number of Hispanic health care workers will increase significantly soon, the language barrier will continue to be a nationwide problem, especially in areas with large Hispanic populations (Root, 1987). Language and cultural barriers in health care must be given a much greater priority in the service provision to the elderly. Bicultural patient representatives and interpreters of the same ethnic background will help solve part of the problem and remove some of the institutional obstacles to higher quality health care for minority elderly (Quesada, 1976).

Minorities will constitute an ever larger share of the new entrants into the labor force in the 1990s. Immigrants will constitute the largest share of the increase among workers since World War I. Unless this country makes a concerted effort now to improving education for minority youngsters and to training young Hispanics and other minority persons for paraprofessional and skilled health care jobs in aging, the combination of escalating numbers of older people requiring long-term care and a poorly educated work force will be disastrous.

CONCLUSIONS AND RECOMMENDATIONS

As a nation we must develop comprehensive community-based care and alternatives to institutionalization as a more balanced approach to meeting the health needs of the minority elderly and other older Americans. Alternatives are particularly important for the Hispanic community, for whom nursing homes (asilos) are often a dreaded place of last resort when no other health care alternative remains (see Espino in this volume for more detailed information regarding these issues). A comprehensive continuum of long-term care services should be available, including in-home and community-based care for the "at-risk" aged and disabled population. This could be achieved by increasing the federal Medicaid match for these services for at-risk persons if states (1) provide a comprehensive assessment of individuals who probably need long term skilled nursing or intermediate care facility services if in-home or community-based services are not available; (2) provide a wide range of home and community-based services for at risk persons who can continue to remain in their communities; (3) establish reimbursement limits at a rate not exceeding the level for nursing home care; and (4) coordinate long-term care and community-based services with similar services provided under other legislation. Assisting elderly Hispanics to become eligible for hospital insurance such as Medicare or Medicaid, or to enroll in health maintenance organizations, should become a top priority. These actions would enable older Hispanics and other elderly minorities to receive more appropriate long-term care and in-home services.

The lack of alternative community-based long-term care programs that give informal medical and nonmedical services (assistance with activities of daily living) is a persistent problem. Special consideration for the needs of low-income, minority urban and rural older Americans should be taken into account in the design and implementation of such programs. Respite care and home health care, whether available through community agencies, volunteer service groups, hospitals, or nursing homes, will become ever more important as the demographics and employment profiles of younger Hispanics change in the future and the amount and degree of informal care available changes. Ideally, this comprehensive, community-based, long-term care system should be incorporated in a national health insurance program. Government funding of home health care and respite care will need to be introduced to make these services available to the people who need them. Congress must look for ways to improve Medicare to achieve this goal in a fiscally responsible manner.

REFERENCES

Acosta, T. (1987). Retention and articulation: Issues and recommendations for increasing Hispanic representation in the health sciences. A Paper Presented at the Hispanic Health Status Symposium. San Antonio, Texas.

Andersen, R., Lewis, S. Z., Giachello, A. L., Aday, L. A., & Chiu, G. (1981). Access to medical care among the Hispanic population of Southwestern United States. *Journal of Health and Social Behavior, 22*, 78–89.

Aday, L. A., Chiu, G. Y., & Andersen, R. (1980). Methodological issues in health care surveys of the Spanish heritage population. *American Journal of Public Health, 70*, 367–374.

Commonwealth Fund Commission on Elderly People Living Alone. (1989). *Poverty and poor health among elderly Hispanic Americans.* Baltimore: The Commonwealth Fund Commission on Elderly Living Alone.

Donabedian, A. (1972). Models for organizing delivery of personal health services. *Millbank Memorial Fund Quarterly, 50*, 103–154.

Dowd, J. J., & Bengtson, V. L. (1978). Aging in minority populations: An examination of the double jeopardy hypothesis. *Journal of Gerontology, 33*, 427–436.

Eribes, R. A., & Bradley-Rawls, M. (1978). The underutilization of nursing home facilities by Mexican American elderly in the Southwest. *The Gerontologist, 18*, 363–371.

Espino, D. V., & Burge, S. K. (1989). Comparisons of aged Mexican American and non-Hispanic white nursing home residents. *Family Medicine, 21*, 191–194.

Espino, D. V., Neufeld, R. R., Mulvihill, M., & Libow, L. S. (1988). Hispanic and non-Hispanic elderly on admission to the nursing home: A pilot study. *The Gerontologist, 28*, 821–824.

Greene, V. L., & Monahan, D. J. (1984). Comparative utilization of community based long-term care services by Hispanic and Anglo elderly in a case management system. *Journal of Gerontology, 39*, 730–735.

Kurtz, S. (1970). In other Americas: Mexican Americans. *New York Times Encyclopedic Almanac*. New York: Times Book and Educational Division.

Lacayo, C. G. (1980). *A national study to assess the service needs of the Hispanic elderly: Final report*. Los Angeles: Asociacion Nacional Pro Personas Mayores.

Lacayo, C. G. (1982). *A national study of Hispanic support systems and the chronically ill older Hispanic*. Los Angeles: Asociacion Nacional Pro Personas Mayores.

Lopez-Aqueres, W., Kemp, B., Staples, F., & Brummel-Smith, K. (1984). Use of health care services by older hispanics. *Journal of the American Geriatrics Society, 32*, 435–440.

Muñoz, E. (1988). Care for the Hispanic poor: A growing segment of American society. *Journal of the American Medical Association, 260*, 2711–2712.

Newton, F. (1980). Issues in research and service delivery among Mexican American elderly: A concise statement with recommendations. *The Gerontologist, 20*, 208–213.

Quesada, G. M. (1976). Language and communication barriers for health delivery to a minority group. *Social Science and Medicine, 10*, 323–327.

Root, R. K. (1987). Issues in Latino health care. *Western Journal of Medicine, 146*, 213–218.

Santos, R. (1987). Education and employment in the health care industry: A Texas perspective. A paper presented at the Hispanic Health Status Symposium. San Antonio, Texas.

Schur, C. L., Bernstein, A. B., & Berk, M. L. (1987). The importance of distinguishing Hispanic subpopulations in the use of medical care. *Medical Care, 25*, 627–641.

Strauss, A. L. (1969). Medical organization, medical care, and lower income groups. *Social Science and Medicine, 3*, 143–177.

Trilla, F. (1982). The plight of the elderly Puerto Rican. *The Journal of Latin Community Health, 1*, 89–91.

U. S. Department of Commerce, Bureau of the Census. (1988). *United States population estimates by age, sex, and race: 1980 to 1987*. Series P-25, No. 1022. Washington, DC: U. S. Government Printing Office.

U. S. Department of Health and Human Services. (1985). *Report of the Secretary's Task Force on Black and Minority Health*. Vol. I, Executive Summary. Washington, DC: U. S. Government Printing Office.

U. S. Department of Health and Human Services, National Center for Health Statistics. (1986). Current estimates from the National Health Interview Survey. *Vital and Health Statistics*. Series 10, No. 164. Washington, DC: U. S. Government Printing Office.

U. S. Department of Labor, Bureau of Labor Statistics. (1989). New labor force projec-
    tions, spanning 1988 to 2000. *Monthly Labor Review*, *3*, 12. Washington, DC: U.
    S. Government Printing Office.

16

Community-Based, Noninstitutional Long-Term Care Service Utilization by Aged Blacks: Facts and Issues

Cary S. Kart

Recent and current debates over longterm care policies for an aging society have, for the most part, failed to consider the unique lifetime circumstances and special health care needs of blacks and other ethnic minorities (Gibson & Jackson, 1987). This is especially problematic given that the population of black elderly is growing more rapidly than the white elderly population (Siegel & Taeuber, 1986). Increasing numbers of black elderly, with chronic, activity-limiting illnesses, will place burdens on their families and force long-term care service providers to be more sensitive to racial and cultural diversity in the client base than has hitherto been the case.

Very little is known about the use of long-term care services by aged blacks, especially noninstitutional services. Writing in the early 1970s, Butler and Lewis (1973, p. 85) remarked that "it appears that staying out of institutions is not as big a problem for older blacks as is getting into them when they are needed." Analyzing data from 1950, 1960, and 1970 Census subject reports, Kart and Beckham (1976) found that older blacks were overrepresented in state mental hospitals and underrepresented in homes for the aged. They concluded that socioeconomic status and racial discrimination accounted for some of this pattern.

Blacks in general and old blacks in particular are not monolithic. Policymakers, service providers, and researchers must be sensitive to heterogeneity within this as well as other minority aged populations. Much overlooking of diversity or heterogeneity within specific minority aged populations likely results from concern with documenting social inequities between dominant and minority aged (Jackson, 1985). Further, as Wilkinson and King (1987) point out, even when diversity among blacks is acknowledged, it is often perceived as less consequential than their common phenotypic traits or shared group history.

The diversity of experience represented in the age distribution of older blacks cannot be overstated. Each cohort of blacks in the United States has been exposed to different cultural practices and social and political conditions (Greene & Siegler, 1984; Wilson, 1978). As well, people of different ages experience shared historical events differently (Riley, 1971, 1985). A black man who was 85 years of age in 1985 was already completing his work career by the time of the passage of the Civil Rights Act of 1964. Many in the younger cohorts of black aged have benefited from this legislation, however, so that social and economic differentiation is greater among the young-old than the old-old. This trend is likely to continue into the foreseeable future. This chapter highlights the diversity among older blacks in the United States through its very specific focus on the facts and issues involved with long-term care service use in this population.

Recognition of the diversity within the minority aged population should lead us away from the comparisons of double jeopardy and toward a sharper focus on minority aging itself. This sharper focus may help us distinguish those health and illness behaviors that may be explained by individual attributes such as race and sex from those better explained by basic socialstructural and organizational variables such as availability of quality health care and healthprovider patterns.

THE FACTS

The Data Set

The 1984 National Health Interview Survey's (NHIS) Supplement on Aging (SOA) provides a unique opportunity to observe patterns of long-term care (LTC) service utilization among older blacks in cross-sectional perspective. The SOA includes a nationally representative sample of approximately 16,000 adults aged 55 and over who responded to a myriad of demographic, health-status, health-service utilization, and health-belief questions. A subset of the SOA, including all 1,217 blacks, is the focus of this chapter. The median age of blacks in the SOA is 69 years. Almost 60% (59.2%) of the respondents are female and almost 47% (46.6%) are married. On median, black sample respondents have completed eight years of school and have family income between $7,000 and $7,999.

Measures

For our purposes here, long-term care services are defined in the broadest terms to include help given at home by relations, friends, or neighbors or by paid professionals, as well as use of a broad array of community services (in-home or not). Nursing home institutionalization is excluded because only three black respondents in the SOA reported spending time in a nursing home in the 12 months prior to being interviewed. Only 13, or 1.1% admitted *ever* being a patient in a nursing home. Four more black respondents reported being on a wait list for nursing home admission. Use of medical services including doctor visits and shortstay hospitalizations are also excluded from this analysis.

Measures of LTC service use include indicators of receiving help for difficulties in activities of daily living (ADLs such as bathing or showering, dressing, eating, toileting, getting into or out of bed or chairs, walking, and getting outside) or instrumental activities of daily living (IADLs such as meal preparation, shopping, money management, using the telephone, and doing light or heavy housework). Also included are community services tapped by indicators of going to a senior center or using special transportation services, meals delivered at home, special meal programs, homemaker services, telephone check services, visiting nurse service, health aide at home, and adult day care.

Need for LTC Services

The SOA allows us to make a preliminary assessment of the possible need for long-term care services in the black community. On the one hand, the majority of black SOA respondents have no difficulty in carrying out their ADLs or IADLs. Almost 75% (74.3%) report no difficulties in carrying out their activities of daily living; 67.9% report no difficulties in carrying out their instrumental activities of daily living. On the other hand, more than one third (36.6%) of all older blacks report difficulty in carrying out at least one ADL or IADL. And among those 75 years and older, this figure is 52.2%, or almost twice the proportion aged 55 to 64 years (26.9%) reporting difficulty with at least one ADL or IADL.

In each case, the proportion of older black SOA respondents reporting difficulty with an ADL or IADL is greater than the proportion reporting receiving

TABLE 16.1 Proportion of Older Black SOA Respondents Receiving Help with ADLs or IADLs or Utilizing Community and Social Services.

ADLs	Percentage
Bathing	6.2
Dressing	4.9
Eating	0.9
Getting out of bed	2.6
Walking	4.5
Getting outside	5.2
Toileting	2.9

IADLs:	
Preparing meals	7.4
Shopping	12.7
Managing money	5.1
Using the telephone	2.8
Doing heavy work	22.6
Doing light work	7.4

Community and Social Services	
Senior center	11.9
Special transportation	6.7
Meal delivered at home	2.1
Special meals program	7.9
Homemaker services	3.1
Telephone check	0.8
Visiting nurse service	3.6
Health aide at home	1.5
Adult day care	0.1

help. Only in the cases of two IADLs, shopping and heavy work, do more than 10% of older blacks report receiving help (see Table 16.1). Still, about 27% report receiving help with at least one ADL or IADL; this increases to 40.7% among those 75 years of age and older. Also, 11.9% of older blacks report using a senior center, the highest percentage of use of any of the listed community and in-home services (see Table 16.1).

While help received with ADLs and IADLs was broadly defined to include that provided by relatives, friends and neighbors, and paid professionals, most help received was *not* paid. Across all ADLs and IADLs, the median proportion of help received that was paid was 14.5%. Only 6.5% of those receiving help to manage their money paid for that help; 23.8% of those receiving help to get outside also used paid help.

Kart (1990) identified five underlying factors of noninstitutional long-term

TABLE 16.2 Long-term Care Constructs Resulting from Factor Analysis and Factor Correlation Matrix

Factor 1 (ADL Help)		Factor 2 (Community Services)		Factor 3 (Home Health Services)		Factor 4 Home Management Services		Factor 5 (Personal Services)	
Toileting	.910	Special meals program	.895	Home health aide	.892	Heavy work	.703	Telephone	.678
Getting out of bed	.893	Senior center	.874	Visiting nurse	.876	Shopping	.670	Managing money	.659
Getting outside	.777	Special transport	.661			Homemaker services	.602		
Walking	.765								
Bathing	.715								
Dressing	.572								

	Factor	Correlation	Matrix		
	Factor 1	Factor 2	Factor 3	Factor 4	Factor 5
Factor 1	1.000				
Factor 2	.006	1.000			
Factor 3	.318	.065	1.000		
Factor 4	.322	.065	.197	1.000	
Factor 5	.359	−.088	.018	.079	1.000

care, after subjecting the ADL help, IADL help, and community services listed above to a factor analysis. The five factors are ADL Help, Community Services, Home Health Services, Home Management Services, and Personal Services. Table 16.2 shows the factors with items included (those with factor loadings of .50 and above), as well as a correlation matrix of the factors. Five dependent variables were constructed from the five factors with each separately indexed to form a continuum from little or no service or help used to extensive use.

Regression analyses were employed, using independent variables following Andersen and Newman's (1973) health-behavior model, in order to separately identify the strongest correlates of each of the noninstitutional long-term care service constructs. This model, sorting independent variables into those that predisposed an individual to use services, those that enabled the securing of services, and those that indicated need or illness level, is commonly used in research efforts to understand variation in health service utilization among different groups including the elderly (e.g., Bass & Noelker, 1987; Coulton & Frost, 1982). In this case, we employ the model to focus on LTC service use among aged blacks.

Correlates of LTC Service Use

Illness level or so-called need factors dominated the findings. Activity limitation was negatively correlated with ADL Help, and use of Home Health Services, Home Management Services, and Personal Services. Older blacks with
major activity limitations were more likely to report receiving ADL help and to
use home health, home management, and personal services. Also, those who
evaluated their health-status in negative terms were more likely to say they receive help with home management services such as shopping and heavy
housework.

Use of Community Services, including special meals programs, a senior center, and special transportation programs, was noteworthy for the absence of
need factors that help explain variation. Nonmarried individuals, those who
attend church, and individuals who perceive themselves as having little control
over their health were most likely to report use of these community services.

At best, Andersen and Newman's health-behavior model provided varying
utility in the explanation of noninstitutional long-term care service use by
older blacks. It was most efficient for explaining use of Home Management Services ($R^2 = .304$), where predisposing, enabling, and need factors entered the
equation. It was weakest in explaining use of Community Services, Home
Health Services, and Personal Services; in each of these cases explained variance was less than 6%.

THE ISSUES

Generally, not all individuals having difficulty with an ADL or IADL require
help with that activity. As well, no established standard of percentage difference between those with ADL or IADL difficulty and those receiving ADL or
IADL help is available to index a special problem for aged blacks or any other
population for that matter. As was indicated above, 37% of blacks aged 55
years and over reported difficulty with at least one ADL or IADL, while 27%
reported receiving help with at least one ADL or IADL. And for those 75 years
and older, 52% reported difficulty with one ADL or IADL while 41% report
actually receiving such help.

With almost eighty percent of blacks 75 years and older who appear to need
help receiving at least some of it, we might be expected to question the very existence of this problem and not just its scope. On the other hand, we know
very little about the quantity of help received—how frequently and consistently
help is provided, or how many different individuals provide help—or about the
quality of help received.

As described above, we do know that few formal noninstitutional LTC services are being used by aged blacks and most of the help they receive is unpaid.
And as we know from other studies (Gibson & Jackson, 1987; Soldo & Man-

ton, 1985; Taylor & Chatters, 1986), informal support networks in the black community are generally seen as vital and responsive to the changing needs and abilities of household and community members. As one author puts it (Harper, 1990, p. 240):

- Blacks have always cared for the sick at home, yet it was never labeled "home care."
- Blacks have been dying at home and receiving care in the process, yet it was never called "hospice care."
- Blacks have relieved each other from the caring and curing processes, yet it was never seen as "respite care."
- Blacks have cared for each other in their homes, in their neighborhoods, and throughout their communities, yet it was never referred to as "volunteerism."

BARRIERS TO LTC SERVICE USE AMONG AGED BLACKS

Still, barriers to help and help seeking may be social psychological, social structural, and/or physical. From a social psychological orientation, Mechanic (1978) has offered ten determinants of help seeking in an effort to explain variation in response to illness and/or disability. While these determinants include recognizing the salience of symptoms, their seriousness and persistence, as well as the cultural assumptions employed by the evaluator, they can generally be classified into four categories: (1) perception and salience of symptoms that may be determined by sociocultural orientation; (2) disruptive and persistent nature of symptoms; (3) competing needs that allow for reinterpreting observed symptoms; and (4) the availability of treatment resources.

Cultural Barriers

These categories suggest potential barriers to aged blacks in their use of community-based noninstitutional long-term care services. For example, the life experience and culture of aged blacks may provide them with little formal knowledge about disease as well as a skepticism about formal care services. These factors may affect the meaning attached to illness and disability symptoms. In addition, participation in lay referral structures may extend periods of symptom experience and assumption of the sick role and thus extend the time to formal care contacts (Suchman, 1965a,b). As Freidson (1989) points out, one type of lay referral structure is an indigenous, extended system that shows a high degree of resistance to using professional practitioners. This may result from cultural definitions of illness that are at odds with those of the professional culture. According to Freidson, in the United States, members of the lower class are more likely to participate in lay referral structures resembling the indigenous case.

On the other hand, Colen and Soto (1979) identified the importance of "natural leaders" in the community (persons who act as brokers between community members and the larger social service system) in conducting outreach activities. Such individuals, including ministers and other church officials of particular importance in the black community, may help overcome the effects of attitudes toward formal services rooted in slavery, discrimination, and a dual system of health care with one system aimed at upper- and middle-income groups and another geared toward poor and minority groups (Harper, 1990).

Social Structural Barriers

The low median income of older blacks reported in the SOA ($7–7,999) and the high rate of poverty among aged blacks generally (about 31% in 1986) suggests that many in this population group face other needs that can lead to denial of or competition with the need for health and/or community-based long-term care services. Low income reduces the capacity to deal effectively with a host of major concerns including health, housing, transportation, nutrition, and personal safety. And if the choice is between paying the monthly rent and/or putting some food on the table and paying for transportation to the senior center or homemaker services, the former are likely to win out. Women, the nonmarried, the oldest-old, those with fewer years of formal education, and Southerners are particularly vulnerable in this regard (Taylor & Chatters, 1988).

Social Psychological Barriers

While long-term care services may simply not be available in many of the neighborhoods in which aged blacks reside, even where such services are present in the broader community, social psychological as well as bureaucratic and physical barriers may exist. Many older blacks are reluctant to seek or ask for help, especially from a formal service agency. For many, use of such services is a reflection of defeat or powerlessness. Others may have a mistrust of helping professionals. One study notes that blacks drop out of treatment earlier and more frequently than whites because of earlier and negative experiences with helping professionals (Sue, McKinney, Allen, & Hall, 1974). McCaslin (1988) points out that historical cohort experiences may play a role in shaping an older persons' view of help-taking and traditional outreach and education efforts may not be sufficient to change these decision-making patterns.

Many older people have limited knowledge or are simply unaware of the availability of needed services. In her study of knowledge of services for the elderly among a statewide sample of Michigan residents aged 60 and over, Chapelski (1989) found being black to be an inhibiting factor to service awareness. Chapelski speculates that this may reflect or even add to the vulnerable position of elderly blacks in Michigan, where being black is associated with lower education and income, reported physical health problems, mental health problems, increased transportation and neighborhood problems, and fewer available kin. Interestingly, there is a strong interaction effect in this study between race and education; older blacks with higher education were more aware of services to the elderly. In a review of four important studies of service use among community-based elderly, McCaslin (1988) identifies self-perception of service knowledge along with need as the most consistent explainer of variation in service use. As she points out, however, we still do not know very much about the reasons why elderly persons do or do not know about the service system or why they do or do not view formal community-based service programs as particularly meaningful in their lives.

Organizational and Physical Barriers

As Ward (1978) notes, many fail to consider how the bureaucratic nature of service-delivery settings and organizations can serve as a barrier to utilization. Poor management and staffing problems present barriers that make it difficult for many elders to access otherwise available services (Wallace, 1990). In effect, there are "bad" agencies. According to case managers in a Missouri metro area, bad agencies are undependable and provide inadequate care (Wallace, 1990). Wolinsky and his colleagues (Wolinsky, Coe, Miller, Prendergast, Creel, & Chares, 1983; Wolinsky & Arnold, 1989a,b) point out that absent from research have been measures of the characteristics of service delivery systems to which the elderly have access. This may be especially telling in trying to understand the use or nonuse of public benefits by older blacks (Jacobson, 1982) and of social service agencies identified as "white" (Colen, 1982; Dancy, 1977; for more on this issue see Hernandez-Gallegos, Capitman, & Yee in this volume). As Colen (1982, p. 183) points out, there is a tendency "to focus on individual rather than organizational pathologies that often render services inaccessible to elderly minority clients."

Finally, real physical barriers may exist to accessing available services in a community. If the senior center is out of the immediate neighborhood and away from a mass transportation line, it may be available but not accessible. Also, accessing one available service may require several others—with difficult multiplicative arrangements. For example, in order to attend the lunch meal at the nutrition site, Mrs. K., a widow, may require some ADL help with dressing and getting outside as well as transportation service.

SUMMARY AND CONCLUSION

This chapter employs data from the 1984 Supplement on Aging to the National Health Interview Survey to assess the utilization of community-based, noninstitutional long-term care services by aged blacks, and the variation in LTC service use by this population. In addition, an array of issues or "barriers" to LTC utilization by this population group is discussed. While need for LTC services is difficult to assess, generally speaking, in absolute terms, it seems that aged blacks do not utilize a great amount of LTC services. About 27% report receiving help with at least one ADL or IADL, and this increases to about 41% among those 75 years and over. Approximately three of four elderly blacks who report needing help with at least one ADL or IADL receive some such help. Further, only small percentages of aged blacks report using formal community-based and in-home services. Also, factor analysis identifies five different clusters of services used and, while illness-level or need factors dominate, diverse characteristics of the aged black population are useful for explaining variation in service use. In part, this highlights the diversity that exists among elderly blacks.

Among aged blacks, barriers to help seeking, use of informal help from relatives, neighbors, and friends, and awareness and utilization of formal services may be social psychological, social structural, and/or organizational or physical. In attempting to remove or overcome such barriers, policymakers and program directors must take care not to offer disincentive to continuation of the strong reliance by many elderly blacks on family and extended kin. New programs or policies ought to supplement and not substitute for the importance to many of the extended family system.

The SOA data employed in this analysis is cross sectional in nature. Given that those aged presently institutionalized were excluded, the sample was biased toward better health and functioning. No doubt, prior to institutionalization, many of the institutionalized black elderly excluded from the SOA were utilizers of community and in-home formal and informal LTC services. A longitudinal study will be required to pick up these experiences, identify the causal ordering among correlates of long-term care service factors, and disentangle the relationships among use of community and home-based LTC services, health-status, and institutionalization.

Finally, Andersen and his colleagues (Aday, Andersen, & Fleming, 1980; Aday, Fleming, & Andersen, 1984) have used the health-behavior model to assess the equitable nature of the health-delivery system. They employ evidence that utilization appears to be primarily a function of need to conclude that equitable access to health care exists. Others disagree (Berki et al., 1985; Mechanic, 1985). Following Wolinsky et al. (1983), this author suggests that until more is known about why people use community and home-based long-term care services, it is premature to declare the health-care delivery system generally and the long-term care system specifically to be equitable.

REFERENCES

Aday, L. A., Andersen, R. M., & Fleming, G. V. (1980). *Health care in the U. S.: Equitable for whom?* Beverly Hills: Sage Publications.

Aday, L. A., Fleming, G. V., & Andersen, R. M. (1984). *Access to healthcare in the U. S.: Who has it, who doesn't.* Chicago: Pluribus Press.

Andersen, R. M., & Newman, J. (1973). Societal and individual determinants of medical care utilization in the United States. *Milbank Memorial Fund Quarterly, 51,* 95–124.

Bass, D. M., & Noelker, L. S. (1987). The influence of family caregivers on elder's use of in-home services. *Journal of Health and Social Behavior, 28,* 184–196.

Berki, S. E., Wyszewianski, L., Lichtenstein, R., Gomotty, P., Bowlyow, J., Papke, E., Crane, S., & Bromberg, J. (1985). Health insurance coverage of the aged. *Medical Care, 23,* 847–854.

Butler, R. N., & Lewis, M. I. (1973). *Aging and mental health.* St. Louis, MO: C. V. Mosby..

Chapelski, E. E. (1989). Determinants of knowledge of services to the elderly: Are strong ties enabling or inhibiting. *The Gerontologist, 29,* 539–545.

Colen, J. N. (1982). Using natural helping networks in social service delivery systems. In R. C. Manuel (Ed.), *Minority aging: Sociological and social psychological issues.* Westport, CT: Greenwood Press.

Colen, J. N., Soto, D. (1979). *Service delivery to aged minorities: Techniques of successful programs.* California State University.

Coulton, C., & Frost, A. (1982). Use of social and health services by the elderly. *Journal of Health and Social Behavior, 23,* 330–339.

Dancy, J. (1977). *The black elderly: A guide for practitioners.* Ann Arbor, MI: Institute of Gerontology, University of Michigan–Wayne State University.

Friedson, E. (1989). Client control and medical practice. In E. Freidson (Ed.), *Medical work in America: Essays on health care.* New Haven, CT: Yale University Press.

Gibson, R. C., & Jackson, J. S. (1987). The health, physical functioning, and informal supports of the black elderly. *The Milbank Quarterly, 65* (Suppl. 2), 421–454.

Greene, R. L., & Siegler, I. C. (1984). Blacks. In E. Palmore (Ed.), *Handbook on the aged in the United States.* Westport, CT: Greenwood Press.

Harper, B. C. O. (1990). Blacks and the health care delivery system: Challenges and prospects. In S. Logan, E. M. Freeman, & R. G. McRoy (Eds.), *Social work practice with black families.* New York: Longman.

Jackson, J. J. (1985). Race, national origin, ethnicity, and aging. In R. H. Binstock, & E. Shanas (Eds.), *Handbook of aging and the social sciences* (2nd ed.). New York: Van Nostrand Reinhold.

Jacobson, S. G. (1982). Equity in the use of public benefits by minority elderly. In R. C. Manuel (Ed.), *Minority aging: Sociological and social psychological issues.* Westport, CT: Greenwood Press.

Kart, C. S. (1990). Variation in long-term care service utilization by aged blacks: Data from the SOA. Paper presented at annual meeting of The North Central Sociological Association, Louisville, KY, March 22.

Kart, C. S., & Beckham, B. L. (1976). Black–white differentials in the institutionalization of the elderly: A temporal analysis. *Social Forces, 54,* 901–910.

McCaslin, R. (1988). Reframing research on service use among the elderly: An analysis of recent findings. *The Gerontologist, 28,* 592–599.

Mechanic, D. (1978). *Medical sociology: A comprehensive text.* New York: Free Press.

Mechanic, D. (1985). Cost containment and the quality of medical care: Rationing strategies in an era of constrained resources. *Milbank Memorial Fund Quarterly, 63,* 453475.

Riley, M. W. (1971). Social gerontology and the age stratification of society. *The Gerontologist, 11,* 79–87.

Riley, M. W. (1985). Age strata in social systems. In R. H. Binstock, & E. Shanas (Eds.), *Handbook of aging and the social sciences* (2nd ed.). New York: Van Nostrand Reinhold.

Siegel, J. S., & Taeuber, C. M. (1986). Demographic perspectives on the long-lived society. *Daedalus, 115,* 77–118.

Soldo, B., & Manton, K. (1985). Changes in the health status and service needs of the oldest old. *Milbank Memorial Fund Quarterly, 63,* 286–323.

Suchman, E. (1965a). Social patterns of illness and medical care. *Journal of Health and Human Behavior, 6,* 2–16.

Suchman, E. (1965b). Stages of illness and medical care. *Journal of Health and Human Behavior, 6,* 114–128.

Sue, S., McKinney, H., Allen, D., & Hall, J. (1974). Delivery of community mental health services to black and white clients. *Journal of Consulting and Clinical Psychology, 42,* 794–801.

Taylor, R. J., & Chatters, L. M. (1988). Correlates of education, income, and poverty among aged blacks. *The Gerontologist, 28,* 435–441.

Wallace, S. P. (1990). The nocare zone: Availability, accessibility, and acceptability in communitybased long-term care. *The Gerontologist, 30,* 254–261.

Ward, R. (1978). Services for older people: An integrated framework for research. *Journal of Health and Social Behavior, 18,* 61–70.

Wilkinson, D. Y., & King, G. (1987). Conceptual and methodological issues in the use of race as a variable: Policy implications. *The Milbank Quarterly, 65* (Suppl. 1), 56–71.

Wilson, W. J. (1978). *The declining significance of race: Blacks and changing American institutions.* Chicago: University of Chicago Press.

Wolinsky, F. D., & Arnold, C. L. (1989a). A birth cohort analysis of dental contact among elderly Americans. *American Journal of Public Health, 79,* 47–51.

Wolinsky, F. D., & Arnold, C. L. (1989b). *Health and illness behavior among elderly Americans.* Detroit: Wayne State University Press.

Wolinsky, F. D., Coe, R. M., Miller, D. K., Prendergast, J. M., Creel, M. J., and Chavez, N. (1983). Health services utilization among the noninstitutionalized elderly. *Journal of Health and Social Behavior, 24,* 325–337.

17

Economic, Health, and Service Use Policies: Implications for Long-Term Care of Ethnic Elderly

Roosevelt Wright, Jr.
Charles H. Mindel

The projected increases in the ethnic minority older population (as detailed in the editor's introductory chapter), along with expected increases in the number of ethnic minority elderly surviving into the upper age ranges (75+ years), are creating concerns about the nature and extent of long-term care services that ought to be provided to them. Since the 75+ population is one of the fastest growing age groups among the minority elderly and since more and more of them will have extensive long-term care needs, especially in view of their greater prevalence of chronic conditions and declining health, it can be expected that there will be increasing demands and utilization of all types of human services and, ultimately, increasing expenditures out of public funds.

Few would deny the fact that we are living in a period in which governmental fiscal austerity and a pervasive mood of conservatism toward formal human services prevails. In this connection, serious issues are being raised about the degree to which our piecemeal system of long-term care can effectively meet the needs of the ethnic minority elderly (Federal Council on the Aging, 1979; Wright, Saleebey, Watts, & Lecca, 1983). Not only are many of the long-term care needs of the ethnic minority elderly not being adequately addressed, but in many cases, current policies and programs, at all levels of government, work against the best interest and well-being of these elderly. Like older people in general, the ethnic minority elderly face formidable challenges to their survival and day-to-day existence. But, unlike most white elderly, their most fundamental problems (i.e., inadequate incomes, inadequate health care, poor and inadequate housing, limited access to needed social services, etc.) are all too often intensified by their ethnic minority status. Admittedly, many of our nation's elderly spend the last years of their lives in environments characterized by poverty, inadequate access to needed human services, poor housing, isolation and loneliness, and so on. However, the likelihood of being in such an environment increases dramatically for elderly members of ethnic and cultural minority groups. For many of these older people, the factors that have contributed to a lifetime of economic, social, and psychological deprivation and anguish are exacerbated in old age.

Three issue areas dominate the current debate over the future direction of long-term care policies for the ethnic minority elderly: (1) economic issues, (2) health issues, and (3) utilization of services issues. These issues will be addressed by examining the critical factors that affect the ethnic minority elderly and are common, for the most part, to each group with respect to national public policy.

ECONOMIC ISSUES

With the possible exception of the Japanese elderly, members of other ethnic minority groups suffer from greater economic hardships and distress than do the white elderly. Monetary statistics (i.e., income figures) are the usual measure by which to judge the older population's financial situation. In this connection, available statistical evidence indicates that, as a group, the ethnic minority elderly have substantially lower money incomes than their white counterparts (U. S. Bureau of the Census, 1987). In 1986, for example, the median income of black elderly males ($6,757) was 56% of white elderly males ($12,131), and that of Hispanic elderly males ($7,369) was 61% of white older males. A similar picture emerges for black and Hispanic females. The median income of black women age 65+ ($4,508) was 67% of white older females ($6,738) and that of Hispanic females of the same age ($4,583) was 68% of white elderly females (U. S. Senate Special Committee on Aging, 1988).

As we would expect, poverty rates (which use real income as their primary measure) are substantially higher among the ethnic minority elderly than among the white elderly. To illustrate, in 1986, the United States Bureau of the

Census (1987) reported that the poverty rate among black elderly (31%) was nearly triple, and among Hispanic elderly (22.5%) more than double the poverty rate among white elderly (10.7%). Forty-eight percent of all black older persons and 33% of older Hispanics had money incomes below 125% of the poverty level (the poor and near poor) compared to about 18.3% of older whites.

The ethnic minority elderly population, as a whole, has a higher poverty rate than the general population of elderly, but some discrete subgroups within this population have even higher poverty rates. For example, the subgroups that have been growing most rapidly among the ethnic elderly (i.e., ethnic minority women, single elderly, those who live alone, and the old-old) have poverty rates well above the average for all older ethnic minority people. In 1986, over half of elderly black women (59.8%) and older Hispanic women (55.1%) not living with families had incomes below the poverty level. Furthermore, nearly two of every three (64%) black elderly women who lived alone and were 75 years of age or older were poor. In addition, other subgroups with high poverty rates within the ethnic minority older population include people who did not work in the previous year, residents of nonmetropolitan areas, residents of poverty areas in large cities, widows, people with little formal education, the ill, disabled, or frail, and those who rely on Social Security as their sole source of expendable income (U. S. Senate Special Committee on Aging, 1988).

With regard to types of income that the ethnic minority elderly have available to them, there are differences between them and the white elderly population. For example, in separate analyses of black men and women, Stokesberry (1985) noted that 39% of black elderly women received Supplemental Security Income (SSI) in addition to Old Age Survivors and Disability Insurance (OASDI) and income from continued employment after age 65. Among black elderly males 27% were receiving SSI, indicating that their OASDI payments obviously were so low that they were also entitled to SSI. For elderly white males, however, only 12% were receiving SSI and only 11% of white elderly females were receiving SSI. The three major sources of income for elderly blacks (and for other ethnic minority groups), whether they were living alone or in a family situation, were, in order, OASDI, earnings from employment, and SSI. For the white elderly who were living alone, the three major sources of income were OASDI, dividends, and pension incomes; and for the white elderly who were living in a family situation, the three main sources of income were OASDI, dividends, and earnings from outside employment.

Almost all of the ethnic minority elderly have some access to Social Security and Medicare. The poorest among them may also be eligible for income-tested programs in the form of SSI, Medicaid, Food Stamps, and housing subsidies. A relatively small number of the ethnic elderly have private pensions and health insurance to complement their Social Security and Medicare benefits. A much smaller segment of the group have some personal financial assets that generate significant income to help meet their needs. This combination of income and assets, for the most part, meets the needs of many older ethnic minority elderly, but far too many are still left in financial poverty. If it were not for Social Security benefits nearly 60% of the ethnic minority aged would live in poverty. Despite the rising standards and economic security of the elderly in the aggregate, a large group of ethnic minority elderly lack adequate resources to meet basic housing, food, and health care needs—a situation that is absolutely deplorable in a society that is as economically and socially affluent as ours.

Without doubt, inadequate resources is an obvious and unfortunate reality of life for a large number of ethnic minority aged. As the different subgroups among the ethnic minority elderly population age in the years ahead, their plight and economic conditions are only going to become worse. Yet, as a nation, we have not developed workable and efficient policies and programs to cope with their long-term care needs and problems. Long-term care initiatives to improve the basic income support of older ethnic minorities, especially those that are destitute and impoverished, must be developed.

HEALTH ISSUES

According to Liang (1986), there are three major conceptualizations and measurements of physical health in social gerontology. First, the physical definition or medical model of health conceptualizes health as a residual category defined by the absence of disease. The presence of a disease is determined by the symptoms reported by the patient and signs detected by observation, examination, and laboratory tests. Second, the social definition of health or the functional model views physical health as a state of optimum capacity for the performance of roles and tasks. The functional model of physical health has been operationalized in terms of mobility, self-maintenance, role performance, and disability. The third approach focuses on the subjective evaluation of physical health or the psychological model. According to the psychological model, physical health rating is the individual's perception and evaluation of his or her overall physical health.

Literature on the health of older Americans from a variety of ethnic and racial groups consistently portrays the Japanese elderly as exceptionally healthy and vigorously more active than their other elderly counterparts including whites (Gordon, 1967; Kiefer, 1974). Age-specific or age-adjusted morbidity and mortality rates are generally lower among the Japanese elderly than the white elderly, and many specific disease and illness rates are significantly reduced. Thus, the literature indicates that health status is not a special problem for the vast majority of Japanese elderly. On the other hand, the literature clearly indicates that on virtually every indicator of health (i.e., morbidity and mortality rates, life expectancy, functional health, and psychological health), the health status of all other ethnic minority elderly groups consistently ranks well below that of the white elderly. For example, Markides and Mindel (1987) note that the ethnic minority elderly were expected to live an average of 69.2 years in 1978, 4.8 years less than the white elderly. More recent statistics, however, indicate that at age 65, ethnic minorities could expect to live 15.5 more years, 1.3 years less than whites at that age (National Center for Health Statistics, 1986). In relative terms, white life expectancy at age 65 is about 8% higher than ethnic minority life expectancy (U. S. Senate Special Committee on Aging, 1988).

Mortality (i.e., cause of death) data indicates that heart disease was the major cause of death among the elderly in 1950. This is still the case today, even though there have been rapid declines in death rates from heart disease since 1968, especially among elderly males. Death rates from cancer, however, continue to rise in comparison to heart disease, especially deaths caused by lung cancer (National Center for Health Statistics, 1984, 1986, 1987). Cerebrovascular diseases (strokes), the third leading cause of death among the elderly, have been decreasing over the past 30 years. Recent mortality data show that the six leading causes of death among the elderly are (in rank order): diseases of the heart (especially ischemic heart disease), malignant neoplasms, cerebrovascular diseases, chronic obstructive pulmonary diseases, pneumonia and influenza, and diabetes (National Center for Health Statistics, 1986, 1987). Although these conditions are the most prevalent health problems for all elderly persons, there is some evidence to suggest that they are disproportionately higher, in terms of their prevalence and incidence, among the elderly in ethnic minority groups (Markides & Mindel, 1987; McNeely & Colen, 1983; U. S. Senate Special Committee on Aging, 1988). It should be noted, however, that available data indicate that racial or ethnic group membership per se does not appear to be the determining factor in explaining differences in the health status of the ethnic minority and white elderly (a similar point is made regarding the use of social services among ethnic minorities by Wood and Wan in this volume). Rather, as Morrison (1983:162) notes: "it is the disproportionate representation of minority aged in the lower socioeconomic strata that appear to explain much of the variance in health status . . . ." Additionally, as in the areas of morbidity, mortality, and life expectancy, the ethnic minority elderly are consistently more disadvantaged on a variety of functional health indicators (i.e., subjective health status, limitation of activity, restricted activity days, bed disability days, etc.) than are the white elderly (Markides & Mindel, 1987; McNeely & Colen, 1983; Soldo & DaVita, 1977).

UTILIZATION OF SERVICE ISSUES

The array of services developed as a consequence of long-term care legislation has been frequently targeted at certain needy populations as well as the general population of the elderly. Key questions are: How successful have these programs been in reaching elderly who are members of certain ethnic minority groups? Do ethnic minority elderly use services to the same degree that majority elderly do? And if not, what are the factors influencing utilization?

Since the 1970s a considerable amount of research has been accomplished examining the utilization patterns of health and social services by the elderly. The predominant model for assessing the use of health and social services was pioneered by the work of Andersen and Newman (1973), who examined the utilization of health services in terms of predisposing factors, enabling factors, and need factors. Ward (1977) suggested that the Andersen and Newman model of utilization be tested out on older, low-income, and ethnic minority populations to see if differential patterns of use of social services existed. A number of studies have shown in fact that different patterns of use do exist by ethnic group. Ralston and Griggs (1980) found that for older blacks (in contrast to whites) different patterns of use of services existed when sex, marital status, education, homeownership, and length of residence were taken into account. In general, it has been found that many of the same predisposing factors that influence the majority of the elderly's use of health and social services also affect minority elderly's use of health and social services (see Andersen & Aday, 1978; Andersen & Newman, 1973; Haug, 1981; Hershey, Luft, & Glanaris, 1975; Mindel & Wright, 1982; Rundall & Wheeler, 1979; Starrett, 1983; Wolinsky , 1978; Wright, Creecy, & Berg, 1979).

An area that has been identified as important in determining the use of services is family factors. Certain consistent findings concerning the ethnic minority elderly are their close ties with their families. Many references have been found regarding the importance of the ethnic family in caring for the needs of their elderly members (see, for example, Bell, Kasschau, & Zellman, 1976; Cantor, 1979; Mindel, Habenstein, & Wright, 1988; Valle & Mendoza, 1978). A somewhat contrary view of the relationship of the elderly to their family has been offered by other writers (see Wood and Wan and Lacayo in this volume). For example, Gallego (1980) and Jackson (1980) have argued that statements about how ethnic groups "take care of their own" are often based on cultural myths. They argue that this myth have been historically invoked as an excuse for not providing services to ethnic elderly. They maintain that the ethnic family may provide certain services to their members, but this serves to excuse the formal system from making services appropriately available to these individuals.

Formal versus Informal Systems

This issue raises the larger matter of the role of the informal system vis-à-vis the formal support system in the care of the elderly. A closer examination of the actual way in which the informal system relates to the formal system of support has been the source of considerable research. Mindel and Wright (1982) in a study comparing the black elderly to white elderly in a probability sample from Cleveland, Ohio, identified an important role for the informal family support system among the black elderly as contrasted to the white elderly. Among the black elderly, they found a causal link between the use of formal services and contact with the informal kinship group, a link not found among the white elderly. This relationship suggested that the aid to the elderly by the family is supplemental to the seeking of help from institutional sources. The family system or informal support system provides certain kinds of services for elderly family members, but there is also a strong reliance on the formal system for assistance in certain other areas such as health care, nursing services, and financial aid. Moreover, it has also been found that the informal support system, particularly the family, has been an important source of information regarding availability of formally provided social services and health care services. The family is frequently the first source of care that the elderly turn to. If the family can provide the care, it often will. However, it also often acts as an information and referral source (Ciccerilli, 1981). In this connection, Starrett, Mindel, and Wright (1983) in a study of over 1,800 Hispanic elderly found that the knowledge and awareness of the availability of services was crucial to the utilization of such services and that this awareness was most frequently provided by other family members. Additionally, Mindel, Wright, and Starrett (1986) examined the actual expenditures on social and health care services by black and white elderly and found that the formal and informal systems actually act in a complementary manner.

Underutilization of health and social services with respect to the ethnic elderly have also been found to be related to language and cultural differences (see for example, Lee, 1960; Sue & Kitano, 1973; Valle & Mendoza, 1978). Clearly a continuing role for the children of the ethnic minority elderly will be that of intermediaries between the formal system of services and their aged parents. The extent to which the younger generation ethnic group members are willing and able to provide for their elderly parents is a debatable matter. However, a willingness to help in the roles of intermediary, broker, and advocate may well be increasingly common among these groups.

Barriers to Service Utilization

An important issue in the utilization of services by minority elderly concerns the barriers that stand in the way of effective use. Guttman (1980) found that minority group membership was a significant factor in the under- and nonutilization of public human service programs (see also Lacayo, in this volume). Difficulties with procedures, eligibility requirements, and lack of knowledge of the existence of benefits and programs are identified as significant causes of low levels of use. In addition, many elderly members of minority groups have been reluctant to participate in social programs. For example, Watson, Well, Hargett, and King (1981) found that many elderly black individuals feared a loss in social security benefits if they participated in Area Agency on Aging programs. Bell et al. (1976) described similar factors when they examined why ethnic minority elderly failed to apply for benefits. It has been noted by many researchers that effective delivery of services to ethnic minority elderly requires a conscious effort to be responsive to the cultural uniqueness of their ethnic populations. When program staff reflect the ethnic background of their elderly clientele including being bilingual, the utilization of human service programs is positively affected (Bell et al., 1976; Wright et al., 1983; Wylie, 1971; for more on this issue see Hernandez, Capitman, & Yee in this volume).

Increasing Utilization of Services

Difficulties in access to services for the ethnic minority elderly tend to fall into two broad categories. The first category concerns issues in cultural awareness, while the second category concerns issues regarding the use of support systems, including the family and local community resources.

It has been suggested that ethnic considerations should be a part of the design and delivery of all health care and social service programs. Age-specific programs must take into account the cultural uniqueness of the older groups they are to serve at the time of their design and in the development of the procedures for the implementation of the program (McCaslin & Calvert, 1975). It has often been noted that the cultural perspective of the policymakers, planners, and service providers often differ substantially from that of the service recipients in that the "experts'" perceptions of the world are shaped by their own social and cultural milieus, which are frequently different from those they are planning to serve (Colen, 1983; McConnell & Davis, 1977; Riesenfeld, Newcomer, Berlant, & Dempsey, 1972). Other studies have found that the involvement of the black elderly in the design and establishment of their own services has been an effective means of securing utilization of services (Sainer, Schwartz, & Jackson, 1973). Colen and Soto (1979) in their study of aging Mexican- and Native American elderly found similar results. It was strongly recommended that cultural values and practices, such as food preferences, relationships between males and females, sex roles, and language differences, be considered and planned for if programs are to be useful. When potential recipients of service have input and are active participants in the program planning and development process, the resulting programs are more successful than when they are simply presented to a group. Sensitivity with respect to cultural differences that exist are crucial for programs to be successful.

In addition to the need for ethnic cultural influence in the design of helping programs, it is also important that services be delivered in such a way that the dignity of the recipient is preserved (Stanford, 1977; White, 1977). The incorporation of cultural practices into the actual delivery of service [regardless of the type(s) of service] should be an accepted practice. For example, many ethnic minority groups have strict definitions of where and when men and women should interact with one another, with the marital status of the individuals being an important factor (Barresi, 1987). To design activities and/or programs that violate these cultural norms is to show disrespect for the individuals and their culture. With a genuine sensitivity to the cultural practices of the client or client group, no matter how "strange" or "old fashioned" these might seem, a program is much more likely to be successful and appealing.

The second major area regarding access to services concerns the role of the informal support system in providing access and reducing barriers to formal service utilization by the ethnic elderly. Family members, friends, and neighbors can often identify persons at risk, determine culturally appropriate help seeking behavior, and be a resource themselves in the provision of services (Barber, Cook, & Ackerman, 1980; Erikson, 1975; Gallego, 1980; Safier & Pfouts, 1979; Staples, 1976). Research has shown that the informal ethnic support network is not necessarily an alternative to the formal support system, but depending on the family and ethnic group, a complement and/or supplement to it (see for example, Mindel & Wright, 1982; Mindel et al., 1986). The family frequently serves as facilitator, linking the elderly to the "system." If practitioners are seriously interested in serving the ethnic minority elderly, they need to understand the place of the family in the helping process. Aguilar (1972) and Vontress (1976) described the importance of the climate of trust that needs to develop between practitioners and clients and their families, including the need to be cognizant of the cultural roles of various family members and cultural styles of communication, both verbal and nonverbal.

In addition to the use of the family and friendship network, it has been suggested that the use of ethnic community resources including churches, minority newspapers, community centers, neighborhood organizations, and social clubs might be useful in securing participation in important long-term care programs and services. The common denominator in these alternative resources is that they are all indigenous cultural institutions that exist in the ethnic community. Knowledge of the ethnic community and an identification of the indigenous institutions will provide channels to the ethnic minority elderly that would otherwise be untapped.

GOVERNMENT POLICY FORMATION AND LONG-TERM CARE FOR MINORITY ELDERLY

Federal long-term care policy has been reflected in two important areas: in the public arena, where representatives of competing interest groups have come together to debate and exchange positions on the needs of the elderly, and in the legislative arena, where many of these publicly debated ideas reach the status of law. The dynamic political processes that have occurred in these two arenas has resulted in significant and monumental changes in government policies toward the elderly in general and, more importantly, toward the ethnic minority elderly.

Historically, important developments and changes in policy have often come as a response to the several White House Conferences on Aging that have been held in 1961, 1971, and 1981. These conferences, which have brought together representatives of the various consumers and providers of services to the elderly, have been critical in mobilizing and crystallizing attitudes toward programs for the elderly. They have reflected, in part, the consciousness of the times, but they have also provided important ideas and opportunities for development of policy. The first White House Conference in 1961 occurred just prior to the period of intense legislative activity in the area of civil rights, health, and education. The enactment of the 1965 Older Americans Act was in part an outcome of the activities of this conference, as was the passage of Medicare and Medicaid. The first White House Conference began the process of moving toward a national social policy on aging. The second White House Conference in 1971 attempted to identify important areas of need and means through which actions could be taken to address important needs. It is also important to note that it was at the 1971 White House Conference that representatives of ethnic minority elderly began to assert themselves and to request special consideration in light of the particular conditions of life that they endured. As a result, specific recommendations were made in what was referred to as "special concerns," one of which concerned ethnic minority elderly.

The special concerns section on *The Elderly Among the Minorities* contained 153 specific recommendations and numerous other suggestions and commentary concerning the special needs of Asian, Hispanic, Black and Native American elderly (White House Conference on Aging, 1971). Some of these recommendations included guaranteed annual incomes, expansion of the Medicare program, in particular the need to fund health and home based services for elderly who did not require hospitalization, and the need for more culturally sensitive health care services. It was felt that there was an underutilization of health care services by many minority and ethnic elderly due to the insensitivity of the dominant culture's service delivery personnel (who are generally middle-class Anglos) to the culture of the ethnic elderly client. Recommendations that more age-specfic and culturally sensitive programs be developed was strongly urged.

As a result, during the 1970s it was found that ethnic cultural elements became a meaningful part of many of the public programs and services provided to the ethnic minority elderly. For example, there was more hiring by the government in Social Security district offices of ethnic minority service delivery personnel, including bilingual staff. In addition, program benefits and eligibility materials began to be translated into Spanish and other ethnic languages. Advocacy groups began to pressure state and local governments to develop senior centers and other services for Chinese, Japanese, Puerto Rican, and other ethnic groups. Local Area Agencies on Aging began to become more sensitive to the ethnic dimension in their senior centers.

The 1981 White House Conference on Aging was disappointing from an ethnic minority standpoint. In particular, minority and ethnic elderly were not given the special status they had in the 1971 Conference, and none of the committees of this conference was directly charged with the concerns of minority elderly.

Beginning in the 1980s the direction in public policy toward the ethnic minority elderly (as well as the aged population in general) began to shift. The federal government began to move away from vigorous enforcement of much of the civil rights law, and the notion of "set-asides" for targeting and preferential treatment for ethnic and other minorities began to disappear or to be considered less important. The notion that the federal government or the state government was the party primarily responsible for the needs of the elderly began to shift in a direction of families and voluntary groups, corporations, and other individuals, who were now expected to take the lead in caring for older persons.

The expansion of federal benefits and programs for the elderly ended owing to budget deficits, and the government use of race, gender, and ethnicity in determining where and how human services would be placed disappeared. In fact, the 1980s was a period of serious federal fiscal retrenchment and scaling back. As Torres-Gil (1987, p. 250) has stated:

> during the 1980s those aging programs that were universal and were not means tested carried popular support. Social Security, Medicare, and the Older Americans Act maintained their basic structure and benefits although some of their benefits were scaled back and greater costs were placed on beneficiaries. On the other hand programs that were means tested and targeted toward low income elderly took deeper cuts during this period. Food stamps, low income energy subsidies, Section 202 and Section 8 housing supports were all drastically affected by cutbacks. Medicaid programs in many states were either frozen or reduced. Those programs that disproportionately aided low income (and hence minority) elderly, were scaled back at the very time when they were in great demand because of the increase of poverty among minority elderly.

LONG-TERM CARE LEGISLATION

At the federal level, programs created for long-term care of the elderly and particularly the ethnic minority elderly, have been affected through several very important pieces of legislation. Two of the most important, the Social Security

Act of 1935, with its various expansions and amendments over the last 50 years, and the Older Americans Act of 1965 and its amendments, are discussed in detail below.

Since its enactment in 1935, the Social Security Act has been amended and expanded in both its breadth and depth of coverage. In 1965 the Medicare (Title 18) and Medicaid (Title 19) provisions were added as amendments to the Social Security Act. In 1974 the Supplemental Security Income (SSI) program under Title 16 of the Social Security Act was implemented. This program replaced the older means-tested programs of welfare to the aged, blind, and disabled. In terms of long-term care, the addition to the Social Security Act of the Medicare and Medicaid programs in 1965 have been crucial. Medicare provides medical coverage for the elderly, covering most hospital and physician expenses. Medicaid has been an especially important program for many ethnic minorities. It is a cooperative federal/state medical assistance program for the needy and poor, many of whom are ethnic minority elderly.

Whereas Medicare is a program of entitlement based on participation in Social Security, Medicaid is a welfare program in which eligibility based on need must be shown. The range of services covered under Medicaid is considerably broader than that of Medicare. For example, Medicaid covers inpatient hospital services as well as outpatient hospital services, physician services, prescription drugs, X-ray, and skilled nursing home services. While states are required to provide the above, they can at their own option offer additional benefits under this program, including home health care and private nursing services, dental care, hearing aids, eye glasses, mental hospital care, and prostheses.

The benchmark legislation of the 1960s and the one that directly attempted to create a national social policy for the elderly was the Older Americans Act. This Act was initially passed in 1965 and amended in 1967, 1969, 1972, 1973, 1975, and finally in 1978 The Older Americans Act declared broad objectives concerning the responsibility of the government to assist older people. The various amendments both realigned and consolidated various programs and structures and expanded services toward particular populations. The Act also created an Administration on Aging to oversee the programs it had created. The Older Americans Act has funded, among other things, nutritious meal services to elderly, transportation services, and various other community and social services. In addition, it has provided and served as a planning and research arm of the federal government in the areas of long-term care to the elderly.

Social Support for the Minority Elderly

The dominant approach to the long-term care of the ethnic minority elderly in recent years has been what is termed the "social services strategy." Behind this approach is the idea that aging, especially among ethnic groups, is a process of progressive dependency and incapacity. Thus government policy should aim to alleviate or postpone this dependency and to enhance the social integration of the elderly, their morale, and their adjustment to old age. Clearly the issue of increasing dependency is one of the dominant themes that organized many of the health care and social service programs that are currently available to the ethnic aged. Consequently, a large number of innovative health and social service programs have been created over the past 20 years. These have included home health services such as nursing, physical therapy, occupational therapy, speech therapy, medical/social services, home health aid, homemaker services, and medical supplies. Additionally, two nutrition programs were added: congregate meals at a centrally located nutrition sites and the Meals on Wheels program through which meals are delivered directly to the individual's home. Both were funded primarily through the Older Americans Act. Many of the traditional social services such as casework and psychotherapy, as well as assistance given through local community mental health centers, crisis intervention services, self-help groups organized within various clubs and organizations for the elderly including senior centers, telephone reassurance, and friendly visiting programs, were also developed. Although these programs were perhaps not developed explicitly for ethnic elderly, they did target many of the unmet needs of the ethnic minority elderly—needs caused by the higher likelihood of disadvantaged socioeconomic status associated with ethnic minority group membership.

CONCLUSION AND RECOMMENDATIONS

This discussion has examined long-term care policies as they have affected the ethnic elderly. Economic issues, health issues, and issues concerning the utilization of services developed to deal with these policies have been discussed.

Economically, the ethnic minority elderly continue to have substantially higher poverty rates than the general population of elderly. For those above 75 years of age, problems are especially severe. Similarly, it was shown that on every indicator of health status, morbidity, mortality, and life expectancy, ethnic minority elderly rank well below the general population of elderly. The problems that these issues detail have led in turn over the past generation to a series of important legislative initiatives, in part sparked by the advocacy of key groups and individuals. This legislation, especially crucial amendments to the Social Security Act, including Medicare and Medicaid, and the enactment and amendment of the Older Americans Act have led to a wide range of potential solutions to the needs of the elderly and of the ethnic elderly in particular. However, it has been found that in spite of the development of many services and programs, the needs of this population continue to remain unmet in many cases.

Future social policies to address the many unmet needs of the ethnic minority aged must be directed toward the dual goals of developing specific program initiatives for improving their basic income levels and enhancing their accessibility to adequate long-term care health and social services. These goals can be accomplished, in part, if the following policy options and program modifications are seriously considered and, ultimately, implemented:

1. expanding OASDI program coverage and simultaneously increasing cash benefit levels to the minimum poverty levels,
2. developing new or innovative cost-control measures and providing additional monetary support for the Medicare and Medicaid health insurance systems,
3. using Federal government subsidies to encourage the development and spread of private industry long-term care insurance as well as targeted subsidies to help the destitute ethnic minority aged to purchase private insurance,
4. increasing SSI benefits to assure, at the very least, poverty-level incomes for those ethnic minority elderly without other sources of income,
5. eliminating or easing restrictive limits on income and liquid assests in order to qualify for SSI and Medicaid,
6. expanding Medicaid coverage to all uninsured ethnic elderly persons who are poor and categorically ineligible for cash assistance,
7. developing more effective outreach programs to increase participation of the ethnic minority aged in existing human service programs, especially the SSI and Medicaid programs,
8. improving the organization and coordination of both public and private sector acute- and long-term care services and benefits for the ethnic minority aged.

The solutions proposed above to meeting the long-term care needs of large segments of the ethnic minority elderly are complex, multifaceted, and elusive, but they are readily attainable. They will require, however, a reemphasis and rededication by the political sector to finding the tax revenues and other resources necessary to support these changes. In times of increasing budget deficits and scarce resources such as are being experienced in the 1990s one has to be cautious in predicting a successful outcome in the near future.

REFERENCES

Aguilar, I. (1972). Initial contacts with Mexican American families. *Social Work, 17,* 66–70.

Andersen, R., & Aday, L. A. (1978). Access to medical care in the United States: Realized and potential. *Medical Care, 16,* 533–546.

Andersen, R., & Newman, J. F. (1973). Societal and individual determinants of medical care utilization in the United States. *Milbank Memorial Fund Quarterly, 51,* 95–124.

Barber, C., Cook, A., & Ackerman, A. (1980). *Attitudes of Navajo youth toward supporting aged parents.* Paper presented at the annual meeting of the Gerontological Society of America, San Diego, CA.

Barresi, C. M. (1987). Ethnic aging and the life course. In D. E. Gelfand & C. M. Barresi (Eds.), *Ethnic dimensions of aging* (pp 18–34). New York: Springer Publishing Co.

Bell, D., Kasschau, P., & Zellman, G. (1976). *Delivering services to elderly members of minority groups: A critical review of the literature.* Santa Monica, CA: Rand.

Cantor, M. H. (1979). The informal support system of New York's inner city elderly: Is ethnicity a factor? In D. E. Gelfand & A. J. Kutzik (Eds.), *Ethnicity and aging: Theory, research, policy* (pp. 153–174). New York: Springer Publishing Co.

Ciccerilli, V. (1981). *Helping elderly parents.* Boston: Auburn House.

Colen, J. N. (1983). Facilitating service delivery to the minority aged. In R. L. McNeely & J. N. Colen (Eds.), *Aging in minority groups.* Newbury Park, CA: Sage.

Colen, J. N., & Soto, D. (1979). *Service delivery to aged minorities: Techniques of successful programs.* Sacramento: California State University.

Erikson, G. (1975). The concept of personal network in clinical practice. *Family Process, 14,* 487–498.

Federal Council on the Aging. (1979). *Policy issues concerning the elderly minorities: A staff report.* DHHS Pub. No. (OHDS) 80-20670, U. S. Department of Health and Human Services. Washington, DC: U. S. Government Printing Office.

Gallego, D. (1980). *The Mexican American elderly: Familial and friendship support system . . . fact or fiction.* Paper presented at the annual meeting of the Gerontological Society of America, San Diego, CA.

Gordon, T. (1967). Further mortality experience among Japanese Americans. *Public Health Reports, 82,* 973–984.

Guttman, D. (1980). *Perspective in equitable share in public benefits by minority elderly: Executive summary.* DHHS/ADA Grant No. 90-A-1617. Washington, DC: Catholic University of America.

Haug, M. (1981). Age and medical care utilization patterns. *Journal of Gerontology, 36,* 103–111.

Hershey, J. C., Luft, H. S., & Glanaris, J. (1975). Making sense out of utilization data. *Medical Care, 13,* 838–854.

Jackson, J. J. (1980). *Minorities and aging.* Belmont, CA: Wadsworth.

Kiefer, C. W. (1974). *Changing cultures, changing lives: An ethnographic study of three generations of Japanese Americans.* San Francisco: Jossey-Bass.

Liang, J. (1986). Self-reported physical health among aged adults. *Journal of Gerontology, 41,* 248–260.

Lee, R. H. (1960). *The Chinese in the United States.* Hong Kong: Hong Kong University.

Markides, K. S., & Mindel, C. H. (1987). *Aging and ethnicity.* Newbury Park, CA: Sage.

McConnell, S., & Davis, W. (1977). *Social and cultural contexts of aging: Decisionmaker survey report.* Los Angeles: University of Southern California, Andrus Gerontology Center.

McNeely, R. L., & Colen, J. L. (1983). *Aging in minority groups*. Newbury Park, CA: Sage.

Mindel, C. H., & Wright, R. (1982). The use of social services by black and white elderly: The role of social support systems. *Journal of Gerontological Social Work, 4,* 107-126.

Mindel, C. H., Habenstein, R. W., & Wright, Jr., R. (1988). *Ethnic families in America: Patterns and variations*. New York: Elsevier.

Mindel, C. H., Wright, R., & Starrett, R. (1986). Informal and formal social and health service use by black and white elderly: A comparative cost approach. *The Gerontologist, 26,* 279-285.

Morrison, B. J. (1983). Physical health and the minority aged. In R. L. McNeely & J. L. Colen (Eds.), *Aging in minority groups*. Newbury Park, CA: Sage.

National Center for Health Statistics. (1984). *Health indicators for Hispanic, black, and white Americans*. Vital and Health Statistics, Series 10, No. 148. Washington, DC: U. S. Government Printing Office.

National Center for Health Statistics. (1986). *Health, United States, 1986*. DHHS Pub. No. (PHS) 87-1232. Department of Health and Human Services. Washington, DC: U. S. Government Printing Office.

National Center for Health Statistics. (1987). *Vital Statistics of the United States, 1984*. Vol. 11, Section 6 (Lifetables). Washington, DC: U. S. Government Printing Office.

Ralston, P. A., & Griggs, M. B. (1980). Factors affecting participation in senior centers: Race, sex, socio-economic differences. *Journal of Minority Aging, 5,* 209-217.

Riesenfeld, M. J., Newcomer, R. J., Berlant, P. V., & Dempsey, W. A. (1972). Perceptions of public service needs: The urban elderly and the public agency. *The Gerontologist, 12,* 185-190.

Rundall, T. G., & Wheeler, J. R. C. (1979). The effect of income on use of preventive care: An evaluation of alternative explanations. *Journal of Health and Social Behavior, 20,* 397-406.

Safier, E., & Pfouts, J. (1979). *Social network analysis: A new tool for understanding individual and family functioning*. Paper presented at the annual meeting of the Council on Social Work Education, Boston, MA.

Sainer, J. S., Schwartz, L. L., & Jackson, T. G. (1973). Steps in the development of a comprehensive service delivery system for the elderly. *The Gerontologist, 13,* 98.

Soldo, B. J., & DaVita, C. (1977). *Profiles of the black aged*. Washington, DC: Center for Population Studies, Georgetown University.

Stanford, E. P. (1977). *Comprehensive service delivery systems for the minority aged*. San Diego: University Center on Aging, San Diego State University.

Staples, R. (1976). *Introduction to black sociology*. New York: McGraw-Hill.

Starrett, R. A. (1983). *The utilization of social services by the Hispanic elderly population*. Unpublished doctoral dissertation, University of Texas at Arlington.

Starrett, R. A., Mindel, C. H., & Wright, R. (1983). Influence of support systems on the use of social services by the Hispanic elderly. *Social Work Research and Abstracts, 19,* 35-40.

Stokesberry, J. (1985). New policy issues in black aging: A state and national perspective. *Journal of Applied Gerontology, 4,* 28-34.

Sue, S., & Kitano, H. H. L. (1973). Asian Americans: A success story? *Journal of Social Issues, 2,* 1–209.

Torres-Gil, F. (1987). Aging in an ethnic society: Policy issues for aging among minority groups. In D. E. Gelfand & C. M. Barresi (Eds.), *Ethnic dimensions of aging.* New York: Springer Publishing Co.

U. S. Bureau of the Census. (1987). *Current population reports. Series P-25, No. 1000* (February 1987). Washington, DC: U. S. Government Printing Office.

U. S. Senate Special Committee on Aging. (1988). *Aging America: Trends and projections.* Washington, DC: U. S. Government Printing Office.

Valle, R., & Mendoza, L. (1978). *The elderly Latino.* San Diego: Campanile Press.

Vontress, C. E. (1976). Counseling middle-aged and aging cultural minorities. *Personnel and Guidance Journal, 55,* 132–135.

Ward, R. A. (1977). Services for older people: An integrated framework for research. *Journal of Health and Social Behavior, 18,* 61–70.

Watson, W., Well, R., Hargett, S., & King, S. W. (1981). *Study of minority elderly utilization of social services in the Commonwealth of Pennsylvania.* Washington, DC: National Caucus on Black Aging.

White, E. H. (1977). Giving care to minority patients. *Nursing Clinics of North America, 12,* 27–40.

White House Conference on Aging. (1971). Toward a national policy on aging. Final Report, Vol. 11. *Proceedings of the 1971 White House Conference on Aging,* Washington, DC: U. S. Government Printing Office.

Wolinsky, F. D. (1978). Assessing the effects of predisposing, enabling, and illness morbidity characteristics on health service utilization. *Journal of Health and Social Behavior, 19,* 384–396.

Wright, R., Creecy, R. F., & Berg, W. E. (1979). The black elderly and their use of health care services: A causal analysis. *Journal of Gerontological Social Work, 2,* 11–28.

Wright, R., Saleebey, D., Watts, T., & Lecca, P. (1983). *Transcultural perspectives in the human services: Organizational issues and trends.* Springfield, IL: Charles C. Thomas.

Wylie, F. M. (1971). Attitudes toward aging and the aged among Black Americans: Some historical perspectives. *Aging and Human Development, 2,* 66–70.

18

Ethnic Seniors' Preferences for Long-Term Care Services and Financing: A Case for an Informed Choice

Donald E. Stull

Something seems amiss if the predominant form of long-term care is inconsistent with the preferences of its clients and the public. (Kane & Kane, 1987, p. 357)

This powerful statement captures quite well one of the ironies in the development, expansion, and funding of long-term care services. Kane and Kane point out further that available evidence, though scant, strongly suggests that the development of long-term care services is not consistent with the personal preferences of the elderly and their families. We can assume that this is also true for ethnic elderly, however, research on long-term care preferences for different ethnic groups is virtually nonexistent.

This study was conducted under the auspices of the Fellowship Program in Applied Gerontology of the Gerontological Society of America and jointly funded by the the Cleveland Foundation and the Federation for Community Planning through its William C. and Elizabeth M. Treuhaft Chair for Health Planning.

Research has shown that elders prefer to remain in the community when possible and avoid entering a nursing home (e.g., American Assiciation of Retired Persons, 1984; Kulys, 1983). Most (80%) of the older respondents interviewed in the American Association of Retired Persons (AARP) 1984 study preferred home health services to living in a nursing home. Currently, many initiatives and programs are being developed around the country that attempt to delay or prevent nursing home placement of older persons by substituting less expensive community-based home services. These programs, which often use Medicaid 2176 waivers to purchase community-based home care services, are generally targeted to low-income elderly as a response to the large amount of federal and state Medicaid dollars spent on nursing home care. This leaves a large portion of the older population without these same opportunities to obtain community-based long-term care services.

Much of the development of long-term care services appears to be done from the top down, often with financing a main concern. Indeed, more salient questions in developing, implementing, and expanding long-term care services include: What are the most cost-effective services, and what services are reimbursable? One of the problems with this top-down approach is that it ignores the preferences of the elderly and their families about long-term care services, as well as their ability and willingness to pay for those services. Thus, development of services as well as funding and reimbursement methods often do not take into account the particular circumstances of the consumer, except at the most aggregate level, through such means as service use, as reported in the National Health Interview Surveys.

The purpose of this chapter is to present information derived from an urban sample on: (1) their current use and anticipated need for long-term health and social services, (2) their preferences for various long-term health and social services, (3) their ability to pay for the services, and (4) their willingness to purchase insurance that covers many long-term care services not normally covered by Medicare. Information regarding ability to pay and willingness to purchase insurance that covers long-term care services is relevant to preferences. If the ability and willingness of seniors to pay coincides with their preferences for programs or services, then a much stronger case can be made for developing or expanding long-term care services plus ways to finance them.

The study was conducted in Cleveland, Ohio, an ethnically diverse midwestern city, as part of a larger study of ethnic diversity in health and impairment, service use, Medicare knowledge, and health and long-term care financing. The sample includes whites, blacks, and Hispanics. Findings for the total sample will be presented, followed by differences between the three groups for each of the above dimensions. A key assertion of this chapter, as noted in many of the other chapters in this volume, is that consideration of the ethnicity of elders is critical to appropriate long-term care planning, policy, and practice. Focusing on the aggregate level of data masks many important differences between the three ethnic groups compared in this chapter. These differences would suggest varying strategies for planning, implementing, and financing long-term care services for different ethnic groups.

METHODS

Sample

The data were collected from seniors in the Greater Cleveland area as part of the Gerontological Society of America's Fellowship Program in Applied Gerontology in the summer of 1987. Cleveland has been the site of several large-scale surveys on health and service use over the last several decades, including the "Study of Older People in Cleveland, Ohio, 1975, 1976" conducted by the Government Accounting Office (GAO) (also see Coulton & Frost, 1982), and a 1984 re-interview of surviving seniors from the original 1975 GAO study (Ford, Folmar, Salmon, Medalie, Roy, & Galazka, 1988).

The ability to assess the level of use of (and potential need for) services and to develop good consumer education programs (a focus of the original study from which these data come) required that a reasonably representative sample of elderly, 60 years of age and older, be obtained. Cost considerations, however, ruled out a strict probability sampling. Census tracts were randomly selected within the Cleveland SMSA. Several different sources of respondents were then arbitrarily solicited, one from each selected census tract: (1) clients of community-based services (such as senior centers, nutrition sites, neighborhood centers, local offices on aging, and agencies providing home care for homebound frail elderly), (2) senior adult education programs at two community colleges, (3) members of local ethnic organizations, and (4) patients at an Alzheimer's clinic who were not too impaired to participate.

Every attempt was made to obtain a proportionately representative sample of black and white elders. To achieve this, two senior/neighborhood centers with predominantly black clients were selected. Hispanics were oversampled from an Hispanic senior center to obtain a large enough sample for comparison with the other two ethnic groups.

In general, the questionnaires were self-administered, except for clients who were incapable of completing them on their own (e.g., those with impaired vision, arthritis, Alzheimer's or other dementia); these were completed by caregivers or other close relatives. One agency, the Hispanic Senior Center, had the questionnaire translated into Spanish to facilitate the data collection. In that way, the instrument was translated only once, guaranteeing consistency of questions and answer choices, and speeding up the process of data collection. A total of 1,647 questionnaires were sent out for completion.

Measures

Respondents were asked how many times in the past six months they had used each of 28 health and social services listed (e.g., hospital, physician, nursing home, senior center, group meals, home delivered meals, chore/homemaker services, visiting nurse, senior transportation, foot care, physical therapy in a hospital, physical therapy at home). A separate set of questions for the same list of services asked respondents to indicate how likely it was (very unlikely, somewhat unlikely, somewhat likely, very likely) that they would use each service in the future. In addition, they were asked if they would be willing to pay for insurance that included coverage of each service.

Another set of health and social service use questions asked respondents how important (not at all important, somewhat important, very important) they found a number of features of health care services and medical coverage. The purpose of these questions was to get at the relative importance of traditional features of health care and medical coverage (e.g., fee-for-service, choosing your own doctor, seeing the same doctor every time) and alternative health care coverage and service delivery (e.g., a single fee and use the facilities as often as needed, having a variety of medical and long-term care services covered by the insurance). These questions were modeled after questions used by Ward and Bryant (1986).

Respondents were asked whether they had purchased Medicare supplemental insurance (medigap). If respondents indicated that they had purchased such a policy, they were asked how many policies they had purchased, how much per month they cost, why they bought them, and whether or not they were satisfied with the coverage of the policy (policies). Respondents were also asked what health insurance, if any, they currently had.

In addition to these questions, respondents were asked an extensive set of questions about their health, chronic illnesses, and functional ability. Along with these health measures, information on basic demographic and background characteristics was elicited. For the purposes of this chapter, these health measures and demographic questions allow us to compare our sample with other, nationally representative samples.

RESULTS

A total of 1,016 completed questionnaires were returned. Thirteen of these were completed by people under the age of 60 (the lower limit for inclusion in the study). This left 1,003 usable questionnaires for analyses. Of the respondents, 83% are white, 13% are black, and 4% are Hispanic. Only 10% of the Hispanic seniors speak English.

The average age of the sample is 71. In many ways, the sample is nearly identical to older persons in the population. For example, fewer than 25% of the respondents indicate that they needed help with any of the seven personal care tasks, and fewer than one-third reported needing help with any of the five instrumental activities of daily living. This is in line with findings from nationally representative samples (National Center for Health Statistics, 1987a). Use of health and social services is similar to that of nationally representative samples. For example, the five most commonly used services were physician, senior center, eye care, dental care, and group meals. National data indicate that use of senior centers and senior center meals (group meals) were the highest among the community-based services examined (National Center for Health Statistics, 1986).The sample reflects the economic and ethnic diversity of the Greater Cleveland area. Representation of black and white elderly in the sample is close to population proportions for Cleveland and the surrounding county. The representation of blacks is somewhat higher for this sample, compared to national figures (13% vs. 8% respectively; U. S. Bureau of the Census, 1987). Representation of Hispanic elderly in the sample is higher than population proportions for Cleveland, but close to national figures. Median education for this sample is in line with national figures. However, the proportion who graduated from high school is about half the national figure. Incomes for this sample tend to be lower than those reported in national samples. According to census data, about 13% of all persons 65+ are below poverty level. In this sample 25% of persons 65+ are below the poverty level.

In general, characteristics of the sample indicate that these seniors are very similar to seniors nationally, with three exceptions: (1) a larger proportion of this sample is black, (2) these seniors are not as well educated, and (3) they have a lower median income than seniors nationally. These differences are likely the result of the greater ethnic diversity and the economic history of Cleveland.

Seniors' Current Use and Anticipated Need for, Long-Term Health and Social Services

Respondents report using an average of four health or social services during the previous six months. The four most commonly used services were physician (72% used physician services in the previous six months), senior center (45% used them), dental care (35%), and eye care (34%). The next most utilized services were group meals (27% used them), foot care (26%), public transportation (25%), hospital (23%), senior information (23%), and health clinic (22%).

At first, it was thought that the somewhat high use of senior centers and group meals is partly a reflection of half the sample coming from senior centers and neighborhood centers. However, as noted above, national data (National Center for Health Statistics, 1986) indicate that utilization rates of senior centers and senior center meals (group meals) were the highest among the community and in-home services examined.

There are some interesting racial differences in service utilization. In general, Hispanics use more services and use them more often than either whites or blacks (an average of eight services vs. four and five, respectively). The greater use of health services on the part of Hispanics in this sample may be due, in part, to their poorer functional health. They also have higher rates of social and long-term care service use, suggesting that they not only have knowledge of, but access to, these services. Black respondents tend to have higher rates of health and social service utilization than white respondents. While we can only speculate, it may be that the black and Hispanic respondents in this study, who came primarily from senior centers, are already tied into the network of social services. These people may have a better idea of the services available to them and how to gain access to those services. Unfortunately, since most research on service use among seniors does not disaggregate results by race, it is unclear if the higher rates of service use among the nonwhites in this sample is reflective of service use among nonwhites in the general population.

Respondents were also asked about the likelihood of using those same health and social services in the future. Not surprisingly, medical services (hospital and physician) are the services with the greatest likelihood of being used. Nearly three-fourths indicate that it is likely that they will use these services in the future. Over half of the respondents report that it is likely that they will use other medical-related services, such as eye care, foot care, and dental care. Fifty-nine percent indicate that it is likely that they will use senior transportation, and 48% report that they will probably use senior centers in the future. Interestingly, about one-third report that it is likely that they will use long-term care services in the home (e.g., chore/homemaker service, home health aide, visiting nurse).

Despite the fact that Hispanics report higher use of hospitals than either blacks or whites (53% have used a hospital in the past six months vs. 28% and 20%, respectively), they indicate only slightly higher levels of expected use than do whites (77% of Hispanics expect to use the services vs. 72% of white elderly) and slightly lower levels of use than blacks (83% expect to use the service). They consider it more likely that they will use a health clinic than either blacks or whites (80% vs. 69% and 43%, respectively). Hispanic respondents, compared with black and white respondents, also feel that it is more likely that they will use a nursing home at some time in the future (50% versus 35% and 31%, respectively). Similar patterns exist for use of mental hospital and mental health clinic. In general, Hispanic respondents indicate a higher likelihood of service use than either blacks or whites.

Seniors' Preferences for Long-Term Health and Social Services

Respondents were asked to indicate how important nine features of health care services and medical coverage were to them: Seeing the same doctor every time, being able to choose the doctor who treats you, receiving all health care at a single place, paying one monthly fee and using the medical facilties as often as you need, paying only for the services you use, having nursing home care paid for by your insurance, having your insurance pay for health services provided in your home, having dental care paid for by your insurance, and having social services (such as counseling for you or your family; senior transportation) paid for by your insurance. This question was a variation of one used by Ward and Bryant (1986) in their study of HMO enrollment. Not surprisingly, all respondents consider these features important. In fact, with the exception of two features (single fee and social services paid for by insurance), the majority of respondents indicate that the features are very important.

Realizing that this approach to understanding the relative importance of these features could raise some problems, in particular, treating this list as a "wish list," a second question was used. This question was also modeled after one used by Ward and Bryant (1986). Respondents were asked to rank the three most important features from the list of nine features.

A number of interesting findings come out of this question. The most important feature is "seeing the same doctor every time." The second most important feature is "being able to choose your own doctor." It is clear that having a "family doctor" is important, and that it is important to choose this physician. In terms of potential HMO or Social/HMO enrollment, these findings are not necessarily bad news. If the choice of physician is up to the client, and the client is able to see that physician every time, he/she may be willing to join an HMO or a Social/HMO.

The third most important feature is "having nursing home care paid for by your insurance." This is very useful information in light of current concerns about financing long-term care. People are clearly concerned about the coverage. The fact that it is exceeded in importance only by physician characteristics indicates the central importance this feature has. This information should be of interest to the insurance industry and developers of SHMOs.

There are some substantial ethnic differences in ratings of importance of the features. For example, Hispanics consider it much more important than blacks or whites to see the same doctor. Seventy-five percent of Hispanics consider this the most important feature of health care and medical coverage versus 48% and 40% for blacks and whites, respectively. In fact, they are more concerned about that than being able to choose their own doctor. Blacks report a greater importance attached to seeing the same doctor compared to whites, while at the same time they report a lower importance attached to being able to choose their own doctor (17% vs. 23%, respectively, chose this as the most important feature).

Ability to Pay for the Services

Respondents were asked how they paid for hospital stays and visits to a physician. The majority (86%) of hospital stays were paid for by Medicare, with another large proportion (56%) paid for by private insurance. Many respondents use both sources to cover the costs of hospital stays. Fifteen percent report that Medicaid paid for hospital stays; 17% indicate that they paid for hospital stays with their own money; 12% report that their visits were paid for by a Health Maintenance Organization (HMO).

Visits to a physician show somewhat different methods of payment. Medicare was used in the majority of cases (70%), with private insurance used in 50% of the cases. A sizable number (34%) paid for visits to a physician with their own money. Only 9% used Medicaid, while 13% said that their HMO paid for the visits.

A substantial proportion (41%) of the respondents report that they have purchased medigap policies. This figure is somewhat lower than that of other research. For example, one study found that 59% of persons 65+ with Medicare also had private insurance (Health Insurance Association of America, 1984). In the present study, if we look only at those seniors with Medicare, the percentage with Medicap policies increases slightly to 43%. Of those that have purchased such a policy, 85% have purchased one policy, and 14% have purchased two policies. Over half (56%) are paying $50 a month or more for those policies. Forty-four percent are paying $60 a month or more. Several respondents wrote in the amount they pay for their policies. The amounts were as high as $147.50 every two months, or about $74 per month.

The reasons for purchasing these policies are varied. Slightly over half (53%) say they are afraid of using up their savings in a medical emergency. Nearly three-fourths (73%) are afraid of the high cost of medical care. Over one-fourth (27%) report that they are afraid of losing their home in a medical emergency. Seven percent indicate that a relative recommended that they purchase such a policy.

Over three-fourths (76%) of those who purchased a medigap policy say they have used the policy. Of those that used it, 25% are not satisfied with the coverage of their policies, and 75% are satisfied. Interestingly, 44% are only somewhat satisfied with the coverage of their policies.

There are some significant ethnic differences in medigap purchase and experience. Blacks are much less likely than either whites or Hispanics to have purchased medigap policies (25% vs. 43% and 43%, respectively). They are also much more likely to have purchased less expensive policies. Hispanic respondents report different reasons from the other groups for purchasing medigap policies. For example, they less often express fear of using up their savings or of losing their home in a medical emergency. However, they more often have purchased a medigap policy because a relative recommended that they buy one. White respondents are the most likely to have used their policies, followed by blacks and then Hispanics. Hispanics tend to be more satisfied with the coverage of their policies than either blacks or whites.

Willingness to Purchase Insurance That Covers Many Long-Term Care Services Not Normally Covered by Medicare

Respondents were asked whether they would be willing to purchase insurance that provides coverage for the various health, social, and long-term care services discussed earlier. Nearly two-thirds (63%) say they would purchase insurance that provides coverage of nursing home care; 44% would purchase insurance that covers chore/homemaker services; 56% would purchase insurance that covers visiting nurse; and 50% would purchase insurance that coveres home health aide.

On average, then, at least *half* of the respondents to this question are willing to purchase insurance that includes coverage of long-term care services. This indicates a rather large potential market for insurance that provides this coverage—coverage that for the most part is not provided by Medicare. The other side of the issue, however, raises the question of whether the 41% who purchased medigap policies did so with the mistaken understanding that long-term care services are covered. Unfortunately, there are no data to substantiate this assumption. In addition to this question, seniors were asked how much they would be willing to pay to have financial protection for long-term care. *One-fourth* of the seniors indicate a willingess to pay $40 per month or more for long-term care coverage.

White and black elderly in the sample indicate a greater willingness than Hispanics to purchase insurance that covered the long-term care services mentioned above. For example, 87% of Hispanic elderly versus 36% of white and 35% of black elderly report that they would not purchase insurance that covered nursing home care. Similarly, 92% of Hispanics versus 58% of whites and 37% of blacks stated that they would not purchase insurance the covered chore/homemaker services. None of the Hispanic elderly reported a willingess to purchase insurance that covered visiting nurse services or home health aide.

There is great variation by ethnic group in response to the question asking about how much they would be willing to pay for long-term care coverage. Twenty-seven percent of white elderly indicate a willingess to pay $40 per month or more for such coverage, with 24% replying that they would not pay anything for such coverage. Thirteen percent of black seniors responded that they would pay $40 per month or more for long-term care coverage, with 19% indicating that they would not pay anything for such coverage. Only 6% of Hispanic seniors would pay $40 per month or more for long-term care coverage. Nearly half (49%) would not pay anything for such coverage. For all three groups, the modal response was that they were willing to pay $10 per month for long-term care coverage.

DISCUSSION

One important finding from this study is that ethnic groups cannot be combined when looking at preferences for long-term care services and financing. Each of the three major ethnic groups sampled was substantially different from the others on these dimensions. Indeed, if the standard white/nonwhite comparison had been performed, as is often the case with government reports, the distinctions between black and Hispanic elderly would have been masked. The consequence could be inadequate planning, implementation, and financing of long-term care services for one of these groups, while for another the implementation and financing could be more than sufficient.

Data on the utilization of health and social services indicates that none of the services go unused by seniors. Each of the 28 services listed have been used by about 1% of the sample or more. Use of senior centers and group meals was highest of all services examined. This is congruent with national data. With one in four seniors reporting having used a senior center at least once during the past six months, the data indicate a reasonably strong need for that service. While these data showed relatively high utilization rates for some services for the total sample, there were substantial variations by ethnicity. Clearly, health related services (physician, hospital, health clinic, eye care, foot care, and dental care) are important and show relatively high utilization rates.

Interest in Purchase of Long-Term Care Insurance

An important issue for development or expansion of long-term care services and their financing concerns the interest seniors have in purchasing insurance that covers long-term care, such as nursing home care, visiting nurse, home health aide, and chore/homemaker services. Since nursing home care is the most costly of these services, we will focus on that. Nearly two-thirds (63%) of the seniors indicate that they would purchase insurance that included coverage of nursing home care. This indicates a large market for insurance policies that actually cover this care, and a large number of potential customers for a Social/HMO or some form of community-based long-term care (e.g., "Nursing Homes Without Walls," Lombardi, 1991).

Those interested in developing community-based long-term care programs, or alternative delivery and financing systems such as SHMOs, or at least looking more closely at the feasibility of such an organization can take this as one good indicator of interest among seniors. Insurance companies considering long-term care insurance could also use this as a good indicator of interest and ability to afford such policies: *one-fourth of these seniors indicate a willingness to pay $40 per month or more for such protection.* This could be an important opportunity for a public–private partnership. Through expanded Medicare and Medicaid coverage, perhaps along with private insurance, a large proportion of seniors could receive long-term care and remain in their homes, the preference of seniors and the government.

These seniors, regardless of ethnicity, report that having long-term care services (nursing home and home health care) is important. Moreover, we know that the amount these seniors are paying for medigap insurance falls in the range of current costs for such programs as SHMOs. For example, according to Leutz and his colleagues (Leutz, Abrahams, Greenlick, Kane, & Prottas, 1988), the monthly premium for the four demonstration sites for SHMOs ranges from $29 to $47. Over 75% of the seniors who have purchased medigap policies in this sample could pay for the coverage provided in a SHMO instead of purchasing medigap, and they would be purchasing long-term care coverage at the same time.

Interestingly, the Hispanic elderly in this sample are more likely than either black or white elderly to expect to use a nursing home sometime in the future. At the same time, Hispanic elderly are the least willing to purchase insurance that covers nursing home care. They are, however, similar to white elderly in the purchase of medigap insurance. Could it be that they believe their medigap policies will cover the costs of nursing home care? In other data from this study reported elsewhere (Stull, 1987) Hispanic elderly had the poorest knowledge of Medicare coverage. It may be, then, that a belief that Medicare and medigap policies will cover nursing home and other long-term care leaves Hispanic elderly with a false sense that long-term care will be financially covered.

Black elderly were somewhat more likely than white elderly to anticipate using a nursing home. This is in contrast to actual utilization rates for nursing homes (National Center for Health Statistics, 1987b; also see Wood & Wan and Kart, in this volume). National data have shown that blacks have lower nursing home utilization rates than whites—14% versus 23%, respectively. In addition, the 1982 National Long-Term Care Survey found that a higher proportion of blacks and other nonwhite elderly were functionally impaired and still living in the community.

IMPLICATIONS FOR LONG-TERM CARE

There are several implications of these findings for the development, expansion, and financing of long-term care services and programs. Each of these requires special considerations for ethnicity.

First, education regarding Medicare and medigap coverage is needed. Medicare is a complex program of entitlements, purchased coverage, deductibles, and copayments. Many seniors, unfortunately, believe that Medicare covers long-term care, including nursing home care. In fact, many seniors often think that Medicare and Medicaid are the same. Added to this issue is the complexity of medigap policies, each of which has its own special qualifications and reimbursement methods. Some states, such as California and Ohio, have implemented medigap education programs that try to educate seniors about features, and pitfalls, to consider when purchasing medigap insurance. These programs also require some discussion of Medicare coverage. Such educational programs should be expanded, with special consideration for seniors who do not speak English or ethnic communities that may not establish strong ties outside of their own communities. For example, use of community leaders to gain entree into ethnic communities and lend credibility to the education programs is one way to establish such programs in these communities. Moreover, conducting these programs at churches and neighborhood centers lends credibility and makes them more accessible. Announcing Medicare and medigap programs in foreign-language newspapers and church newsletters will often reach the seniors themselves or their relatives.

Second, there is a need for development and expansion of community-based long-term care programs. This is not a new idea; scholars and practitioners have been addressing this issue for years. However, a greater emphasis must be placed on the preferences for features and financing as it varies by ethnic group. This will require greater sensitivity to ethnicity of respondents, including explicit sampling of ethnic seniors and retaining ethnic identification of respondents. That is, it is important not to reduce ethnicity to white–nonwhite when coding or analyzing data. The development or expansion of programs on the basis of aggregate data (e.g., by state or national data without regard to ethnicity, or a focus on only white–nonwhite differences) will hamper development of programs that are in line with the preferences of the intended clients. For example, black–Hispanic differences noted in the present study would have been masked if white–nonwhite comparisons had been made. Related to this is that consideration of ethnic differences for features, financing, and ability to pay will allow for more efficient targeting of resources and increase the odds of providing services that clients will use and can benefit from. Similarly, conducting small area surveys or needs assesments will help local and state agencies develop more efficient and carefully targeted resource allocation. Instead of relying on national data for development or expansion of programs, local and state units on aging could use information from their actual or potential clients.

Finally, this area appears to be an important one for considering public–private partnerships in service delivery and financing, including expansion of public and private financing of community-based long-term care. The present sample indicates that many of the seniors have the financial ability to meet copayments for some form of capitated health and long-term care delivery system. Many of these seniors anticipate using long-term care services and are willing to purchase some form of insurance that covers these services, should they need them. Nearly half of these seniors have purchased some form of private medigap insurance. These premiums could be used as private copayments for health and long-term care services. Alternatively, perhaps an expansion of the

Medicare system could be used to cover or offset costs of long-term care. The development of an optional "Medicare Part C" for long-term care could operate much as capitated, risk-pooling delivery systems (e.g., HMOs) do now. However, developing such private–public financing mechanisms will require sensitivity to ethnic differences in financial ability and preferences for services.

From both the consumer's and provider's position, an informed choice will help in the development, delivery, and financing of long-term care over the next decade or two. Informing seniors of Medicare and medigap coverage and gaps will help them make better decisions about what medigap policies to purchase, if any, or how they can prepare financially for anticipated long-term care costs. Information on seniors' ability and willingness to pay for coverage of long-term care services will help in the development of new methods of financing. Moreover, informing policymakers and planners of ethnic seniors' preferences for long-term care services can lead to development of more comprehensive and ethnically sensitive programs.

REFERENCES

American Association of Retired Persons. (1984). *Long-term care survey.* Washington, DC: American Association of Retired Persons.

Coulton, C., & Frost, A. K. (1982). Use of social and health services by the elderly. *Journal of Health and Social Behavior, 23,* 330–339.

Ford, A. B., Folmar, S. J., Salmon, R. B., Medalie, J. H., Roy, A. W., & Galazka, S. S. (1988). Health and function in the old and very old. *Journal of the American Geriatric Society, 36,* 187–197.

Health Insurance Association of America. (1984). *Source book of health insurance data, 1982–1983.*

Kane, R. A., & Kane, R. L. (1987). *Long-term care: Principles, programs and policies.* New York: Springer Publishing Co.

Kulys, R. (1983). Future crises and the very old: Implications for discharge planning. *Health and Social Work, 8,* 182–195.

Leutz, W., Abrahams, R., Greenlick, M., Kane, R., & Prottas, J. (1988). Targeting expanded care to the aged: Early SHMO experience. *The Gerontologist, 28,* 4–17.

Lombardi, T. (1991). The Nursing Home Without Walls: State of New York. In J. A. Miller (Ed.), *Community-based long-term care: Innovative models.* Newbury Park, CA: Sage.

National Center for Health Statistics. (1986). Aging in the eighties, age 65 and over— Use of community services, preliminary data from the Supplement on Aging to the National Health Interview Survey: United States, January–June, 1984. *Advance Data from Vital and Health Statistics.* No. 124. Hyattsville, MD: U. S. Public Health Service.

National Center for Health Statistics. (1987a). Aging in the eighties, functional limitations of individuals age 65 years and over. *Advance Data from Vital and Health Statistics.* No. 133. Hyattsville, MD: U. S. Public Health Service.

National Center for Health Statistics. (1987b). Use of nursing homes by the elderly, preliminary data from the 1985 National Nursing Home Survey. *Advance Data from Vital and Health Statistics*. No. 137. Hyattsville, MD: U. S. Public Health Service.

Stull, D. E. (1987). *Long-term care service use among elderly in Greater Cleveland: Methods of payment, knowledge of Medicare coverage, and interest in Social/HMOs*. Final Report to the Fellowship Program in Applied Gerontology of the Gerontological Society of America.

U. S. Bureau of the Census. (1987). *Statistical Abstracts of the United States: 1988*. (108th ed.). Washington, DC: U. S. Government Printing Office.

Ward, R. A. & Bryant, E. (1986). A case study of HMO Medicare enrollment. *The Gerontologist*, 26, 655–662

Index